A Cappella Arranging 2.0

A Cappella Arranging 2.0

The Next Level

Deke Sharon and
Dylan Bell

ROWMAN & LITTLEFIELD
Lanham • Boulder • New York • London

Published by Rowman & Littlefield
An imprint of The Rowman & Littlefield Publishing Group, Inc.
4501 Forbes Boulevard, Suite 200, Lanham, Maryland 20706
www.rowman.com

86-90 Paul Street, London EC2A 4NE

British Library Cataloguing in Publication Information Available

Library of Congress Cataloging-in-Publication Data

Names: Sharon, Deke, author. | Bell, Dylan, author.
Title: A cappella arranging 2.0 : the next level / Deke Sharon and Dylan Bell.
Description: Lanham : Rowman & Littlefield, 2024. | Series: Music pro guides | Includes
  bibliographical references.
Identifiers: LCCN 2024005860 (print) | LCCN 2024005861 (ebook) | ISBN 9781538172650 (cloth) |
  ISBN 9781538172667 (paperback) | ISBN 9781538172674 (ebook)
Subjects: LCSH: Arrangement (Music) | Vocal groups. | Choral music.
Classification: LCC MT70.5 .S53 2024 (print) | LCC MT70.5 (ebook) |
  DDC 782.5/137—dc23/eng/20240209
LC record available at https://lccn.loc.gov/2024005860
LC ebook record available at https://lccn.loc.gov/2024005861

♾™ The paper used in this publication meets the minimum requirements of American National Standard for Information Sciences—Permanence of Paper for Printed Library Materials, ANSI/NISO Z39.48-1992.

Contents

Introduction

When we first published *A Cappella Arranging* in 2013, we knew there was no book of its kind out there, but we had no idea how much it was needed: since its publication, it has gone through multiple reprintings, made its way everywhere from the halls of academia to Hollywood movie screens, and been translated into multiple languages and enjoyed by arrangers and singers around the world.

And yet we knew there was still more to be said.

Books on arranging are practical, whether they inform you how to arrange instruments, voices, flowers, or deck chairs on the *Titanic*. Perhaps a few words wax poetic in the introduction, but by chapter 1 you'll find yourself neck-deep in chord progressions and exceptions to the rules you learned in basic music theory. That's all well and good: we like chord progressions and music theory. But we've never come across a book that explains what it's like to be an arranger. We tried to give some insight in our book *A Cappella Arranging*, but the book was at its core practical, about getting down to business, so we did, as well. The same concept has been bandied about through the ages, be it in Latin (*ars longa, vita brevis*) or on radio stations ("Less talk, more rock"), and so in this book we do just that: rock, instead of talk.

A Cappella Arranging 2.0 picks up where our first book left off. Whereas our first book discussed principles at length, we assume that by now you have many of these definitions and descriptions under your belt and would rather see them in action.

And yet there is a time for talk, at least for those of us prone to overthinking the creative act. As authors, we're rather fond of reading essays, and some of the best are about reading, and writing, and writing about reading, and reading about writing. It would follow that as musicians we should simply create music about music, but that quickly grows tiresome as music is best when grounded in emotion, not intellect. Sure, there may be a place for "pure" music without an emotional component, but we're more interested in making people feel something. As far as we're concerned, all the theory and technique in the world is the mere resounding of gongs and clanging of cymbals if there is no heart and soul behind it.

In Section One: Creative Principles, we attempt the nearly impossible: putting into words the overarching "why" that hopefully drives all your work as an arranger. If you were an institution, this would be your mission statement. If you were writing an essay, this might be your thesis. If it's a sonnet, these are the emotions—or even, your beloved—that inspires your words. Whatever metaphor you want to use, reading this section can refocus your energies to make sure the "why"—not just the "how"—is the primary force behind your work.

One can simply and effectively express "I love you," but a poet can breathe a universe of life into the same sentiment with wide-ranging and layered vocabulary, rhythm, and inspiration. Once the "why" is firmly front of mind, we can move on to the "how." Section Two: Theoretical Techniques gives an advanced look at many of the tools of the trade, with a deep dive into a cappella-specific techniques and usage beyond what most theory books can offer.

A Cappella Arranging focused primarily on ensemble writing, but this book goes further and deeper, looking at specific arranging situations and contexts beyond standard arrangement writing. These can be found in Section Three: Beyond the Ensemble: Specialized Arranging.

You've undoubtedly been inspired by other vocal arrangers and wondered what makes their arrangement style unique . . . and more importantly, *How can I do that?* Section Four: Arranging "In the Style Of . . ." gives you a baker's dozen of the most influential arrangers/groups in the contemporary a cappella world and takes you under the hood with an in-depth analysis of their arranging styles and techniques. If "good artists borrow and great artists steal," we hand you the keys to the vault . . . or at least a good set of blueprints.

For all the "how-to" verbiage, nothing beats getting into the mind of the arranger. Section Five: Reimagining Arrangements is a personal and anecdotal analysis of some of our own works, why we made the choices we made, and how we created what we did. As we said earlier, no one really talks about what it's like to be an arranger. Here, we open our heads and explain the thought processes: you might be surprised to see how similar they are to your own.

So, welcome back . . . or simply welcome, if this is the first book of ours you're reading. Either way, we hope you find it helpful, useful, informative, and full of ideas that will help expand your creativity and effectiveness as an arranger.

A quick word on nomenclature . . .

This is *A Cappella Arranging 2.0*, so when we make references to instruments ("the drummer," "the horns," etc.), unless specified otherwise, we're talking about singers singing instrumental-type parts, not the instruments themselves. Using terminology established in our first book, "BGs" are background vocal parts (which can sound vocal or instrumental: think of it as "just about anything that isn't lead or bass"), and "VP" means "vocal percussionist," a.k.a. your "drummer."

Creative Principles

If you're just dying to get started, or you're looking to use this book as a reference resource, thumbing through for a new technique or idea, you could skip this chapter and get straight to the "what" and "how." But even the most experienced arrangers need to take a moment to get themselves in the frame of mind to be creative. And anytime you need to see the forest and forget the trees, come back and visit this section again.

This section looks at creative principles from three perspectives. The first, and most straightforward, is chapter 1: a revisiting of the Ten Step Method that defined our first book. If you've read any good novel or watched a great movie, you'll recall that each time you experience it, you find something new. So did we, and we offer a decade's worth of fresh insight into the process. We also explore what might be different for an advanced arranger and how you may even question or challenge these onetime instructions.

Chapter 2, "The Creative Process," explores this challenging, elusive subject through the use of allegory. In our first book, you met our friends the Dreamer, the Editor, and the Critic, and you learned how they can work together to guide your process. Now, we meet a few of their friends, and we learn how they can take our arrangements to the next level or, if misunderstood, how they can stifle the process. You had the basic set; now enjoy the expansion pack!

Chapter 3, "The Most Important Thing," is a reminder of, for all the "what" in this book, it is meaningless without the "why." The story, the emotional connection between the artist and the listener ... this is The Most Important Thing, the reason we love vocal music and why we pour so much energy into making sure our arrangements are just right.

Pull up a chair, dim the lights, settle in, and stay awhile. Close your laptop, open your mind and heart, and let's get started.

CHAPTER 1

The Ten Steps, Revisited

At the core of our first book, *A Cappella Arranging*, is a ten-step method, designed to help both the first-time arranger as well as experienced arrangers, as it starts with the largest decisions and moves down to minutiae. Each step was cracked open further with its own chapter, going into great detail. "Step 5: Prepare Your Materials," for example, looked further at notational styles and conventions. "Step 6: Write Out the Melody" became an in-depth look at using lyrics as inspiration. And so on. If you don't have our first book, if you haven't taken the time to glance at this recently, or if it's not a part of your normal process, we suggest you take a look at Appendix A: Basic Arranging in Ten Steps.

A decade (and likely, many arrangements) later, is there anything more to learn? We think so, and it's time for a fresh look to see what may have changed in that time.

First of all, you may now be skipping through some steps, or doing them in a different order, or combining them, or revisiting steps along the way. This is great, and it means you're moving deeper into your own individual process. The more experienced you are, the more you may question or alter the process. That's great, as well: no questioning means no growth!

1. Choose a Song

If you're arranging frequently, this has likely become second nature, and you have a series of unconscious considerations when deciding what to arrange. Now is a good time to question those assumptions, because you've become an experienced arranger. These could be questioning "givens," such as:

» *Closing a set with a slow song.* Who says you have to end with a bang? How could you close a set with a slow song? What song might truly be a show-stopper, even if it's a ballad?
» *Your soloists.* What assumptions are you making when considering your soloists regarding who can/should be challenged, to strike unexpected gold in

a performance? Do they have something to offer that you're unaware of, or never thought to bring to light?

» *That song you didn't want to arrange.* When might it benefit you to arrange that song a group member is pestering you about that you're sure will be a dud ... and how could you use your magical arranging mojo to turn it into a hit?

You've answered the easy questions; now answer the difficult ones, and those that you can't answer, keep in the back of your mind. Any song can work a cappella, perhaps not every song for every group, but as an experienced arranger, you should consider how to push yourself to expand your and your group's abilities.

2. Listen to the Original—Repeatedly

Let's be honest: you're probably not doing this anymore. You don't need to. You can hear a song once or twice, get the gist of it, and dive right in. At the very least, you're probably working on the next steps ahead while listening. We know—we do it all the time, too. But there still is great value in listening in the background, having the song "soak in," and letting your subconscious work while you're sleeping.

3. Look at—and Listen to—Other Arrangements

This originally applied to other well-known covers of the song by other (non–a cappella) bands, assuming that in Step One you were choosing a song that wasn't overdone. If you were looking at other a cappella versions, it was to make sure yours was at least somewhat original. You know enough now to make your arrangement original enough, but there's even greater value, now that you better understand the characteristics and parameters of arranging, in listening to a wide variety of different versions, good and bad. Especially bad. Look for what doesn't work and look beyond why into what choices were being made that led there, how the arranger was expecting something to work that didn't, so you can avoid the same mistakes. Plus, the good stuff? Steal, per usual. Your job will be made easier, and better.

This time, we also encourage you to take a YouTube deep dive into other vocal arrangements. Again, pay as much attention to the things you don't like as much as the things you do, such as:

» *Poor intonation.* Yes, we know you can tell when a group is out of tune ... but can you tell *why* they are out of tune? How could your arranging skills have helped them be in better tune? What choices will you make that will save your singers from the same fate?

» *"Questionable" choices.* What choices were too much, too busy, too complicated? Rarely will you find arrangers who appreciate and employ simplicity, yet that is exactly what is often needed.
» *Bad use of vocal range.* Listen for the moments when extended range gets the group into trouble. We've all done it; now soak in it: the bass is too low and inaudible, the soloist too high and screechy. The BGs are badly voiced around the lead and take up too much space.

Awkward syllables, sloppy polyrhythms, overly dense chord voicings—listen and learn. Plus, the good stuff? Steal, once again.

For that matter, if you've been arranging for a long time, take a look at your own first arrangements. Knowing what you know now, what would you have done differently?

» *Dylan Says: My 1980s Top 40 cover group, Retrocity, has been around for twenty-five years. We recently pulled out some charts I wrote way back when. They still hold up—I was already an experienced arranger by then—but with a quarter century of hindsight, I'd still make a few changes, be kinder to the voices . . . and definitely improve my notation etiquette!*

4. Decide on a Form

In *A Cappella Arranging*, we talked mostly about form-as-function, altering the form primarily to "trim the fat" from a chart. But there's more to choosing a form than simply removing extra choruses and instrumental passages. It can be used creatively and artistically, as well. You're an advanced arranger, so you can start making some unexpected choices. Quote the bridge to craft an introduction, layer elements of the chorus into the verse, and so on. Use a piece of the song as a "thesis" or thematic core and rebuild the arrangement around that.

And master the art of the "cutdown." Many televised music shows find ways to distill songs into ninety-second gems. Commercials, social-media reels, and other short-format media may work best with a fifteen- to thirty-second clip. As an arranger, this is a very useful—and marketable—skill.

5. Prepare Your Materials

If you're like us, you may find the tools you use for arranging end up impacting your choices. Copying a passage, repeating a section, transposition, and so on: there are choices we make now that we didn't make when arranging with pencil and paper (if you remember those days). Even more so, arranging into a DAW (digital audio workstation) will likely result in different choices, as you'll be guided more by your ear than your eye. If you're stuck, or want to breathe new techniques into your practice, change your medium.

>> *Dylan Says: My father was an author, and for one of his novels he switched media, from using a word processor to writing by hand. The result on his writing was immediately obvious: handwriting made his prose clearer, punchier, and more visceral.*

6. Write Out the Melody

This was always the first step in the actual writing process because a) you need the melody anyways, and it's the least likely to be altered; b) it helps "map out" the chart as you are writing; and c) it's great-but-necessary busywork, allowing your arranger brain to work in the background. Perhaps by now you're no longer doing this; maybe you likely just dive in wherever you're inspired, with the melody in mind. But is the melody still the most important aspect of your arrangement?

Writing the melody first may also box you in. If you put it in the soprano line, maybe you're less likely to move it around to other parts, only from the sheer inertia of "it's already there." At this advanced stage, you can likely easily hold and manipulate the melody in your head, bending it and mentally reorganizing it at will, and you no longer need it in the chart to know where you are. See what happens if you hold off writing the melody until you really know what you want to do with it and where it will go. How does that shape your arrangement?

7. Write Out the Bass Line

We described the bass line as the "secondary melody" in our first book, and we still like that description. So, is the bass line a true countermelody and not just a collection of boring tonic notes that provide the foundation for everything else, and is it fun to sing? Maybe the original bass line was boring: writing a new, active bass line could open up new avenues of creativity for the arrangement and breathe new life into the song.

8. Write Out the BGs

First of all, why wait till the melody and bass line are done?

Steps six through eight, in sequence, are a surefire method to writing a workable arrangement, in particular when you are early in your arranging career. But as you get more experienced, we suggest seeing these three steps not only as interchangeable in order, but don't even worry about finishing one factor before working on another. Start with the first factor that strikes your fancy in the moment, work on another, then go back to another, as your creative ideas develop. See what happens when you dive in with a cool block texture or countermelody in an upper voice, even before you add the melody or bass line. How does that affect the melody or the bass line? Challenge your assumptions and reimagine your process to shake things up.

For these three now-interconnected steps, imagine that you're writing a play: the melody is the protagonist; the bass line is a secondary main character, maybe a sidekick; and the BGs are supporting characters. A standard arrangement puts the main character front and center pretty much always, with the faithful sidekick beside them. The supporting roles know their place, and everyone's job is to serve the main character. In drama, that would make for a pretty one-dimensional play. Why not play with that in music?

Take, for example, the play *Rosencrantz and Guildenstern Are Dead* by Tom Stoppard. It takes an interesting approach: it reimagines Shakespeare's *Hamlet* from the perspective of two minor characters. The whole pecking order is flipped upside down: the focus is "backstage" on the two minor characters, and Hamlet and the others are relegated to fragments of scenes. You may not want your melody to be a bit player in your arrangement, but who says it has to be the star, all the time? Maybe the BGs can steal the spotlight, or the bass line.

9. The Final Touches

This was mostly described from a technical and musical perspective: looking for "weak spots" in the arrangement and fixing them. Now that you're probably pretty good at this, expand this further to include more aesthetic, artistic, and emotional characteristics. And, as always, challenge your usual assumptions and processes.

What exactly are your final touches, and what process do you use to decide what to add or remove? Are you singing through each line? Are you playing the arrangement back and improvising over the top of it to see what else occurs to you? Do you have enough "moments" in it, so it doesn't just chug along? Are you using all of your group's talents? Do you have the song's overarching emotional character driving all your decisions, even if that means removing a cool chord you really love?

This step is where you have an opportunity to revisit your arrangement almost as if it was sent by someone else, trying to find what you might do differently to make it better. Unless you're in a rush, it can help to have some time and distance between you and the work you've created. Set it aside to revisit, once you've forgotten a bit of what you did. You may find you can look at it more dispassionately, and let go more easily of creative ideas that you were once attached to. They say an artist never finishes their work; they just walk away from it. In this case, walk away first, come back and give it one last look over, then walk away for good. That is, until Step Ten.

10. Record/Rehearse

Remember that your arrangement isn't music. It's notes on paper, sounds in an audio file, and otherwise just a road map to get your singers to connect with the audience. That's when it becomes music.

By rehearsing and recording the song, you take the ideas in your head, which you put on paper, and see what they really become when put into voices, either live or in the studio. Don't be precious, don't lose focus, and don't take it personally when anyone recommends changes. Appreciate the insight and honesty, and remember that everyone's on the same page; they, too, want this to be music. Learn from this process, as it will get you one step closer to hearing their voices in your head as you arrange.

Finally, we'll add one more step.

11. What Do You Do Differently?

There must be steps in your own process that vary from this, ways in which you make arrangement choices, both conscious and subconscious. Try to first identify and then challenge that process, as by doing so you'll unlock different ways of tapping in to your creativity (just as the difference that occurs when moving from arranging with a notation program to arranging into a microphone). There's nothing wrong with how you're doing things; it's simply that the act of doing things differently will "shake the tree" and some new ideas will fall out.

Remember, these Ten Steps, while effective, are designed to help arrangers learn a process. They are not commandments, nor are they laws, just guidelines to help you get started. Now that you're well on your way, keep them in mind, assimilate your own processes, and most importantly, continue to reflect, question, challenge, and grow.

CHAPTER 2

The Creative Process

In our first book, we looked a little at the creative process, challenging as that may be. We framed the creative process as a continuous dialogue (sometimes an argument) between three Jung-style archetypes—the Dreamer, the Editor, and the Critic—and we offered suggestions for getting to know them, understanding them, and learning how to make them work together. In the same way that Jung's archetypes can help us make sense of the immense complexity of the human psyche, these three characters help us personify, and better understand, this ultimately unknowable Thing we call the Creative Process.

A decade or so later, they continue to serve their roles well. But it turns out they have friends, and these friends can help or hinder the process. As with all these archetypes, the key is to understand them, learn to love them, and let them know their place.

We imagined the creative process as being a room where two of these characters can work together—occasionally three, but it tends to get crowded. Different characters will come in and out at different stages of the game. First, a reminder of who our three main archetypes are.

The Dreamer

The Dreamer is raw, unpolished creativity. The Dreamer is the part of you that generates ideas, simple or crazy. The Dreamer isn't practical: they're not the type to figure out how to make things work. Someone else can do that.

The Dreamer needs a lot of space and time to do their thing. They don't understand time or deadlines: sometimes they only work when they feel like it. And the Dreamer is a sensitive soul. Interrupt them, analyze their work, or criticize them, and they'll run out of the room and disappear for a while. And you don't want that: without the Dreamer, you have nothing to work with. They can create something from nothing, and that is their greatest power.

The Editor

We all know the Editor well: they get things done and make things go. They're practical and logical (if a little stodgy and boring sometimes). The Editor loves to tinker and execute, and this is their big skill. The Editor has an eye for the big picture, and they are excellent at assimilating different ideas and making them work together.

But the Editor is useless without something to work on. And they're not the one who creates it: that's the Dreamer's job. Sometimes the Editor is a little myopic: they can't see beyond what's in front of them. They need help on either side to make things go—raw material to work with, and someone to look it over and help make it better.

The Critic

The Critic looks for faults. Like a detective with a magnifying glass, or a tax auditor, they're looking for things that aren't right. They're looking for weakness, and if it's there, they'll find it.

Sounds like a nasty character. Why include them at all?

At first glance, the Critic seems like a negative type . . . but really, they're not. Their end goal is the same as that of the Dreamer and the Editor: they want to make the best arrangement possible. They just have a very specialized tool set, useful at very specific times. Unlike the Editor, simply working with what they have, the Critic can see what's missing and, thus, help to find it. But like a person with a chainsaw, you want to be careful where they're allowed to roam.

There's a quick look at our main characters. Now let's look at their friends, starting with the friends of the Dreamer.

The Joker

The Joker is that impish character who sits on your shoulder and whispers silly nothings into your ear while you're working. What use do they have?

First, they're exceptionally creative. They can take an ordinary idea and juice it up with a little fun. If you've ever added a sly music quote to your arrangement, or a fun little Easter egg meant only for the repeat listener, that's your Joker at work.

》 *Dylan Says: I'm a naturally playful person, with a prominent Joker. I give them free rein in my creative process, even if many of their ideas aren't put into play. In my arrangement for Cadence of "The Dry Cleaner from Des Moines," when the lead sings, "he picked out a booth at Circus Circus, where the cowgirls fill the room with their big balloons," the BGs sing a comic "doot doot doodl-oodl-oot doot doo doo" quote from the circus song "Entry of the Gladiators," rhythmically displaced and reharmonized to jazz chords. A good friend called up sometime later and bellowed, "Ha! I've been listening on repeat for months and FINALLY heard that bit!"*

» *Deke Says: Musical Easter eggs are always fun to weave into arrangements, and you never know when you'll spark a moment of insight . . . like when I got an email years later from a singer who realized and yet wondered if the syllable I chose for the B section of "I Want a Hippopotamus for Christmas" wasn't just a nice ringing and resonant sound, but indeed had an additional layer of meaning. I replied proudly that yes, indeed, I was fully aware of the layers of meaning when I chose the syllable "dung."*

Second, they don't take themselves too seriously. Remember, we're creating art, not performing heart surgery. A little sparkle and levity never hurt anyone, and a work that takes itself too seriously may fall under the weight of its own self-importance.

Third, even in tragedy, we need humor. Watch any drama, and you'll see a little comic relief sneak in here and there.

While they may not drive the process, and you don't really need them, it's nice to have the Joker around.

The Procrastinator

Who doesn't know this character—all too well? They barely need an introduction. The procrastinator waits, delays, and seems to do Nothing. At first glance, the Procrastinator serves no useful purpose, and your first instinct will be to curse their name and banish them forever.

But please don't. Not until you get to know them and understand them.

The Procrastinator isn't a bad character. Believe it or not, they are a guardian figure. Sometimes the Procrastinator's job is to protect the Dreamer from our other main characters, the Editor and the Critic. As mentioned earlier, the Dreamer is a bit of a fragile creature sometimes, and their work is easily disturbed by an overeager Editor or Critic barging in. Sometimes they hide . . . and they hide behind the Procrastinator.

Sometimes creativity comes from conscientious hard work: imagine the author pounding out their daily one-thousand-words-of-raw-material, working that creative muscle until it can present itself on command. We believe in flexing the creative muscle this way. But we equally believe in the idea of creativity "working in the background." Have you ever had a brilliant, creative idea just appear from thin air? Have you ever felt inspired and didn't know why? More importantly, when did these ideas appear? Chances are, they appeared when you were doing Nothing Important: taking a walk, cleaning your house, or even while sleeping. More often than not, that's the work of the Procrastinator: they take you out of the forced-creativity laboratory and set aside—often, seemingly, against your will—time and space for the Dreamer to work in secret. John Cleese's book *Creativity* has at its core a very helpful concept: spend some time musing a problem, then walk away from it. Read, take a shower, sleep. Your mind is working in the background, and the answer will often present itself to you in time.

The Procrastinator can also protect you from the Demon Doubt, whom you will meet shortly.

» *Deke Says: I'm not usually a procrastinator; I'm the opposite (we don't have a word for it in English—the guy who read his textbooks at the beginning of the semester before class started, and the like), but sometimes I'm just not feeling creative. When that's the case and I'm on a deadline, I sit down and do all the non-creative steps of the ten-step formula: listen to the track while doing something else, and sit down to lay out the sheet music, figure out the form, and put the melody in place. This way, when creativity strikes, I'm able to just dive right in and make creative choices.*

Recognize the Procrastinator as a (usually) helpful figure, and you'll save yourself a lot of wasted angst and guilt. You don't need to answer them every time they call, but in their own way, they're usually trying to help.

The Editor also has some friends to bring to the party . . .

The Referee

The referee has one job: keep the process running smoothly and on time.

Very often, you're working to some sort of deadline. It may be the needs of a client, or your own group, or just a self-imposed deadline. You'll need the Referee to help you.

The Referee keeps things moving forward, mindful of the time a particular process takes. They are the one who decides when the Dreamer is done spinning raw material and (hopefully with the Dreamer's blessing) allows the Editor in to stitch it together. The Referee often has to settle disputes between the characters, making a judgment call to avoid endless dithering. The arranging process, like any game or sport, is the sum total of an untold number of actions and micro-decisions, and the Referee makes the calls and keeps the play moving.

Not all characters play together well. Some, like the Dreamer and the Critic, shouldn't even be in the room at the same time at all: each may undo the others' work. The Referee and the Procrastinator are typically at odds with each other: one is trying to move forward while the other is calling for a time-out. Most of the time, you'll want the Referee to tell the Procrastinator to get lost: there's work to be done! But once in a while, if you don't have a real deadline to meet (or even if you do, but you're not too close), or if you're at a creative impasse, let the Procrastinator win the fight. Put the arrangement in a drawer, close the laptop, go to sleep, or just walk away. Chances are, your arrangement will be the better for it.

Professor Should

Professor Should is actually a friend of both the Editor and the Critic. Professor Should is that seemingly fussy type, usually wagging a finger and sermonizing on How Things Should Be Done. We'll be honest: we know them all too well, but we really don't like them that much. However, they do serve their purpose.

Professor Should tends to hover over you while you work, checking your work like any nosy micromanager might. Sometimes they think they have a better idea. Maybe they're right; maybe they're wrong. Professor Should, like the Critic, is in opposition to the Dreamer, who prefers the open word *could* to the limiting word *should*.

At worst, Professor Should is a wet blanket on creativity, stifling interesting ideas that may fall outside the norm. On the other hand, Professor Should can also keep you in line. Got a great creative idea, but you're writing for an amateur group? They'll let you know if it's realistically achievable. Is your Superstar getting out of line? (Who's that? Read on. . . .) The Professor knows how to talk them out of their flights of self-indulgence and keep the arrangement doing what it should: serving the music and the singers. Take everything they say with a large grain of salt, but if they insist, listen to what they have to say. They just might be right—this time.

The Superstar

The Superstar is a manifestation of (or maybe a cousin to) Freud's Ego. They're always shouting, "Check me out!" On the opposite shoulder from Professor Should, they're often looking for places to be seen: a clever reharmonization here, a moment of technical fireworks there. The Superstar has been around as long as art has been, and many great works bear their signature. A great composer wrote a theme subject around the letters of his own name, B-A-C-H (B natural); artists paint themselves into their works; and so on. The artist, however humble, still wants to be seen: that's the Superstar.

Scattered throughout this book are reminders of our role as arranger: to be invisible, to serve the music, the story, the emotional connection between performer and listener. We remain behind the curtain. You'd think the Superstar has no place here, and, to be honest, the Superstar can be a bit of a hindrance. Depending on the dominance of your Superstar, you may spend some or much of your time keeping them at bay for risk of turning your sublime work into a self-aggrandizing folly.

(That last paragraph sounded an awful lot like Professor Should, didn't it?)

But the Superstar has a place, too. They can nudge the Dreamer into amazing flights of fancy, or enable the Editor to brilliance beyond their self-limiting seriousness. The Superstar can tell the Professor to take a hike, and sometimes they will. Arrangements need moments, especially if it's a performance on a competition stage or designed to grab attention as people pass by on an outdoor stage, and the Superstar—being a showoff—can be your best friend here.

And let's face it: ego, the sense of self, can be a powerful and positive driver, which, in its best form, can build pyramids, spaceships, and symphonies—driving us to greatness.

Demon Doubt

Finally, we've reached the toughest one to deal with, and we don't use the term *demon* all that lightly. We all have this one inside us. Demon Doubt tells us it can't be done, or that we're not capable enough. It tries to feed us poison: "Your creative well is running dry" . . . "You're out of ideas" . . . "You've nothing left to offer . . . if you ever did" . . . "Your work isn't good enough" . . . "You can't do it" . . . If you have a writing block, that's the demon squashing all the other archetypes flat.

Writing about them is painful enough, but it has to be done.

Demons can't be slaughtered, but they can be kept at bay. Here are a few suggestions as to how.

» *Realize you're not alone.* Demon Doubt's biggest lie is that you're in this alone, that you're the only one who risks failure. Everyone—and we mean everyone—has to face the demon at some point, no matter how famous, accomplished, or brilliant they may be. While the Tortured Artist stereotype may not be all that constructive, it's a reminder that creating art can be a difficult process at times, for everyone. Read up on some of the struggles and doubts the great artists have gone through, and remind yourself that you're in good company.

» *Understand it's not that big a deal.* This isn't rocket science, and no one's life hangs in the balance. For that matter, not every decision will make or break an arrangement. If you don't have a genius choice, pick the best one you can come up with and move on. Arranging is sometimes art, sometimes craft, and sometimes just a simple task of lining up voices. If you're questioning yourself, you're taking it all too seriously. Sometimes choices you think aren't great end up shining onstage. Just pick something and move on.

» *Let the Procrastinator take over.* Sometimes you can't fight: you need to take flight, seek shelter, and regain your strength. That's when the Procrastinator can protect you. Walk away, let them seduce you into a night of Doing

Nothing. It's okay . . . there's a good chance things will look better in the light of a new day.

» *Look back.* This advice is best for more experienced arrangers, but if you're reading this book, that should include you. You can build walls to protect you, and those are built from your own past works. They can remind you of what you have created and what you're capable of. These works exist, they're alive, and they are demon-proof.

» *Understand that it means you care.* Think about this: a synonym for *doubt* is *concern*, and being concerned means you're invested, you're engaged, and you want to do your best. Imagine if you didn't have a doubt in your mind: it would mean that you're either confident beyond reality, or maybe it just didn't matter enough to you.

» *Remember: creativity doesn't die.* A common feeling/fear with creativity is, *I've used it all up. There's no more.* This is a myth: it's demon-jive. You are alive, living and evolving, changing and growing, in a world that is also living and changing. The same atoms and molecules have been endlessly recombining for billions of years into new life, new things, and new people, and you're part of that swirling momentum of constant change. Life is creativity in itself, and as you plug into this, you'll realize that you are constantly experiencing new things and evolving yourself. This will make its way into your work.

Creativity is life: it is momentous, overwhelming, awe-inspiring, and occasionally fickle, inscrutable, and difficult. There will be dry spells and fallow periods: these are necessary for creativity to regroup and regrow. But creativity never dies. Trust us on this one.

CHAPTER 3

The Most Important Thing

At the end of a long day, pretty much nobody says, "Ugh, I'm so wiped out, I just need to listen to some music . . . that's technically flawless." Concert tickets are expensive, and people's free time is limited. What do they choose to go see? Performances that will grab their hearts and minds, transport them to another place, and most of all, make them feel.

What grabs you more: a Photoshopped, blemish-free, picture-perfect fashion spread, or the timeless, 1968 photo *Earthrise*, showing us our planet in all its beauty and fragility? One sells makeup; the other inspired the environmental movement of the 1970s and beyond.

And, of course, with digital retouching software such as Melodyne and Auto-Tune, every recording could be technically perfect, snapped to a grid of perfect tuning and rhythm . . . and that guarantees exactly zero interest. By today's standards, much of the vocal music of the past isn't anywhere close to "perfectly in tune," but ask yourself honestly: Did you even notice? These classic tracks are filled with energy, vibe, and emotion—and they remain beloved: no one would call them "imperfect," nor would they care.

What, then, ties all these examples together and makes them compelling? The act of telling a story: a human, engaging, sometimes-imperfect, always soul-stirring story.

Instrumental music can tell a story, it can be sublime, but vocal music is emotionally visceral: it grabs us by the ears and heart and won't let go. A cappella music, being the sound of voices singing together in harmony, can do this exponentially. The thing that makes a cappella so compelling in our digitally manufactured day and age is not that it's perfect, but rather, that it's human. The flaws and imperfections inherent in an all-vocal performance are almost assured the moment you walk onstage, and yet it doesn't immediately ruin the performance. What does ruin a performance is if the singers are terrified of singing a wrong note or otherwise exhibiting any flaws. If they are so wrapped up in the mechanics that they forget the art—and the heart—they can leave the audience cold.

Do we care that a group of kindergarteners isn't technically perfect? Of course not—they're entirely, completely themselves, and we find this not only charming, but heartwarming: we harken back to our own carefree childhood days. By middle school, expectations of "perfection" (and, sadly, sometimes the directors' egos) can creep in, resulting in choirs that are self-conscious and reserved. We then have to fight our way back to being ourselves onstage, and allowing our inner lights to shine as we offer our best version of truth and beauty and our voices join together in harmony.

If you think this is a problem to be tackled only by the singers onstage—if you think it's their problem to deal with and not yours—you're sorely mistaken. You create the road map they'll follow as their voices align, and the choices you make can put them on the right path, or lead them to get lost in the woods. Are you putting the story and emotion first and foremost in your choices, from chord voicings and syllables to dynamics and nuances? Are you setting them up for success by putting them in the right part of their vocal range to express the song's message effectively? Are you amplifying the best elements of the song, and using all your tools as an arranger to align the song's technical elements and reach the common goal onstage of affecting the audience?

Remember our mantra: we believe that the "what and how" behind all the techniques and methods we as arrangers have at our disposal should always be subservient to the "why"—telling a compelling story and making an emotional connection. This connection—between arranger and artist, between performer and audience—is the Most Important Thing.

Deke wrote a book—*The Heart of Vocal Harmony*—that teaches groups of singers how to perform with consistent, unified emotion and teaches directors how to foster and promote an ensemble atmosphere in which this is possible. We'd like to include two brief chapters from the early sections of this book that we think will have some resonance for you as an arranger, as you contemplate how your decisions affect every singer's ability to powerfully impact their audiences emotionally.

Say Something

> We all know that being able to express deep emotion can literally save a person's life, and suppressing emotion can kill you both spiritually and physically.
>
> —Lisa Kleypas

If you agree that music is a form of communication, then it follows that the most fundamental task you have as a musician, as a singer, is to say something.

If music is a language both embracing and superseding linguistics, a language that is universal and yet very personal, timeless, and timely, what exactly does it mean to say something through music? It means that you can say pretty much anything, so long as it is meaningful to you. You can sing about what it felt like to be relegated to the children's table at Thanksgiving when you wanted to sit with the adults, and you can sing about the deep connection you feel when you stare at the stars on a moonless night. If it's poignant to you, then it's potentially poignant to someone else.

If you're singing music casually, for fun, for friends, then there is no reason you should sing anything other than what you want to sing. If you're a professional, with rare exception you shouldn't try to sing something that you don't believe, that you're not feeling, that you can't infuse with your own experience. It would be the same as a public speaker delivering a speech that she doesn't believe. Unless you and all your singing cohorts are superlative actors, the audience likely will not stay long or remember much. There is too much music, too much media in our world, and if you don't grab someone and hold them, they will change the channel, click away to another video or song, likely never to return.

Therefore, if you want people to hear you, if you want to increase your audience, if you want to touch people, if you want to change lives, if you want music to be your career, your vocation, the task is clear: say something powerful, something meaningful, something that speaks truth. Something that touches people. Something that people will return to and share with friends.

This has never been more important than now, as the world turns its attention to vocal harmony in a way that is utterly unprecedented. My experiences with mass-media vocal harmony began on *The Sing-Off* on NBC, where it was my role to oversee all the performances. There, I quickly realized that each group's competition wasn't the other groups; it was 199 other channels of television plus everything on the internet. I had to ensure that each performance by each group was so powerful and compelling that people wouldn't wonder what was on the other channels.

It became clear, immediately, that we needed each group to find the truth in a song right away, and that no group could afford to sing music that wasn't true for them. A nineteen-year-old can't deliver "Still Crazy After All These Years" with anything approaching believability. Perhaps if the song is reworked and there's a level of irony or a greater meaning, it might be possible (never say never), but that's a high bar to clear, and most singers, especially amateur singers, are wise to stick to their lives, their experiences, their feelings, their reality.

Why? Because when you're performing, you're creating music for others. It's a gift, and that gift is rarely delivered under ideal circumstances. Perhaps you were first captivated by a particular song late at night, when the mood was just right and the music moved you to want to sing the song yourself. Later you will find yourself onstage needing to re-create that feeling in order for the music to have a message, to have validity. Did you choose a song that you have difficulty feeling, an emotion that eludes you when the circumstances change? Then you chose the wrong song.

Too often, groups don't consider this when choosing repertoire. "I like this song" is not the same as "People will want to hear me sing this song because I can make it my own" or even "Lots of people will be drawn to hear me sing this song, despite the countless other versions available to everyone everywhere."

This last point is important to remember: if you're going to sing "When I Was Your Man" by Bruno Mars, you first need to realize there are probably around one thousand different versions already strewn across the internet.

Twenty years ago, everyone was happy to hear your a cappella group sing "The Lion Sleeps Tonight," because it was likely the only version they'd hear an a cappella group sing all year. Now everyone has several versions at their fingertips, all day, every day—and they know it. To make your version stand out, to make your performance compelling, you have to be different. You have to be better. And to be better, you have to be honest.

Never before has it mattered so very much that music have a unique, powerful, transcendent quality driven by emotional integrity. Looking at it from the perspective of economic theory, supply is sky-high and rising daily, so as a result, demand is at an all-time low.

Yet there is always the demand for powerful, awe-inspiring music, there is always the demand for something new, and many people are just now discovering the power in an a cappella performance. The purity of unified expression unmediated by machines and technology—just voices and faces, harmonies and emotions—creates an impact that is simply unforgettable.

With apologies to the movie *Field of Dreams*, if you sing something honest and real and meaningful, they will come. Not always, not right away, but in time, you will build an audience of people who are eager to hear your next creation because they know that no matter what you deliver, you're delivering something real. You're saying something.

Singularity

> We are only as strong as we are united, as weak as we are divided.
>
> —J.K. Rowling

There is nothing more compelling than another person.

We spend our lives interacting with others, watching others, learning from others. With rare exception, the focus of almost every movie, book, story, and song is, in short, another person. We endlessly watch other faces, listen to other voices.

The human voice was the first instrument and remains the most powerful and effective method of musical creation and emotional transference. Certainly other instruments may exceed the human voice in range, but none can make you laugh or cry with the same immediacy.

Whether it be a military display or a marching band, the synchronicity of a group of people is also compelling, but for a different reason. We're awed by the precision of people moving and acting in concert. We are transfixed by the stories and emotions of others, we love the sound of the voice, and we're compelled when we see people acting as one. Put them all together, and you have vocal harmony; you have a cappella.

But for these elements to work together with maximum impact, every person needs to be expressing the same emotion at the same time.

An emotional singularity like this doesn't exist elsewhere. People marching in unison need only get their bodies synchronized. When actors share a scene together, each character has his or her own reaction and path, which generally differs from the others'. Moreover, the power of vocal music comes not from singers acting, but rather from their honest expression of themselves as themselves.

Herein lies perhaps the biggest challenge facing a choral director: How do you get all of your singers to feel and express in synchronicity while maintaining musical excellence? Unfortunately, the topic of emotional singularity is rarely addressed in rehearsals, in music rooms, in education. It is largely assumed that the people singing Beethoven's Ninth will feel joy when they sing about joy. The music is joyful, the lyrics are joyful, and you might occasionally have the director shout, "More joyful!" but that doesn't usually work any more than it works when a loved one tells you "stop feeling so _____ (insert any emotion)."

Perhaps a particular group wouldn't have difficulty expressing the joy of singing while onstage at the end of Beethoven's Ninth (it isn't hard to get swept up into the moment), but what about a wide-ranging concert program in which your group sings a dozen songs, one after another, each with a very different emotional story and journey, and no orchestra onstage playing one of classical music's most iconic celebrations? A solo singer-songwriter is more often than not well-versed at moving from one story to the next, but rarely are group harmony singers so deft. The result is a performance in which the efficacy of each song varies greatly, as your singers try to conjure moments as powerful as your best rehearsal, in rapid succession. It's a near-impossible task when left to chance and circumstance.

Every group is different, every song is different, every situation is different, and yet we can draw upon a variety of principles taken from a range of disciplines to help create a consistent emotional performance in your group, song after song.

SECTION II

Theoretical Techniques

Good arranging requires a deep musical vocabulary. Music theory is, of course, just a theory—an agreed-upon set of "rules" that were derived from excellent musical practices of the past, providing a useful set of guidelines and tools to help you craft your arrangements wisely, creatively, and effectively. In this section, we'll cover a number of arranging techniques that should be in the arsenal of every arranger.

But this is *A Cappella Arranging 2.0*, not a primer, so we'll assume that . . .

a) You're aware of these techniques already. We're not going to explain them entirely from scratch, but rather, take a deeper dive and offer specific written examples. There are many excellent music theory books and references online should you want or need to explore anything mentioned here even further.

b) You use some of these techniques already, but in a more natural, instinctive way, rather than a "studied" way. Perhaps you worked out these ideas in your own arranging practices, or from transcribing existing arrangements. We're fully of the mind that "natural" learning offers deeper and more meaningful insight to the individual; however, knowing the names, parameters, contexts, and principles behind various techniques can allow you to consciously recognize, access, and expand beyond what you've already "picked up" on the way.

c) You're familiar with these techniques primarily from an instrumental perspective. Perhaps you're an experienced arranger/orchestrator but don't specialize in working with voices, or when you have, you've treated the voices in a more choral manner. The explanations provided here will provide deeper insight into what works in a purely vocal context, informed by the best practices across the contemporary a cappella of the twentieth and now twenty-first centuries.

》 *Dylan and Deke Say: Though we both have extensive formal music education from fancy graduate schools, most of what we learn (and are still learning!) is experiential, "on the job" education. The formal education is a useful foundation, and it often fills in a few blanks, but we still consider ourselves largely self-taught. And while theory is useful and interesting, in the end, what works onstage or in the studio is what matters. A book of rules may teach you less than spending a weekend poring over great a cappella arrangements as you listen to recordings of them, then putting those ideas into practice.*

Let's jump in!

CHAPTER 4

Vocal Ranges and Additional Techniques

I n *A Cappella Arranging*, we offered some basic information on vocal ranges and "sweet spots." This is a good place to start, so here's what we said.

Vocal Range Conventions

First, a slew of disclaimers. The conventions listed here are just suggestions; for every one of them, you will find exceptions. These guidelines will suit you well if you don't know the voices you're writing for: stick to them and you pretty much guarantee that anyone will be able to sing your chart. For now, we'll assume you're writing for mixed voices: TTBB, SSAA, and other styles are explained in greater detail later in the book. Also, even though we've discussed the extreme range possibilities of the human voice, right now we are going to work within the standard range of choral singing, since many of the extended technique skills are specialized.

Next, some definitions. These assume amateur singers with a little training and experience. Professional singers will have a more developed voice, meaning a near-inaudible break, wider range, and wider sweet and power spots.

» *Full range*: represents safe extremes for each voice part.
» *Average range*: represents where you'll want to focus most of the writing; you can "dip" into higher and lower ranges, but you may not want to keep people outside the average range for very long, especially on the lower end if the voices aren't amplified.
» *Break:* varies greatly from singer to singer, but this represents a reasonable average. Singing up, down, around, or through the break often means changes in timbre. You may want to avoid this for a main melody part, for example, or you may want to exploit this timbre change, such as when arranging a

song by a singer who deliberately changes his or her voice over the break for a yodeling-like sound.

» *Sweet spot*: where a given voice part sounds most natural and lyrical; good for melodic writing.

» *Power spot*: where the voice starts to sound full to slightly strained in chest voice; good for a strong rock or pop lead, where the singer is typically at the top of his or her chest-voice range.

These timbral ranges are good to know since voice parts have quite a bit of crossover. What sounds sultry for an alto may sound bright and rockin' for a tenor; and what sounds sweet for a soprano may sound full and powerful for an alto. Knowing these differences means you can make artistic choices based on what sound you're after.

Soprano

» Full range:	G3–C6
» Average range:	C4–G5
» Break:	G4–B♭4 (some high sopranos will have a second, higher break around D4)
» Sweet spot:	G4–E5 (primarily in head voice)
» Power spot:	G4–D5 (chest voice)

Alto

» Full range:	F3–G5
» Average range:	G3–D5
» Break:	G4–A4 (some low altos and female tenors will have a second, lower break around A3–C4)
» Sweet spot:	C4–A4
» Power spot:	F4–C5

Tenor

» Full range:	A2–A4 (up to D5–E5 with falsetto)
» Average range:	C3–G4
» Break:	D4–F4
» Sweet spot:	G3–F4
» Power spot:	C4–G4

Bass

» Full range: D2–F4 (notes below F2 will require either amplification or lots of basses to come through)
» Average range: F2–C4
» Break: C4–D4 (lower basses may have a second, lower break around F2–G2)
» Sweet spot: A2–A3
» Power spot: F3–D4

You'll notice there are no definitions for "in-between" vocal parts, such as soprano 2, alto 2, or baritone. As a general rule, for the in-between parts, treat the average range as their full range, and leave the extreme ranges for the outer parts. You can also move the "average range" of these in-between parts down a third for soprano 2 and alto 2 and up a third for baritone.

These ranges are typical of standard singers, but if you find yourself dealing with professionals, you should get their specific ranges. For example, a rock tenor spends more time in what would be considered standard alto range than tenor range. In fact, plenty of pop music lives in the high tenor range for men and the alto range for women—essentially the same place—which is why women can sometimes sing along to the radio more effortlessly than men can.

This is certainly all true, but as you likely know, there's much more that can be said about voice parts, ranges, and "extended techniques" that we didn't cover in the first book.

Tenor/Alto Unison Blending

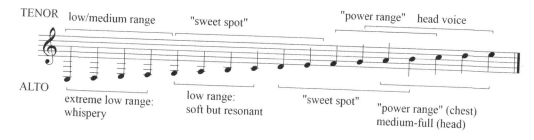

Blending two voices of differing types can offer a richness of tone not possible by blending similar voice types, and this can be used to extend or strengthen the potential vocal range of a given part.

Take, for example, an alto/tenor blend. This gives you a high changed voice, and a low unchanged voice, with plenty of overlap.

In the low-tenor range, an alto can "ghost" or whisper the notes, adding a breathy shimmer. In the mid-tenor range, the alto rounds out the increasingly bright tenor voice. In the upper-tenor chest range, the alto is reaching its own medium-range, usually with a solid tone and consistency. It can also smooth out the tenor's chest-to-head break, which may otherwise sound exposed and potentially fragile.

Conversely, in the alto's low range, the tenor voice adds support and strength. In the alto's midrange, a tenor voice can add edge and brilliance, if sung in chest voice, or a round resonance if sung in head voice. In the alto's upper range and/or over the alto's chest/head break, if the tenor has a well-developed head voice, the tenor can smooth out the alto break.

A mixed voice blend can work as a rich but complementary ensemble sound for a melodic line. It also works particularly well for a lead vocal line, especially if the original vocalist has an exceptionally wide range, but your singers do not. The two voice types can cover the vocal spread, with the extreme ranges of each voice "smoothed out" by the other. Many contemporary male vocal leads, for example, are in tenor to countertenor range, out of reach for the average tenor. A perfect example: Freddie Mercury's lead voice in "We Are the Champions" by Queen:

Using an alto/tenor blend makes the rock lead possible for an amateur group. Overall, an alto/tenor unison blend is a very flexible sound to consider in your arrangement.

Another way the contrast between the parts can be used is in juxtaposition. For instance, if you have a relentless eighth-note figure you need throughout a verse, it can be exhausting and quite boring for one voice part to sing it incessantly. Instead, consider having the alto and tenor lines alternate this vocal part, one measure (or two) of alto, then one or two measures of tenor, then alto again, then tenor again, and so on. The voice part not covering this line is free to sing anything else, and the boring, repetitive part ends up having much more subtle variety as the audience hears the change in texture as the parts alternate.

Soprano/Bass (or Tenor) Octave Doubling

Being at the opposite ends of the vocal spectrum, you don't generally have much crossover in range between soprano and bass . . . but they work well for octave doubling. This is a texture that works well in a few situations:

» For a bass/tenor lead, a soprano octave double, sung softly and in head voice, can add a subtle shine to the lower voice and help it cut through the mix. You often hear pop songs where the lead vocalist sings in octaves with him/herself, which is a lovely sound: this technique replicates that parallel vocal color in a different way.

» For a soprano lead, a bass/tenor octave double can add weight and breadth to the sound. If you want a subtle "octaver" effect, use a tenor voice: it can disappear into the blend more easily as it's more likely to be in a transparent midrange. If you want a fuller, edgier sound, try a bass voice: you're at the upper end of the bass range, so the sound will be brighter and project more. As an experienced arranger, you should be always considering a voice part's vocal color.

Extended Vocal Techniques

So far, everything we've discussed falls within the standard choral ranges and abilities you're likely familiar with. Now it's time to look at techniques beyond those found in your average choral handbook. Many of these are commonly used in the contemporary a cappella landscape, but having been more recently developed, and with fewer text resources (apart from our own!) discussing these in detail, they may be "under the radar" of many vocal arrangers. Some take extensive training, and we'll indicate them as such. Many are acquired skills that, with a little practice, are accessible to most singers. You may find that singers have picked up these techniques, and you simply weren't aware of them!

These don't constitute an exhaustive list, and they are generally useful in a contemporary a cappella setting. We won't describe the "how-to" in great depth: we are not experts, and the purpose here is not to teach these techniques, but rather to make the arranger aware that they exist as we offer suggestions as to how they can be best used.

Overtone Singing

This vocal technique can be found in music from eastern Asian areas such as Mongolia, Tuva, and Tibet, as well as other cultures, but it has spread across the world to be absorbed into contemporary vocal practice. There are a number of methods, but the one we'll discuss here can be achieved without any formal training and with a little practice.

If we think of the different sounds of vowels, from "oo" all the way to "ee," we describe them as "dark to bright": in a more technical sense, we can describe them as having fewer/lower overtones to more/higher overtones. These overtones can be focused even further. Start by singing a note to "oo," but with the tongue moved farther back than usual. To create higher overtones, move the tongue farther back so the sides (not the tip) are touching your back teeth. You may notice that the "oo" starts to sound more like an "rr," as in the word "burr." While doing this, purse the lips even tighter than a regular "oo," like when whistling. The process of doing this changes the shape of the cavity inside your mouth and accentuates different overtones. By moving the vocal tone and tongue farther down into the throat, you can alter the mix of the fundamental and the overtone. The experts can create an overtone far louder than the fundamental. For practice, try whistling: the way you change pitch when whistling is similar to the changes in the lips/mouth cavity for overtone singing.

In contemporary a cappella practice, this can have a few applications:

» *Ambient soundscapes*: overtone singing provides an ethereal, otherworldly effect to soundscapes as the overtones sit far beyond the expected range of the human voice.
» *Solo singers* may use this technique to create a wider sonic palette . . . or to represent two notes at once!
» *Representation of synthesizers and synth pads*: a common sound in synthesizers is the "filter sweep," moving through overtones from low to high, and vice versa. Start with the word "wow," which is really a rapid pronunciation of three consecutive vowels: "oo," "ah," and back to "oo." Slow the word down drastically (taking five to ten seconds to pass through all the vowel sounds in "wow") and focus on those vowels, and the many vowels you pass through between the two. There's your filter sweep. This can be done between any two vowels. "Wow" gives a low-to-medium sweep; "wee" gives higher overtones; and "aye" gives only medium-to-high overtones. While this is commonly achieved easily through the use of vowel smears, this is still a relatively conventional sound. The use of overtones adds an unexpected shine to the sound: if multiple singers overtone-sing, without attempting to synchronize their overtones, the result is a randomized "shimmer" that is nothing short of magical.

Once you start to consider overtone singing, you realize that, in essence, we're playing with overtones every time we make a vowel sound. You've probably also been aware of songs with a lot of a certain vowel sound in a lyric, and you leaned on that vowel or those specific lyrics in your background parts. This sounds good because not only do the fundamental pitches you've written sound good together, but the overtones of these aligned vowels are similarly aligned.

Undertone Singing

This is another extended vocal technique found in eastern Asia. There are multiple techniques that can be used to create a pitch lower than you could normally sing, but we'll describe the simplest one:

You've likely heard of "vocal fry." It's that gravelly sound your voice may have in the morning, or that you're hearing more often when people are speaking at the bottom of their vocal range. One notable example is the voice of Dr. Claw, Inspector Gadget's nemesis (although there have been multiple voice actors, they all live down in that low, choppy/creaky vocal basement). Kurt Cobain used vocal fry when singing; Britney Spears often does, as well; and Kim Kardashian is famous for using it when speaking. It's the "edgy" sound you hear many pop singers use when they start a phrase, and the sound that every vocal coach (including us!) tells you is terrible for you and that you should avoid as much as possible. Well, we can use it here, and if done right and used sparingly, it isn't damaging.

Undertone singing involves relaxing your vocal cords so that they also vibrate an octave below the note you're singing. This usually involves a single note only in your mid-lower range, similar to a drone. Place the tone a little farther down the throat than usual and relax the throat. You may feel the vocal fry "catch" and create the octave below. With practice, you can keep this undertone going.

Further to this, additional overtones can be added by manipulating the vocal cavity. In the previous overtone example, pursing the lips gave high-pitched, "whistling" harmonics. In this technique, the harmonics are an octave or two lower: instead of pursing the lips, shaping the mouth in various vowel shapes from a dark "oo" to a bright "ay" will accentuate lower and higher harmonics respectively.

Undertone singing can add a primal, exciting sound to your tonal palette as an arranger. To learn more about over/undertone singing, and to hear it in various contexts, try the "Overtone Music Network" at https://www.overtone.cc.

Buzz-Bass

Once a fringe technique, buzz-bass is increasingly heard in professional pop a cappella groups. It is practiced primarily by beatboxers who use it to re-create low synth bass lines as well as other musical effects, as well as bass singers (both changed and unchanged voices) looking to extend their vocal range.

The technique involves buzzing the lips, similar to a brass player, but tuning the buzz more precisely to create a low but audible pitch. The buzz should be relaxed, but not so loose that the result is rapid fluttering instead of an audible pitch: think of the embouchure of a tuba player, and you'll have a good starting point. At first, the buzzing range will be limited to a few notes, which can be useful as occasional "bass bombs" or accents, but over time, the range and accuracy improves until a whole bass line can be buzzed. The effect, when amplified and sent into subwoofers, is dramatic, like the drop in a dubstep track: *BOOM!*

Buzz-Bass, *plus Humming*

This addition to the buzz-bass creates a two-tone effect. The humming is generally done in falsetto, farther back in the throat than usual. Why? The placement for normal humming occurs in the front of the face, beneath the nose and behind the lips, but since this conflicts directly with the buzzing lips, it's nearly impossible to do both. A falsetto/back-placement approach is the only way to consistently control both the low and the high notes.

Depending on the relationship of the hummed pitch to the buzzed pitch, this can have different effects:

» An inharmonic relationship gives a sound like a brash lead synth, often found in industrial, techno, and other electronic styles of music. This is a common sound in the beatboxer's palette.

» A harmonic relationship can either function as an overtone-accentuation of the bass note, or even as a consonant harmony (octaves, fifths, and occasionally thirds sound best, with the low, buzzed note on the tonic). An early example is Bobby McFerrin's live version of the song "Drive," where he harmonizes with himself by buzzing a bass riff and humming a third (plus a couple of octaves) above.

To hear this in action, simply search online for beatboxing demonstrations or solo beatboxing sets from competitions.

Beat-Bass

This is simply what it sounds like: the bass singer sings a bass line and covers VP simultaneously. This is a common performance practice, especially for bass singers in small ensembles or songs where there is no dedicated vocal percussionist.

To make this work, the percussion part is usually reduced to a simple kick-and-snare pattern, with the bass humming parts of the bass line "behind" the front of the face, which is handling the kick-and-snare sounds.

This can be used in arranging in several ways:

» *It frees up a voice.* It's a common assumption that VP requires a dedicated voice/person to cover the groove. By recognizing that, in many cases, the bass can handle both, you're now one voice "richer."

» *It allows for a "dynamic allocation" of VP in a song.* Need an extra voice for one chorus? Let the bass singer beat-bass for a section and use your VP singer as an extra voice.

» *It allows for multiple layers of VP.* Let the beat-bass handle the basic downbeat/backbeat, kick-and-snare pattern, and give your dedicated VP an extra, detailed layer of percussion.

There are a few parameters that will help you make the most of this.

A kick and bass note, simultaneously, is easy: a standard "Dm" bass syllable becomes "Bm," with a harder plosive to cover the kick articulation when amplified (as that plosive attack—the puff of air—hitting the microphone diaphragm is what gets amplified and replicates the sound of the foot pedal hitting the kick drum).

A snare and bass note, simultaneously, is more difficult as the articulation of the snare is more involved. A "forward" (plosive) snare requires a tight squeeze and release of the embouchure: no room for the bass note to come out. A "backward" (in-breath) snare leaves the bass note "in the throat" without resonating well. In both cases, the effect is that the bass note sounds delayed behind the articulation of the snare. This works with either the more traditional rock-and-roll "pf" snare or more modern sampled-sounding "k" snare.

This can be dealt with in a couple of ways, depending on the style of the music.

In rock, pop, funk, and other contemporary genres, the bass line can be written or modified to avoid the backbeat. Here's an example of a rock-style, steady-eighth-note bass line. A delayed-sounding bass note on the backbeat would ruin the drive of the line, so the bass note on the downbeat is simply removed.

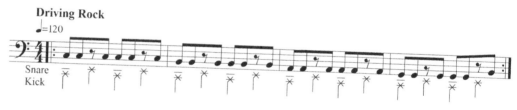

In R&B, funk, and soul, the bass line is often rhythmically active and exciting, and "dances" around the kick and snare. Leaving the backbeat out sounds just as good and even enhances the interplay between bass and drums: this is very helpful when the bassist and drummer are the same person! Here's an example of an R&B/funk bass line working around the backbeat.

In EDM (electronic dance music), the delayed-bass "problem" is not only acceptable; it is part of the style of the music. EDM gets much of its pulsing rhythm from the use of compression on the main mix, side-chained to the kick (and sometimes snare) drum. In layperson's terms, the kick drum "stomps" on everything else, which quickly pulses back up to its usual volume (giving that characteristic "mm-WUH-mm-WUH" sound). This effect occurs naturally in beat-bass: in fact, the singer may accentuate that effect even more.

Pitched Inhale

If you gasp audibly and loudly, you've just done a pitched inhale. This can be used to musical effect, as well. It's particularly useful for a solo singer or very small ensemble where you don't want the sonic continuity interrupted with a prolonged breath. It can give an almost "circular breathing" effect, as the singer can sing at length without the listener hearing the breath as a gap in the sound.

To try this technique, start with a long, loud, audible gasp: imagine a dramatic plot twist in a movie. The sound you made will probably be in your head voice, somewhat gritty-sounding, and fairly wild in pitch. Now try the same, but at a fraction of the intensity. Now you've got a soft, light head-tone. Practice this a few times and eventually you'll get control over the pitch. It's usually best used for a single, relatively quick note at a time.

The master of this technique is Bobby McFerrin, and it allows him to sing long, self-accompanying phrases without pausing. Here's an example of how he uses it:

Vocal drummers use a similar technique all the time: in their case, the breath is unpitched but used as an inward-breathing hi-hat, or the sound of a DJ scratching (as used by Darren Robinson, a.k.a. the Human Beat Box of the Fat Boys).

Humming and Whistling

You don't hear it often, but it's quite useful, and surprisingly not too difficult. It's another technique especially helpful for solo singers, duos, or trios to add an additional note to the sound. We use the term *humming* since there's no words/syllables, but since your lips are pursed for whistling, the vocal tone is actually somewhere between a hum and an "oo" vowel.

Start with humming, somewhere in the lower-middle of your register. Then, purse your lips. If you know how to whistle, you'll realize that—though you probably never really thought about it this way—the pitch of the whistle is controlled, but the shape of the mouth cavity and placement of the tongue is similar to the "whistle-style" overtone singing described earlier. Now, while humming a single long tone, try whistling a few notes. Some notes will resonate more than others: these are likely harmonics of the note you're humming. When you find one of these resonant notes, say, a third, try moving the hum and "taking the whistle with you," up and down a few notes of a scale. Now you've got parallel harmony! You might sound like a flying saucer/UFO initially as you slide around in an attempt to control both your humming and whistling pitch together, but you'll get the hang of it before too long.

Here's an example of this in use, from FreePlay's version of Bill Withers's "Just the Two of Us." The bridge has some nice jazzy harmonies normally out of reach for two voices . . . but possible with the whistle as the third note.

The most surprising thing is that the hum and whistle don't conflict with each other much and can be controlled independently. With enough practice, it's even possible to hum/whistle a Bach minuet!

» *Dylan Says: I learned how to create a "Leslie" tremolo effect, like a Hammond organ, by humming and singing. I could find an overtone and create the tremolo by fluttering my lips a bit. I even learned how to create the "on/off" effect of the tremolo speeding up and slowing down the lip-flutter (#acapellanerd).*

Given that these techniques are not in common use, you may not find yourself using them for generic "off the rack" charts meant for mass consumption. But if you're looking for extra sounds beyond the norm, these techniques can open up exciting new sonic possibilities for your group.

CHAPTER 5

Counterpoint, Polyphony, and Two-Voice Writing

Those of you with formal Western musical training may harken back to the dry and methodical practice of writing of two- and three-voice exercises, memorizing dull rules, and avoiding the dreaded parallel fifths. You're among friends in the twenty-first century now, and we can safely say: you can brush those notions aside. Instead, we'll explain where these traditional classical practices and techniques can be useful in modern a cappella writing, and how they can offer up fresh ways of writing parts.

But What about *The Rules*?

You are familiar by now with our approach to so-called Rules, which range from, "Sure, but . . ." to "Rules? What rules?" In our previous book, we stated, "There are no rules, only contexts," and we stand by this. What doesn't work in one situation may work perfectly well in another. If this strikes you as arrogant, or ignorant, or simply rubs you the wrong way, let us remind you that music theory is the collective accumulation of knowledge that came from studying great music, with the intent of figuring out what is and isn't a good/successful technique, and then codifying these takeaways into a set of "rules" that composers could use to make their music better. There is value to this practice as a learning exercise, but the most innovative composers didn't follow rules, or if they did, they found ways to break them, which led to new, updated rules as music evolved. Student composers who follow music theory mindlessly may find their music to be formulaic and without character, and the same could be said of arrangers. We want you to understand where these theoretical best practices were born, where they can be best used, and when they'll get in your way.

Before jumping into the where and how-to of using these techniques in modern writing, let's quickly examine a few "rules" of counterpoint and polyphony and see what still applies to modern music, and what can be set aside . . . or, at least, be taken with a grain of salt.

Rule #1: *Lines must start and end on "perfect" intervals (unison, octave, fourth, fifth).*

The spirit of this is well-intended. Western music has traditionally been predicated on the idea of "motion and rest" or "tension and release." You could expand this outward to other art forms that tell a story. Cinema, theater, and novels typically start from a static place, something happens, that thing gets resolved, and the story is over. This is the canonical Hero's Journey, as elucidated by Joseph Campbell. It's so baked into Western ideas of mythology and storytelling that it makes its way into music, not only in the macro sense (for example, a song beginning and ending on the tonic chord), but also in the micro sense (musical phrases beginning and ending with "resolution," or in the sonic sense, consonance).

Let's imagine that, for now, we're not looking to upend hundreds of years of listeners' expectations. That said, let's also update our sense of "consonance."

Back when polyphonic music was in its heyday, "consonant" or stable intervals were perfect intervals. A third was considered unstable, an inappropriate place to end a phrase. Put another way, melodic lines were supposed to "come back together" toward a stable, perfect interval. Octaves and unisons achieve this, but so do fourths and fifths: their simple intervallic ratios (3:2 and 4:3, respectively) mean the two sounds practically "melt together" into one. Resolution achieved.

In the several hundred years since, and especially in the last one hundred or so years with the extension of harmony in genres such as jazz, or the demolition of harmony in atonal music, our collective definition of "stable" intervals has expanded considerably. No one hears two voices in harmony, singing in thirds and sixths, and shouts out, "It's too unstable! Please resolve that!" if they end on a sweet-sounding harmony: if that happened, Simon and Garfunkel and the Everly Brothers wouldn't have had much of a career. Add jazz into the mix, and the "accepted-as-stable" intervals keep piling up: songs and phrases may regularly end on just about any upper partial without offending the ear.

So, with this in mind, we can redefine our rule that "lines must start and end on perfect intervals" to something like "lines must start and end on something that sounds nice"—assuming that "nice" is what you're going for, and it won't always be. It wouldn't make much sense if Ives's "Unanswered Question" resolved conclusively on a tonic chord. Paul McCartney's "Silly Love Songs" ends unresolved on the line "and what's wrong with that?"; the Killers' "Mr. Brightside" ends on a IV chord with the lyric "I never"; and the list goes on. Better rule: end the song in the way the song is best ended, resolved or not.

Let's try this next traditional rule on for size:

Rule #2: *Avoid parallel fourths and fifths at all costs.*

Of all the rules about writing harmony, this one probably stuck with you more than any other rule. Quick . . . can you tell us why we have to avoid them?

Again, the spirit of the rule is valid. The general goal of good counterpoint could be summarized simply as "two or more independently functioning voices that sound good together." When two of those voices start running beside each other in lockstep parallel fourths/fifths, the two voices begin to be perceived as one thing, not two. Parallel octaves are a very obvious example of this, and parallel fifths are their frequently misunderstood sibling. With parallel octaves or fifths, your independent lines seem more like "codependent lines," and that richly woven texture momentarily thins out.

Imagine weaving a multicolored tapestry—a real one, not a sonic one. The tapestry probably looks best when all the colors are independent of each other: weave two primary colors together for too long, and the complexity is diminished. Your nuanced color scheme now has a big blotch of blue in the middle.

So, why are parallel thirds acceptable?

This goes back to overtones and ratios. The simple ratios and relationships in fourths and fifths means that the notes "fold into" each other so tightly that they can sound like one note. In fact, since fifths sit so low on the overtone series, the fifth above may just be heard as an overtone of the bottom note. A fourth can suggest a sub-fundamental below. This is the principle behind the sound of organ stops, for example: by layering multiple pipes/notes that line up in the harmonic series, we create one big, complex note instead. And consider that the church organ would have been a common instrument back when these rules were being formulated: on an organ, parallel fourths/fifths may be easily mistaken for a single note.

Thirds, on the other hand, have more complex ratios (5:4 for major, 6:5 for minor), and they are generally perceived as two distinct pitches. Moreover, in any sort of diatonic line, you're likely alternating between major and minor thirds: the intervals are continually changing and therefore stay distinct.

There's the "why." Should we still follow this rule?

If you're looking for a continuous texture without any thinning out, then yes, follow the rule. But perhaps it doesn't matter, or you'd like to use the thinning-and-thickening of texture for a deliberate effect. If so, a run of parallel fourths/fifths can thin out the texture, or even draw attention to itself in an interesting way.

It's also worth noting that, in "free counterpoint," many composers played pretty fast and loose with these rules themselves. And we're no longer in a musical landscape where we're listening to just a few voices as independent lines, but instead we hear a wall of sound, many layers that will vary in complexity as well as timbre throughout the song, with a distinct lead vocal over the top. This rule makes more sense in a style like Dixieland jazz, where it's more exciting and interesting to have the clarinet and trumpet weaving their own lines, but when it comes to rock and roll, it's just fine if Jimmy Page (of Led Zeppelin) or Billie Joe Armstrong (of Green Day) play power chords—open fifths—on their guitars.

This next one's not a rule, but rather a misconception:

Rule #3: *Polyphony and counterpoint are based on, and sound like, early church music.*

They can, but they don't have to. Consider the instrumental interlude in the Beatles' classic "In My Life":

It adds a Baroque flourish to a pop song, just as we expect. The fact that it's played on electric harpsichord only reinforces this. Now try this example:

Note the complex interweaving of voices and the rhythmic interplay. Do you recognize it?

That's right . . . it's Sly and the Family Stone: 1960s funk.

The "voices" are, from top to bottom, lead vocal, guitar, and bass. We'd like to think that Palestrina would have liked this.

Polyphony didn't come from the Western church tradition: it is found in musical traditions all over the world. The example above, like much funk polyphony, is drawn from western African musical traditions.

Now that we've liberated ourselves from some restrictive ideas of what polyphony is and how it should work, let's look at ways in which it can work.

Two-Voice Writing

This one may be obvious, but it's a good place to start. Whether you intend to or not, you'll likely end up using some two-part counterpoint in two-voice writing.
For variety, it can work well to mix and match techniques every four bars or so. In this example, from Don McLean's beautiful ballad "Vincent," as performed by FreePlay, the verses are sung in note-against-note parallel sixths and thirds.

Vincent

Don McLean

To introduce a new texture, the chorus is sung in responsive polyphony.

Here, in Charlie Chaplin's "Smile," FreePlay starts in parallel sixths, then switches to contrary motion for the following phrase. Note that one of the "rules" is broken for deliberate effect: instead of ending on a consonant interval, the phrase ends on a major second, to accentuate the sadness in the line "Smile, what's the use in crying?"

Smile

Chaplin/Turner/Parsons

In this example, from Edvard Grieg's "Anitra's Dance," contrary motion is taken to extremes. Whereas the most academic form of species counterpoint demands no more than a tenth between parts, FreePlay's counterpoint stretches this to three octaves!

Anitra's Dance

Edvard Grieg

For a long-form examination of two-voice writing, as well as more advanced two-voice writing techniques, see the end of this chapter, where this arrangement of "Anitra's Dance" is analyzed in its entirety.

Interlocking/Textured BGs

Polyphonic BGs are a great way to create a sense of depth and texture, particularly if you're looking for something without a defined sense of groove, but still in time.

In FreePlay's arrangement of Neil Young's "Old Man," the intention was to take the original, bouncy folk-guitar part and reimagine it as a floating "spinning wheel," in-time but not groove-based. To do this, they created two responsive parts, which, between them, both outline the minor-major shift in the original guitar part and keep the wheel spinning with responsive movement in both parts.

Old Man

Neil Young

The soprano line is sung in a cross-rhythm of six sixteenths over the ten beats, resolving on beat four of the second bar of the pattern. The bass part is sung in a cross-rhythm of five sixteenths, resolving just before the final beat of the two-bar pattern, meaning the two parts whirl around each other in rhythmic as well as melodic counterpoint.

You can also extend this further to the use of canonic and semi-fugal lines. Later in the same song, a melodic/lyric fragment, "I'm a lot like you were," becomes a sort of theme, or "thesis," for the second verse. This fragment is sung in multiple duets, and one single voice, to create a rich, seven-voice texture. The canonic structure gives it a constant "rolling" effect. Underneath this texture, the bass and drums keep the original drive and groove, the acoustic picking-guitar parts roll gently on, and the lead voice can float, giving the whole section a dreamlike feel. (Note: guitar and lead are not notated here, just the contrapuntal voices and bass line.)

Note another "broken rule": many of these parts are sung in near-parallel fifths. This is used for deliberate effect, as mentioned earlier, as an unconventional possibility. Instead of seven-part polyphony, we have "four-part, harmonized" polyphony: each pair of voices in parallel fifths enriches the harmonic context, but it sounds like one texture rather than two.

Another good time to use counterpoint is to get yourself out of a jam, when what you have won't work. When arranging "Bohemian Rhapsody" for choir back in the 1990s with Anne Raugh, it just wouldn't have worked to have the sopranos, altos, tenors, or basses mimic the guitar solo. It would have been too campy, and that wasn't our desire at all. So instead, the guitar solo that comes before the "I see a little silhouette" section needed a new direction, and making it a contrapuntal choral passage felt right.

Bohemian Rhapsody

It's not in keeping with the original choice that Queen made, but that song changes styles repeatedly, including quasi-classical operatic techniques, and this leaned into something a choir does well. We kept the same chord progression, and the sum total of the interwoven lines told the same characteristic melodic story as Brian May's original guitar solo.

Another thing to consider is that a two-part contrapuntal line can be expanded into a full harmonic part, as Deke did when arranging the end of "Mr. Blue Sky" as an opening number for season two of *The Sing-Off* (United States):

Mister Blue Sky

You might consider this, at its core, to be a three-part counterpoint: the top soprano part, the top tenor part, and the bass line. The soprano part is that soprano line harmonized, the tenor line is the tenor countermelody harmonized, and the bass line outlines the harmonic structure. The alto is chugging away as violins or a harpsichord might. The result is something that feels both contrapuntal and rich, as there are in sum total as many as ten parts happening at once.

Now might be a good time to point out that the human brain can't really parse ten different independent vocal lines at the same time as they all move independently. To this end, the lesson of parallel octaves and fifths can be used to our benefit: by creating parallel block harmonies that move as a unit, we can have both a full, dense sound and a single unit that can be heard as such to listeners. You're, of course, welcome to make your arrangements as complex as you'd like, but if you follow the adage that you should never make anything more difficult to learn and remember than it has to be, keep your writing to something that's impactful without being more than is needed.

"Polyphonic Ostinati": Gospel Choir

Though largely three-part homophonic, a polyphonic repetitive section is a common and interesting convention used in gospel choral music. It takes the form of a "breakdown," after a high point in homophonic singing. The breakdown marks the start of the polyphonic ostinati. Each part will have a short musical phrase taken from the melody or developed from it in some way. The phrase is usually two to four bars long, and repeated. The parts are layered in one by one, building the song back up in dynamic and energy.

Below is an example of a polyphonic ostinato, from the gospel standard "Amazing Grace."

Breakdown: add handclaps

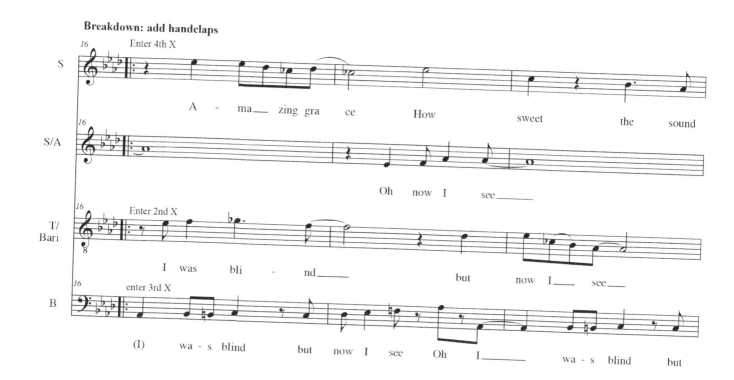

Repeat Ad Lib.

This technique can be used to:

» Give a gospel arrangement something exciting but well within the stylistic parameters of the genre.
» Give a non-gospel piece an additional energetic arc.

"Polyphonic Ostinati": Pop, Rock, and R&B

Sometimes the form of a pop song isn't exactly what will work for your a cappella group, which is what Deke found when arranging "Signed, Sealed, Delivered (I'm Yours)" for the Tufts Beelzebubs. Stevie Wonder can ad-lib over the introduction of the song and lend it immense energy and variety, but when a group of collegiate guys is given the task, unless you happen to have an incredible improvisor in the ranks, the result will fall short.

Enter the polyphonic breakdown. For this moment Deke stripped the song down to a bare four-part figure . . .

Signed, Sealed, Delivered I'm Yours

. . . then slowly made each line more full, more complex, until the last time through, each part had filled out to:

The excitement here is not in one person's virtuosic singing, but in having the audience hear the increasing complexity and interwoven alignment of these four vocal parts, until it launches back into the last verse and chorus (which you can see is led by the lyric in the Tenor 1 part: "I've done a lot of foolish things . . .").

The key to this kind of writing is to write both forward and backward, from the figure you'd like to start with and the one you'd like to end with, adding to the former and subtracting from the latter until you can meet in the middle with a musical "golden spike." You may need to tweak one or the other so you end up with a figure that can start very sparse and eventually build to a full and compelling contrapuntal figure. Can the parts align at times? Of course. Can you write in parallel motion? Why not? What's the guiding principle? As always: whatever can be sung well by your singers, and in sum total sounds great. Don't worry about adhering to any set of rules or era, using anything you studied as a tool instead of a boundary.

"Polyphonic Ostinati": Medleys and Mashups

This idea can be developed further for use in mashups and medleys. In this case, the polyphonic ostinati are used, similar to the gospel example above, but pieces of several (or all) of the songs in the medley are woven in.

The example below comes from the "Michael Jackson Dance Medley" performed by the Canadian "Top 40 of the 1980s" a cappella tribute band Retrocity.

Breakdown and Audience Participation/Mashup

Open repeat between entries as needed. Order of entry:

- break down to VP
- T3 brings in "PYT". Add in Bass after one repeat
- S2/A1 brings in "Workin'"
- S1/T1 brings in "Don't Stop"
- last line: S1/T1 "Don't stop till you get enough" to end

MJ Dance Medley

This excerpt combines all three songs from the medley: "Don't Stop 'Til You Get Enough," "Working Day and Night," and "P.Y.T. (Pretty Young Thing)."

Combining pieces from three different songs can be challenging as they may have different tempi and harmonic structures. In this case, the chord changes are taken from the chorus of "P.Y.T." The song itself is in B minor, with the chorus in a somewhat-neutral-sounding E minor. The excerpt from "Working Day and Night" is in E minor, but the melodic material, with no clear minor third, can work well in an E minor or B minor harmonic space. The excerpt from "Don't Stop 'Til You Get Enough," however, is in B major. In order to make this work, an excerpt had to be chosen that didn't clearly outline a B major tonal center: this would clash with the E minor/B minor material. The excerpt chosen contains the notes F♯-A-B-C♯. This works well in all three key centers: B major or minor (fifth, minor seventh, tonic, ninth, with no third) and E minor (ninth, eleventh, fifth, major sixth, with no third). The tempo for "P.Y.T." is between the tempi of "Don't Stop 'Til You Get Enough" (which is slower) and "Working Day and Night" (which is faster), and makes for a reasonable compromise.

Using polyphonic ostinati is a great to way to "sum up" the medley: rather than ending with just the last song, it recaps all of them. As an added bonus, if you choose the right excerpts of songs, this makes for an excellent audience participation device. Starting with a breakdown, each part can be taught to a section of the audience, repeated *ad libitum*, and even sung by the audience alone. It's a great way to bring the medley—or even a concert set—home with a bang. For more on writing mashups and medleys in general, see chapter 15, "Medleys and Mashups."

This isn't your music professor's polyphony: in fact, we're stretching the definition somewhat beyond what most people would expect. But in doing so, we expand both the idea of what polyphony is and the myriad possibilities it offers in modern arranging techniques.

Two-Voiced Writing Example: "Anitra's Dance" (Dylan)

FreePlay is a duo of Suba Sankaran, an alto with extended range from tenor to soprano, and myself, a tenor with extended range from bass/baritone to alto. As mentioned in chapter 4, "Vocal Ranges and Additional Techniques," this is an ideal combination of voices, with plenty of crossover range for unisons and close harmonies, but enough collective range (in our case, over four octaves) to cover a wide, SATB-style vocal range. Our specialty in live performance is in creating complex, multilayered live-looping creations, but for programmatic variety, we often sing straightforward two-voice arrangements.

FreePlay's two-voice version of "Anitra's Dance" came about when we were asked to come up with a "classical-meets-jazz" piece for a themed concert. When choosing a piece, we wanted something familiar but not overdone. Bach was a natural choice (and we love Bach), but much of his work has been done to death: other interesting pieces, such as Tchaikovsky's *Nutcracker Suite*, posed a similar problem. We settled on this piece from Edvard Grieg's *Peer Gynt Suite*. The music from *Peer Gynt* is generally familiar—especially the iconic "Hall of the Mountain King" as popularized in Disney's *Fantasia*—but "Anitra's Dance" is more of a B-side. So far, so good.

Our goal was not to reinvent this piece: apart from giving it a jazz feel, we chose to follow the original more or less faithfully. The biggest initial challenge was to take a fully orchestrated work and represent it with just two voices. To start, we found a piano reduction of the piece, which made it much easier to extract the essential harmonies. Then, we went through the piece, section by section, to figure out how to create the best representation of melody and harmony. We'll typically take one four- or eight-bar section, sit at the piano for reference, and slowly work out individual parts based on a combination of who covers what, and what is technically reasonable to execute. There's no point in writing something gymnastic if you can't get the notes out properly! The process goes like this:

1. Play a section several times to work out the melody and harmonies. This might mean playing a recording, or playing a piano reduction. Suba and I often work this out where I play the left hand, and she plays the right. It gives each of us a sense of what our voices might cover, and it's easier than sightreading alone!

2. Split it into three "layers": melody, harmony, and bass notes. Depending on the music, harmony-and-bass might just be one and the same. But thinking of it in three layers means that the "third layer" can be assigned to either voice, often switching throughout.

3. Assign the parts. More often than not, there's one melody singer and one person covering harmony/bass. But not always. If the bass part is clear enough, it may outline the harmony well and not require any additional thought. Very often, a harmony part can be sung without a bass part, and the listener fills in the gaps . . . or the root notes may show up in the melody, in which case a bass part isn't needed. If the melody has enough spaces, the melody singer can throw in an occasional bass note or harmony in between phrases. Find the combination that works best in this particular section.

4. Fine-tune the harmonies. With two voices to cover harmonies that usually require three or more notes to sound complete, you're always making choices. Keep the third and drop the fifth? Jam in as many harmonies as possible, or keep it simple for the listener's ear, and let the melody do the work? This will take a little time and will be determined partly by some theoretical knowledge of harmony and voice-leading, but mostly by your ear, and the technical vocal facility needed to execute the parts you're trying to cover.

5. Practice, practice, practice. Run the section many times in a row. You may find, as you do so, that you intended on one particular harmony, but your voice either can't find it or it naturally slips into another harmony. If so, your voice may be telling you something. Follow the "Rule of Three" (or five, or ten, if you prefer): if you can't get it right after three/five/ten attempts, perhaps it's not working. Go where your instincts tell you: as you're practicing, you're also imprinting the part, and if you really want it to stick, go with what works

best for your voice and ears, not what looks best on paper. You may break a few Rules in the process, but if you've read this far into the chapter, you're probably not too concerned.

6. Record the section you just worked out. By the time you do a few sections in a row, you may very well forget what you worked on just a half hour before! Save yourself the head-scratching "what did we do again?" moments, and record voice memos as you go.

7. Move on to the next section, and repeat the whole process.

Writing for two voices is typically more of an experimental, hands-on approach to arranging rather than a score-writing exercise. More often than not, FreePlay doesn't notate our arrangements, unless we do so afterward for posterity or memory. Also, if you're writing for two voices, you're likely arranging for yourselves, or possibly a group you know very well: this allows you to use a less "off the rack" approach and instead take advantage of the unique skill sets of your singers. If you're writing for your own duo, you'll likely want to do this with your singing partner, not alone: they'll find things with their voice you may not have come up with, and they'll learn it much better if they created their own part with you.

So, let's jump in. The full score is found at Appendix B, and as with most examples in this book, a link to the recording can be found in Appendix C.

The beginning of "Anitra's Dance" (mm. 1–8) starts with a simple four-bar accompaniment pattern, repeated twice, to set up the piece: a pedal bass, and two parts covering harmonies that establish the overall tonality. Here, it's important to cover both bass notes and the harmony: not only is it better functionally, but it also establishes a faithful rendition of the work. To do this, I sing "McFerrin-style," covering the bass notes and leaping up to sing the bottom of the harmonies. The leaps are anywhere between an octave and an eleventh, but at least the bottom note is the same each time, making it a little easier to execute. It takes a lot of practice to get this accurate: Bobby McFerrin reputedly spent about six years practicing this technique before bursting on the scene as a solo a cappella superstar. But for solo or two-voice performances, it's an essential skill. Suba covers the top notes of the harmonies before launching into the melody, picking up to m. 9.

From m. 9 to m. 12, Suba covers the melody, and I sing a walking bass. This establishes the jazz flavor, and the walking bass provides enough harmony that a separate layer isn't necessary. That said, note that in beats 2 and 3 of mm. 10–11, my bass line follows the melody in parallel sixths. This fills two roles: we keep the flavor of the walking bass, but we also have some continuity with the accompaniment pattern established in the opening, and that remains throughout this section in the orchestral version.

In mm. 13–16, Suba's melody goes from a fairly scalar shape to something with a more angular melodic arc, and also more harmonic complexity. My part needs to support this, so I transition from a walking bass into something closer to the McFerrin-style technique of the intro. The new harmonies are interesting and unfamiliar, and they deserve to be highlighted: to do this, I sing the first new colors in close harmony thirds with the melody in mm. 13–14, followed by parallel sixths in mm. 15–16 as the melody and harmony invert. Also, in m. 14, we have a great example of representing a four-note chord, B7. Suba's melody covers the dominant flavor with D♯-A-D♯ (third and seventh, the notes commonly used in jazz "shell voicings"), while I sing B-F♯-A in the same rhythm, giving a strong root note on beat one, and ending with a nice third-seventh diad with Suba to clearly spell out the chord.

The next eight bars (mm. 17–24) represented a challenge that took us some time to work out until Suba came up with a clever solution. The original orchestral/piano parts are all in unison, and they look like this:

First of all, with all those descending chromatics and the relentless leap back up to the B, it's really hard to sing accurately. Second, collapsing to unisons at this point just didn't feel right. But Suba observed that the top note is essentially a "soprano pedal," so we broke up the part: I sing the pedal but as a bass, and Suba covers just the descending chromatics without having to keep jumping back up. The result is this:

Apart from being much easier to sing, it also emphasizes the jazz angle we were going for. The bass pedal is a nice jazz convention, and the dotted-quarter cross-rhythm emphasizes the two-against-three rhythm in the original in a much stronger way. Win-win! We also added a variation in the bass part to give it a nice jazz (and contrapuntal) twist: after two bars of unison (mm. 15–16), instead of continuing with Suba in note-for-note unison in mm. 17–18, Suba sings an E-minor scale ascending, while I sing an E-minor pentatonic scale descending, ending on a unison, three octaves apart.

After this is a straight repeat, with Suba adding a few ornaments for variety.

It's worth noting at this point that our "sound/syllable palette" is quite limited: mostly neutral sounds like "doo/doot" and "bah." Some people love the use of different syllables and consider it a part of their arranging creativity, but in this case, it's not really useful. Here's why.

» *We're not imitating instruments.* "Zhing-jenna-joe" is great when you're imitating guitars, and "weeeooooorrrrrnnnn" might be a nice synth sweep, but this music is about the notes, not the tone colors. The beauty is in the melody and harmony, not in some cool sound from a record that needs to be replicated.

» *Accuracy is everything.* This music is harmonically and technically complex, and with only two people, there's little room for error in pitching. There's no strength in numbers here! A lot of "creative syllables" involve dipthongs (which can be hard to tune as the vowel sound shifts) or unusual consonants (which can make the note "onset," and therefore the perception of pitch, shaky). You'll notice that the syllables we chose have little to no diphthong, and simple "d" and "b" consonants that don't interfere with note-onset. It's all about the pure note.

For more on these two particular techniques, see the section on The Swingles in chapter 14, "Around the World: Vocal Sampling, The Swingles, Rajaton, Ladysmith Black Mambazo."

More on note accuracy in two-part writing. As mentioned earlier, with two voices, we're often trying to represent three- or four-note harmony with only two notes. Sometimes this involves "spelling out" the chord in a fairly rapid, semi-arpeggiated way, such as the example at mm. 15–16 referenced earlier. Sometimes it involves rapid color shifts: in mm. 13–16, we're moving from Am♭6-B/A-Am♭6-B7. That's a lot of harmonic ground to cover in a short amount of time. The notes go by fast, and as such, there's no time for the pitch to "settle." The listener's ear needs a little time to recognize the notes, and if the note is still settling, the pitch/harmony will be unclear, and the listener, with no other notes to contextualize, won't hear the harmony as it goes by. Accuracy is everything in two-voice singing, so if you have a choice that's simpler but easier to sing, versus something complex but a little hit-and-miss with accuracy, go simple and clear. And practice—a lot!

Moving on, we're now at the B section (starting at m. 26), in the dominant key. Time for a timbre change, so now I take the melody. Since it's more languid and expressive, there's room for the syllable palette to open up a bit with more "eh" and "oh" vowels introduced, along with some more smear-y consonant blends, giving us the more vocal horn–like "dway" sounds. The overall harmony of E7♭9 is jazzy and a little complex, so Suba's part clearly outlines the harmonic grounding, and she does double duty as harmonizer, mostly in parallel thirds, while also interspersing bass pedals and triadic walking bass lines that clearly outline the E-dominant-ness of this section. The call-and-response of the following four bars is taken directly from the original orchestral version and makes for a nice singing break: up until now, neither singer has had so much as a beat to rest. In the next four bars, we have the same theme modulated, but as an additional variation, we added a four-against-three cross-rhythm at m. 35: it helps the melody flow a little more and adds to the jazzy rhythmic fluidity.

At Section C, we're back to the melodic and harmonic material from the beginning, modulated to D major and D minor. So, we use the same techniques as in the intro and section A. It works well, and there's enough new interest with the new key center.

At Section D, we get into new territory and modulations further away from our original key center: mm. 56–61 are primarily in E♭7 and F/E♭, and mm. 62–68 in F♯m7♭5 (or, if you prefer, Am/F♯, taking us back toward our original key). These modulations are pretty fast and furious in the original, and as we sang through them, we felt there wasn't enough time for the listener to hear the harmonies shift, and barely enough time for us to establish them for ourselves. So, keeping with the "form is flexible" mantra, we added an extra two bars to each new key center, starting with a dominant pickup in the bass at the end of m. 56. This leads us to the first chord of E♭9: Suba holds the ninth, while I spell out the E♭7 chord underneath with E♭, B♭, D♭, and E♭ in the walking line. Once this tonality is firmly established, Suba can start the melody, which I then respond to. The same process is repeated in mm. 62–68, in the tonality of Am/F♯: Suba holds the minor third, while I spell out an F♯m7♭5 with F♯, C, E, and F♯. I then respond with the melody, and we fold this section down into a held unison, holding the entire piece briefly suspended in time.

Because we're in new territory, and hearing more jazz-centred dominant seventh chords, I add in an extra layer of vocal percussion: jazz brushes. This adds some rhythmic propulsion, and despite the fact that I have to hold sustained pitches in the bass to keep the harmony anchored, it isn't too difficult to do. Jazz brushes can be done essentially by expelling air through the teeth, similar to sounding the letter "f." Since it doesn't close the mouth completely like a plosive kick or snare, bass notes can be sung "through" the expelled-f sound. Thus, the "dm .. dm .. dm .. ba-doo-ba dm" pattern starting at m. 56 is really pronounced "tm (ts)f'tm f'tm (ts) bf-tf-f tm," with the sound of stirred brushes under the bass notes. It takes a lot of breath with all those expelled-f brushes, but since it alternates with the melodic responses, it's not exhausting (though it's a lot of pieces to hold together!).

Going back to the "form is flexible" idea: in the original, this section is a bit longer and has a few more developments, and then it recaps the original melody in the original key. We felt that, with two voices, we'd covered enough of it and that replicating the longer section made it less interesting. So, we moved ahead to the end of the recap, but we chose to treat it freely, almost in suspended time (mm. 69–76). There are some additional harmonies, almost a coda, in this section, so we decided to draw it out a bit. It also gives us a break after some pretty constant motion and technically challenging singing.

To finish it off (mm. 77–84), we decided to ramp it up with a *molto accelerando* not found in the original. This is a recap of the melodic material from mm. 17–24, but instead of moving secondary-dominant to dominant (B7 to Em), it moves dominant to tonic (E7 to Am). We used the same break-up-the-melody technique as in the earlier section, but this time, Suba sings the pedal, and I sing the melody, to bookend the piece.

We walked away from arranging this piece surprised and delighted that two voices could cover an entire orchestra. But it goes to show you: with thoughtful arranging and a solid musical knowledge, plus a good awareness of your vocalists' abilities, the voice is nearly limitless.

CHAPTER 6

Harmonic Principles and Techniques

Harmony is at the heart of what we're doing here, and if you're reading this book, chances are you have a pretty good grip on general harmony principles. In this section, we'll go beyond the standard SATB, chorale-style "rules" of harmony and vocal conventions while examining other techniques to enrich your harmonic vocabulary.

This covers all aspects of a cappella arranging, but in particular the writing of BG vocals. If you have our previous book, consider this an extension of our chapter on writing BGs.

Theory purists, take note: we're talking largely about how things sound and work in practical applications, rather than how they function "scientifically." We're drawing from a combination of classical harmonic theory, Lydian-Chromatic Theory, and other techniques we've picked up along the way. Our nomenclature may not follow strict rules. But then, you've seen what we think about "Rules."

Close Harmony Voicing

Standard homophonic SATB writing assumes a few things:

» Four voice parts are spread relatively evenly over one to two octaves, with wider spacing between the bass and upper voices. This is beneficial for tuning a cappella, as it aligns with the harmonic series.
» Intervals between adjacent voice parts can range from a second or third, to up to a twelfth between tenor and bass.
» Each voice generally stays in their "sweet spot" (the comfortable part of their vocal range).
» Melody is usually in the soprano voice, with other voices supporting, as the human ear gravitates to the highest voice.
» While voice-leading within parts remains a valued aesthetic, the overall effect is intended to be homogeneous, and somewhat static, or at least "evenly rolling" without too many peaks and valleys.

» Harmony is largely triadic, with the bass voice primarily offering roots, with passing notes to make the bass line more melodic, as the lowest part is heard as a countermelody. The inner voices—alto and tenor—are the ones who have the least melodic lines, serving mainly to cover chord factors.
» Chord progressions are largely diatonic.
» Most leaps are in singable intervals: fourths, fifths, and sixths, with occasional octaves. Sevenths and ninths are avoided as they're difficult to sing.
» Parallel fifths and octaves are avoided, as the intention is to have four distinct vocal lines that can be heard as such and don't "disappear" in parallel motion.

Close harmony voicing turns these conventions on their head:

» Between three and five voices that are tightly knit, clustered in a range between a sixth and an octave.
» Intervals between adjacent voice parts are as tight as possible, almost always within a second or third.
» Voices may be out of their "sweet spots," with bass and tenor voices in an overall higher tessitura.
» The bass acts as a lower harmony similar to a tenor part, rather than outlining root notes.
» Melody is usually in the upper voice, with parts below often following closely in near-parallel movement, with no intention of making the individual voices heard as separate lines.*
» Voice-leading in parts, while stepwise, may be chromatic and complex. Complex leaps, such as sevenths and ninths, are not uncommon.
» Harmony can involve "upper-structure" partials, such as sevenths, ninths, elevenths, and thirteenths.
» Chord progressions can be diatonic or chromatic, or even purely parallel.

Close harmony voicings are the ambrosia of vocal harmony. The sweetness of the close, stacked intervals, the "buzz" of tones and semitones, and the ring from perfectly tuned tight harmonies can send shivers down the spine.

Barbershop

Close harmony is often associated with vocal jazz, but in contemporary practice it has its roots in places such as traditional barbershop music. Unlike the styles that followed it, such as doo-wop and contemporary pop a cappella, the bass voice is not separated out into its own instrumental-like texture, but rather it serves as the bottom of a four-note stack and is not necessarily the root of the chord. In most barbershop singing, close harmony chords include dominant sevenths (and plenty of them) and major sixth chords, with the occasional diminished chord used in passing. Major sevenths and other upper partials make brief appearances as passing notes, and as dictated by the melody, but they don't feature prominently.

---

* Like any "Rules," these conventions have exceptions: see "Barbershop" below.

Barbershop close harmony does not quite follow the "close harmony" definition listed above: there are a few differences. One notable difference is that, due to its traditional TTBB (and, later, SSAA) format, the melody—or "lead," as it is referred to in barbershop circles—is in the second-to-highest voice, which keeps the voicings from becoming either too dense, or the melody from being too high or strained in the top voice. Instead, the top voice "floats," usually in head-voice, functioning more like an alto voice, but voiced above the lead. While there is some parallelism, chords tend to follow more traditional voice-leading principles rather than the straightforward parallelism seen in other types, such as block-voicing, mentioned below. In addition, not all chords are close harmony, but they are frequently interspersed with more open voicings, where the bass and baritone parts typically drop down (often quite dramatically) to re-voice a chord in open style. The overall effect is to sound much of the time as one voice split into four-part harmony: the lead loudest, followed by the bass, with the top voice (the "tenor") and middle voice (the "baritone") attaching their sound to the lead, following phrasing and even diphthongs. The ultimate goal is to create as many overtones as possible, "ringing" chords, especially at the end of phrases.

Jazz

In the 1930s and 1940s, the relatively new concept of vocal jazz ensemble singing borrowed many techniques from instrumental—in particular, big band—arranging techniques. A typical big band has five saxophones: two alto, two tenor, and one baritone, often voiced as "block" chords, with the melody on top and parts moving in near-lockstep parallel motion. The ranges of the sax section correspond well to voices, so these techniques were reflected in the vocal ensembles of their time.

In a five-voice block, the lower voice doubles the highest, creating a solid "harmonic sandwich," with the melody reinforced on both sides of the block, in octaves.

Here's an example of a diatonic major scale block voicing.

Note that the voicing isn't purely parallel: rather, the chords toggle between an overall tonality of C6 and G7 chords, with the Maj7 voicings "rounded off" to become major sixth chords instead.

Here's the same scale, with some harmonic richness added. In this case, most of the non-chord tones of the tonic chord (2, 4, and 7) are treated as a V7♭9 chord, adding some chromatic passing colors.

Here's an example of a melody using the block-voicing technique:

What'll I Do

Irving Berlin

You'll notice that the top two voices are most often a third apart, occasionally a second. A minor second is usually avoided between the top two voices, as a semitone "buzz" that close to the melody can easily obscure the melody.

Writing in this style isn't too complicated: it's more of a "fill in the blanks" exercise. Start by writing the melody in the top voice, doubled an octave lower in the bottom voice, and fill in the voices from the top down and bottom up. Alto will be mostly a (diatonic) third below, baritone will be a third above the bass, and tenor will be a third above baritone. You'll have to tweak a few notes here and there to fit the chord changes. You'll also have a few choices in the inner voices, depending on the level of chromaticism you are looking for. In the example above, you will notice that the first half of the example takes a more diatonic approach, while the second half adds more chromaticism, and therefore more harmonic movement.

Fewer than Five Voices

While five saxes may be standard in a big band, you may not have five inner voices at your disposal in an a cappella ensemble. The solution is relatively straightforward:

» *Four voices*: simply eliminate the lowest voice. Since it typically doubles the upper voice, you lose the "harmony sandwich" feeling of the block voicing, but none of the notes or colors.

» *Three voices*: your chords will be more triadic, with the interval between the upper voice and lower voice typically a sixth (or sometimes a fifth). Your choices with the middle voice will determine the harmonic richness. The first example leans toward the use of more harmonic extensions, avoiding bass notes to cover as many chord factors as possible.

You'll notice that the voicings aren't always triadic: in some cases, more clustery voicings are used to preserve harmonic richness. Smooth voice-leading becomes more important than the parallelism of five-part block voicing, so the tenor has a nice descending chromatic line that adds plenty of color and voice-leads nicely. In the places where the melody leaps up and down by a fifth or sixth, three voices leaping isn't as smooth as five, so this is resolved by the three voices singing the pickup before the leap in unison: it keeps the voice-leading smooth and highlights the harmonies before and after.

The next example stays triadic: by now, we're moving from a less-jazzy, "reduced" block-chord approach to a more diatonic, gospel/pop approach.

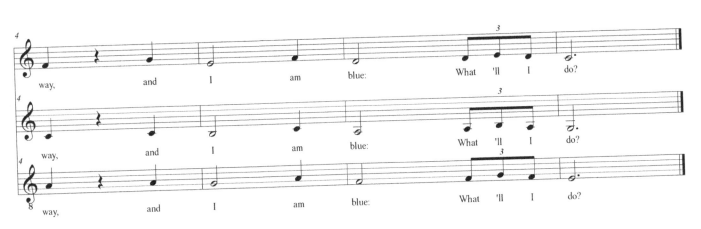

You can think of this as a spectrum, dialing up or down the harmonic color.

If you have a background in piano, this kind of three- or four-note close harmony voicing can be easily replicated with one hand on the piano. For five notes, simply add the left hand doubling the melody below: this technique is commonly used by jazz pianists in performance to represent big band–type block voicing. You can use this instead of the "write the melody and fill in the blanks" approach mentioned above: it gives you easy access, and easy audible feedback, to explore options for voicings.

Block voicing, especially five parts and in longer sections, has a very era-specific, "1940s big band era" sound. If you are looking for this type of evocative association, use it liberally!

Blending the Techniques: The Vocal Jazz Soli

For vocal writing with more variety, you can mix this technique with open voicings and contrary-motion techniques (mentioned earlier in chapter 5, "Counterpoint, Polyphony, and Two-Voice Writing"). This can be particularly striking in a vocal feature such as a jazz soli.

The vocal jazz soli is a convention taken directly from instrumental big band vocabulary, where a section, most often the sax section, does a "group solo" feature. A soli is often a highlight of an arrangement and a great feature for your singers.

In the example below, Dylan wrote a four-part soli over the chord changes for the jazz standard "Hit That Jive, Jack," as recorded by Cadence. The song is in AABA form, and the chord changes (for the jazz-inclined) are roughly "rhythm changes" in the A sections, and "Honeysuckle Rose" changes in B section. (For those unfamiliar, the chord changes are spelled out in the notation.) The soli takes place over the B and final A section.

This soli combines a number of techniques in fairly rapid succession: here's a blow-by-blow analysis:

» Mm. 1–3: four-part, close harmony block voicing.
» Mm. 4–5: moves to open voicings and unison lines.
» Mm. 6–7: contrary motion. For this technique, start with the melody in the top voice, and write an interesting countermelody in the bottom voice. Fill in the remaining voices to taste.
» Mm. 8–9: "two-plus-two" texture. First of all, I decided to reharmonize these bars in a typical jazz way, stuffing an extra "semitone-away" ii–V in the same

space, so that Am7-D7 becomes B♭m7-E♭7-Am7-D7, still over two bars, with the harmonic rhythm doubling as a result. The top two voices repeat a melodic motif for each ii-V, and the bottom voices support this with open shell voicings.

» Mm. 10–11: more contrary motion, starting from unisons and ending on an open voicing. Note that the voicings, while interesting-sounding, aren't necessarily definitive chords with solid roots in the bass. The chord at m. 10 approximates an inverted G6 chord, with the root in the T1 and the fifth in the bass. The chord on the second eighth note of m. 11 is roughly F/E♭: not exactly in standard rhythm changes, but since the soli exists on its own without any other instruments or parts, we can take liberties with the chord changes a bit here, and it sounds interesting.

The rest of the soli is roughly parallel block voicings: some are close, some open, with a unison passage to set us off for the end.

Reharmonization

Reharmonization is worth a textbook of its own (and there are many), and it can take you down a rabbit hole of numbers and theory from which you may never emerge. Rather than reinvent these textbooks, we'll offer some general principles that a) work well for vocal writing, b) don't require a PhD in math or advanced music theory, and c) come from a solid, experiential background. In other words, useful ideas that come more from the ear (aural) than from the brain (cerebral).

Reharmonization is most immediately associated with jazz writing, but it can work in any genre. We touched on some jazz-specific styles in *A Cappella Arranging*, and we'll go deeper here, with additional techniques and moving beyond the context of jazz.

Put in non-musical terms, with reharmonization, you hear something familiar, but from a different aural perspective. It's the musical equivalent of a movie where a scene is replayed from different characters' points of view: with each character, we see something new or find a perspective we hadn't known before. This is the magic of reharmonization.

More Harmonic Movement

Taking its roots from Western classical harmonic principles, many contemporary styles still involve the use of the "primary colors" of harmony: tonic, dominant, and subdominant chords. Fun fact: songs such as "The Book of Love" by the Magnetic Fields are based on the Bergamesca, a harmonic structure (or "chord changes," in modern parlance) from the seventeenth century. So many songs borrow from the chord changes of "Pachelbel's Canon" that it became the subject of a satirical song by musician/comedian Rob Paravonian: his "Pachelbel Rant" takes you through a five-minute medley/diatribe of these songs.

To add more spice to a chord structure, you can start by borrowing from the jazz world.

Basic jazz harmony isn't really a new or different way of conceiving harmony; it is simply an extension of classical harmony. Classical harmony is primarily "tertian," meaning that the chords are imagined by stacking thirds on top of each other. This is usually triadic: major and minor chords with roots, thirds, and fifths. Dominant-sevenths are added for harmonic motion, to help resolve one chord to another. Other notes such as major sevenths and ninths, or other chords such as diminished or augmented chords, may show up, but usually just to add color or to serve as a source of harmonic tension, which is eventually resolved to a more stable major or minor chord.

a "static" major chord   a dominant-7 chord...
                                          which "expects" resolution

Jazz harmony simply extends the limits of what a "normal" chord might be to include sevenths, ninths, even elevenths and thirteenths (a.k.a. fourths and sixths). Well, that's about all the notes in the scale, isn't it? The new "normal" major chord then becomes a major seventh just by piling another note on top of the old major chord, and now it seems that just about every note in the scale is fair game in a static, going-nowhere chord.

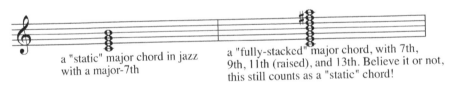

a "static" major chord in jazz   a "fully-stacked" major chord, with 7th,
with a major-7th   9th, 11th (raised), and 13th. Believe it or not,
                                      this still counts as a "static" chord!

In the case of dominant seventh chords, the situation becomes even more varied. In classical harmony, a dominant seventh is usually a "moving" chord, creating tension and resolving to the "resting" major chord: the good old V-I cadence. Keeping with the more-colors-in-the-palette sound in jazz harmony, a moving dominant seventh chord can have its "upper partials" (the ninth, eleventh, and thirteenth) raised or lowered in just about any way you see fit, giving several variations or colors to choose from.

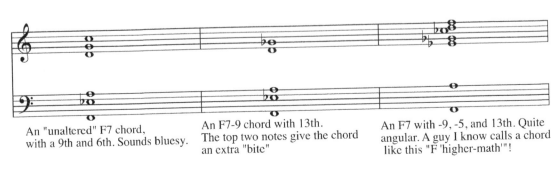

An "unaltered" F7 chord,   An F7-9 chord with 13th.   An F7 with -9, -5, and 13th. Quite
with a 9th and 6th. Sounds bluesy.   The top two notes give the chord   angular. A guy I know calls a chord
                                  an extra "bite"   like this "F 'higher-math'"!

Not only does jazz harmony offer more colors, it offers a finer brush. Jazz harmony uses the same cycle-of-fifths approach to harmonic motion as classical music, but it goes further around the circle. A typical classical cadence needs to get back to the tonic, or I. The usual route: V-I, the perfect cadence, or IV-I the plagal ("amen") cadence. The standard jazz cadence backs up a little further: ii-V-I.

Or it can start from further away: iii-VI-ii-V-I.

A iii-VI-ii-V-I jazz progression. Note that extra partials such as 13th, -9s, etc are common.

Or even further: ♯iv-VII-iii-VI-ii-V-I. Round and round we go.

We'll add an additional twist to this type of progression-building: "Coltrane Changes," so named because they first gained wider popularity with the John Coltrane jazz classic "Giant Steps." In this case, the usual cycle of fifths is replaced by a cycle of V-I cadences, with each new I chord (or temporary key center) a major third away. This has an unusual, angular, and signature sound. It defies the ear's expectations, but since it follows a predicable cycle, the ears will "buy it," accepting it as a different, but workable, progression. It looks like this:

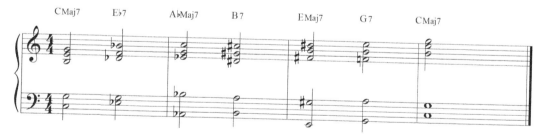

Given the relatively "out there" sound of this progression, it can work well at the end of a song, taking you to some faraway places before gently landing the song home. Note that the chords contain additional upper partials, such as sixths, ninths, and thirteenths, but they aren't specified in the chord symbols. These upper partials are still diatonic to the chord (if not the key) and as such are "natural" extensions of the major/dominant seventh chords: they are implied in the chord and don't need to be explicitly labeled. Such is the extension of jazz harmony.

Used like this, it can act similarly to a tag in barbershop music, where the "hanger," or long tone, is reharmonized at length to bring drama to the end of the song. Since we're used to this convention in a cappella music, you can bring a new twist to it with Coltrane Changes. Here's the end of "Amazing Grace," as a six-part jazz chorale, with "Giant Steps" changes at the end.

In each case, you're adding more harmonic movement by stuffing in more chords. If your song has a harmonically static section, you can dress it up with any of these progressions. Or you can make a section, like a bridge or song end, stand out by adding these additional progressions, while keeping the rest of the piece more conventional. Done well, this can add interest and spice to your arrangement. Overdone, it can be difficult to sing, sound clunky and contrived, and have a feeling of being "clever for cleverness' sake." Like any good spice, use according to taste.

Chord Substitution: Reharmonization by Function

We're used to thinking of "tonic, subdominant, and dominant" as three chords: I, IV, and V. But tonic-dominant-subdominant can be thought of not just as three individual chords, but as functions of harmonic movement. Every chord in a scale can fall under one of these functions, and if you start thinking of the in-between minor/diminished chords and remember your high-school theory "relative minors" (they'll come in handy now, if they didn't back then), you get something like this:

- » I—tonic.
- » ii—relative major of IV: subdominant.
- » iii—an interesting one. It shares most of the same notes as I, so it can be tonic. It's also the relative minor of V—but it doesn't have the definitive-sounding equivalent of the 7 in V7, so it can be a sort of "weak dominant."
- » IV—subdominant.
- » V—dominant.
- » vi—relative minor of I: tonic.
- » vii diminished—shares most of the notes of V7, though the diminished chord gives it a less-defined sound.

If you group those by function, you get:

- » TONIC—I, iii, vi
- » DOMINANT—V, iii, vii diminished
- » SUBDOMINANT—IV, ii

Using the "primary colors" metaphor, we have multiple shades of the same basic colors.

This gives you an easy shorthand for simple, "non-invasive" chord substitutions. Changing an I to vi gives a nice, subtle change. Placed in a chord progression, IV-V-I becomes IV-V-vi, the classical "deceptive cadence." Experiment at will: you won't hurt anything. More likely, you'll refine what you like in a given section by paying attention to the bass movement: remember, the bass is the "second melody," so a nice-sounding bass part also makes for good harmony.

Harmonizing under a Pedal Tone

This is another easy-but-effective way to reharmonize: bypass the harmonic movement in the bottom entirely!

Most chord progressions are defined by root movement, in particular by wide intervals of fifths and fourths in the bass. A pedal tone (taken from organ terminology, the "pedal" being a held bass note, played by foot pedal) keeps the root static, with the chords above perceived as shifts in color rather than as progressions in the typical sense. Over a pedal, the most familiar chord movement above is heard in a different context, with interesting and sometimes-unexpected sonorities as a result.

Substituting Related Key Centers

If your melody is fairly diatonic, you can reharmonize an entire section in a related key, for example a melody in C, harmonized in A minor. Think of this as a "macro" version of substituting individual chords as described above. Take a look at our example, harmonized under a different key center:

This idea of tonic/subdominant/dominant can be extended as well when working in a non-purely-diatonic situation. In this case, we think of a dominant function as a "bright, strong" sound and a subdominant function as a "gentle, rounded" sound. Thinking of them in this way can make it easier to reach for the right harmonic tools according to the sound, effect, or emotion you want to create.

Take, for example, a typical, assertive V7-I cadence. Make the V7 chord minor instead of major, and it takes on a softer, more modal tone.

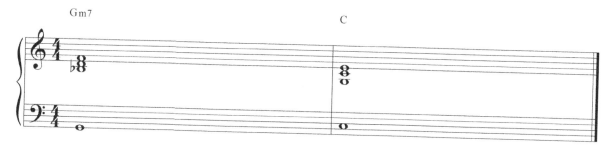

Moving further away from strict diatonicism, another favorite is the "backdoor ii-V-I," borrowed again from jazz. As opposed to the typical "front door" ii-V7-I progression, this comes from the other, subdominant side—iv-♭VII7-I—and it looks like this.

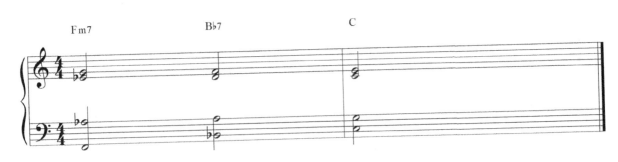

Why does this work? A simple, not-overly-theoretical explanation is this.

In the earlier example, Gm7-C, we shifted colors, turning the stronger G7 into a softer Gm7. Now, imagine if you did this with your overall key center, shifting colors to make it minor:

» In the key of C minor, your relative major is E♭.
» Now try a ii-V-I in E♭, giving us Fm7-B♭7-E♭maj7.
» Next, swap out that E♭ major chord for its relative minor, C minor.
» Finally, replace that C minor with your original C major.

Like the deceptive cadence, leading you somewhere but landing somewhere else, this goes a step further, taking you down a minor-sounding path and pulling a harmonic "bait and switch," taking a sharp turn back to major. It's a surprise, and comes across as an uplifting, "sun coming out from behind the clouds" feeling.

Reharmonization by Melody

This is an opposite approach to functional reharmonization: instead of tinkering with chord progressions, we use the melody as the source of reharmonization. In this case, rather than a steady harmonic rhythm (say, one chord per bar), each melody note is independently harmonized, creating quick, passing harmonies. The choice of notes is wide open, not limited to the diatonic scale. The relationships between the chords as you move through the melody don't matter as much, and they can contain wild chromaticism and rapid-fire color shifts. If we describe reharmonization techniques as color changes, this isn't a momentary change in camera filter: this is a continually shifting kaleidoscope.

The possibilities are nearly endless, and while some harmonic understanding can help to create something workable, the easiest way is simply to experiment. Our ears still love structure, so if we take away the sense of functional and diatonic harmony, while the melody may be enough "structure" for us, we can also look at creating a complementary bass line or bottom voice that either sounds melodic as well, or has some familiar root-movement, even if the chords above don't follow a traditional chord structure.

An effective way to try this is to start with the melody, choose a bass note, and fill in the rest. Here are a few simple examples. The first few stay diatonic, just to get used to the idea.

It's pretty and surprisingly colorful, considering we're only sticking with diatonic notes. While the bass has some root-movement, there's no real sense of functional harmony—more of a shifting of clusters, but at least all in the same key. The next one is chromatic, and now the choices grow exponentially.

While at first it seems like tonal anarchy, there is a little bit of structure coming from the bass, which is singing a straight chromatic descent down a minor sixth, from E♭ to G. With this type of chromatic reharmonization, it's easy to get lost in the weeds, so giving the bass some sort of countermelody can provide you with some direction. Once the bass countermelody is in, fill in the blanks. There are still plenty of choices, but the path becomes clearer.

This example also warrants a side note on enharmonic note "spelling." At first glance, the spelling is atrocious: it follows neither the key center (which it can't, since we've pretty much abandoned the concept of "A♭ major" for the moment) nor the pure vertical spelling of each chord (the first chord has a D♭ in a Dmaj7♯11 chord? Are you serious?). In harmonically ambiguous territory like this, go with your gut and actually read each line individually. Ask yourself, *What would I rather read: a correctly spelled interval or an easy-to-see one?* There are no right or wrong answers here, just what works in the moment. Your rehearsal pianist might hate you, but your singers will be much happier (we speak from experience!).

The following example takes us back into modern music. This is the final few bars of Dylan's arrangement of Stevie Wonder's "I Wish," originally recorded by Cadence on their album *Frost Free*. Dylan will take the story from here.

I Wish

Stevie Wonder

The original song fades out over the same repeated horn melody, but I knew I wanted a "live ending" with as much punch as possible. Prior to this section, the top three voices took the horns, harmonized in triads, supported by two rhythm voices and the ever-present bass line. For this ending, I decided to go for an "all-in" approach with all six voices reharmonizing the horn line. To give the reharmonization some structure, and to build excitement, I chose to have the bass voice continually rising until the very end, dropping to its lowest register for the final two chords. Since the horn line is largely a descending line, this gave some interesting contrary motion, as well.

Once I wrote the "outside voices" (soprano 1, and bass), I filled in each chord from both directions: I built triads and some stacked fourth chords down from the soprano and built open root-fifth-third or root-seventh-third voicings from the bottom up.* I experimented with various options for the inner voices to find the colors I thought were the most interesting, but also reasonable for voice-leading. As the outer voices came closer together, the voicings become denser, with six voices and a very wide range between the upper soprano and lowest bass, starting with over three octaves at the beginning, to a twelfth at its narrowest point.

Looking carefully at the stacked parts, you'll see they follow nothing like a normal chord progression: in fact, they're not really a "progression" at all, so much as a series of colorful chords, given some structure by the melody (which, by now, had been heard several times in its regular, two-chord context) and the countermelodic bass part. I wrote this early in my arranging career: it probably took me a few hours to write these four bars alone, and it's still one of my favorite moments in all my arrangements.

Non-Standard Harmony Techniques

For those who come from a Western music educational background, it can be hard to remember that other forms of harmony existed before the rise of tonal harmony in the seventeenth century. We've had four hundred years of learning one way of hearing harmony, so it's no surprise! It's also a reminder that, while it's often said that many non-Western cultures "don't use harmony," that's not actually true: in most musical cultures, there is still a root note of some sort, from which other notes are derived and usually played against. The melody exists in context with the root note, which is often played as a drone or pedal note: the continually changing relationship of the melody against the drone is, in fact, harmony. Seeing harmony this way can free us from the usual view of harmony as tonic-dominant-subdominant relationships and triadic voicings.

Homophonic Melody-plus-Drone

When we think melody-plus-drone, we typically imagine the drone as a separate, unmoving element: the tamboura in Indian classical music supporting a vocalist or instrumentalist, for example, or the drone of a bagpipe against the melody. But in vocal music, a homophonic drone, singing the same lyrics and rhythms as the melody, provides an active, note-against-note context and interesting harmonic possibilities.

This technique can be found around the world, but it is well-exemplified by music from places such as Bulgaria. This works well with two to three voices: one singer, the "drone," stays on one note (usually the tonic or another "stable" note, but this can vary), while the other moves melodically. Harmonies are implied,

---

* This technique borrows from vocal groups such as Take 6. For more on this technique, see the section regarding Take 6 in chapter 13, "Lush Jazz Harmonies."

and a buzzing tension builds as the melody note approaches the drone in tones or semitones.

Here are two examples of this technique in contemporary use, using the same technique in different ways, from Charlie Chaplin's beautiful standard "Smile," as performed by Dylan's a cappella duo, FreePlay, on the album *Talk to Me*.

In this first example, the "drone" is the third of the chord. The drone is placed higher than the melody, with the melody rising to, or falling away from, the drone. The intervals range from a unison to a sixth away. It provides a degree of tension, as the melody moves closer and further away, but also harmonic stability, allowing us to hear the C major tonality clearly.

In this example, the drone is the root, and the effect is much different. The melody regularly crosses over and under the drone with a range from a third higher to a fourth lower. This regular weaving around the drone creates more tension harmonies, with tone and semitone intervals occurring in rapid succession. The major sonority is less clear, with the melody touching the third, briefly, only once. The emotional effect is a sadder, more wistful feeling. It's no mistake that the "happier" variation occurs first, and the "wistful" one second, echoing the beautifully bittersweet lyrics.

This can be extended to three voices with two drone/static voices against a melody. Unlike a single drone, the note-against-note implied harmony now expands to three-note chords and clusters. The excerpt below comes from FreePlay's reimagining of the Beach Boys' classic "God Only Knows," from the same album.

God Only Knows

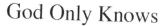

Wilson/Asher

Here, the "drones" move around a little to allow for the harmonic progression of the song but stay about as static as possible, given the relatively fast harmonic rhythm of three chords over four bars. The melody, unlike the example in "Smile," has a wider intervallic range of an octave, and non-stepwise movement. The drone voices help "contain" the melody by sitting in the harmonic middle, while the melody is free to leap around, still supported. The resulting harmonies cover everything from standard triads, to open-fourths and quartal stacks, to tight clusters, creating much more harmonic variety and interest than you might find in a triadic parallel close harmony voicing. As well, with a wide-ranging melody containing arpeggiated leaps, a parallel harmony might sound too jumpy: in this case, the drones-plus-melody technique is both more interesting and more practical.

Blending Techniques: The "Vocal Harmonizer" Effect

Earlier in the chapter, we discussed the idea that vocal techniques of the times often mirror instrumental techniques, using block harmonies taken from big band writing as an example. The same holds true today: modern pop and electronic techniques make their way into contemporary a cappella practice, as well. An interesting example of this is the "vocal harmonizer." In instrumental practice, this involves a solo singer singing into effects box that digitally re-pitches the voice to specific intervals and/or scales and combines them with the uneffected voice. The effected voices "intelligently" follow the melodic contour of the original voice, and the number of voices, as well as the scale, can be controlled. In a simple case, a solo singer can imitate triadic harmony. When more voices are added, the parts become denser and "clustery"… and more static, as the harmonizer avoids crossing voices, and it can't harmonize too far beyond the singer's original pitch without a highly artificial effect. A classic example of a vocal harmonizer, used a cappella, is the song "Hide and Seek," by solo vocalist Imogen Heap.

Imitating this technique creates an interesting "circular-logic" effect: the harmonizer was designed to imitate natural voices, and now natural voices are imitating the harmonizer! However, when the digital idiosyncrasies of a harmonizer are reproduced by human voices, the result is otherworldly.

For a scalar piece to use as an example, look no further than the Christmas carol "The First Nöel." Or we could try some Led Zeppelin instead:

Stairway To Heaven

Note that the melody is in the alto. The harmonizer effect works well when the melody has harmonies both above and below, in a sense "burying" it under the dense harmonies.

The vocal harmonizer effect has the qualities of the lockstep motion of jazz block voicing, combined with the static effect of drone harmonies.

Tintinnabuli

This technique is a compositional style created by the Estonian composer Arvo Pärt, inspired by Gregorian chant. It has an ethereal, "new old sound," combining the simplicity of early-music chant with the interesting rub of tones and semitones. The sound is sweet, easy on the ears, and quite straightforward to achieve.

It involves two voices: the melody, or "M-voice," and the tintinnabular voice, or "T-voice." The technique works best when the melody, like plainchant, is slow and stepwise. The tintinnabular voice sings the tonic, third, or fifth against the melody, in direct relationship to the M-voice. The T-voice can be above or below the melody and can be the closest triadic note up/down (+/-1) or any other relationship, but that relationship is usually kept the same. The result is that the T-voice spells out a triad, sounding a little like the ringing of bells, hence the name tintinnabuli.

Here's "Stairway" with the M-voice in alto, and T-voice in soprano "+1 superior," i.e., singing the closest triad note above.

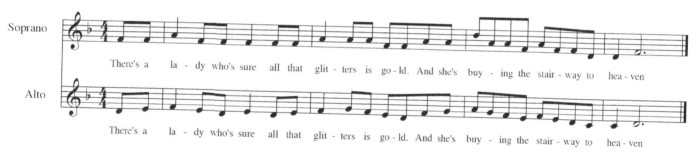

The result is a transparent, yet interesting sound.

This can also be combined with a moving bass line to create additional harmonies or can be used as an additional layer for two BG parts, or as a string-like effect. In the following example, we add a second "M-voice," a descending bass line in half notes. The corresponding T-voice in the tenor is "+2 superior." This relationship, instead of mostly seconds and thirds, gives us more fifths and sixths, a nice open sound for tenor and bass voicings.

You can go quite deep with this, and there are plenty of variations. M-voice and T-voice can be rhythmically displaced from each other; the T-voice can alternate above and below the M-voice note by note; the mode can be shifted, so our D minor melody could be treated as if it were in G mixolydian, starting on the fifth, and the T-voices supporting this. And these are just a few examples.

This chapter is heavy on content, and it can take some time to absorb all these concepts. It can also be seen as a "resource chapter," something to open up when looking for a new technique. Or, if you're coming up against some creative brick wall, look here to remind yourself of what's possible. And remember: despite all the theory, just use your ears. If it sounds good, it *is* good!

SECTION III

Beyond the Ensemble: Specialized Arranging

Writing for ensembles is the heart of what we do as a cappella arrangers, so it's no surprise that our first book focused specifically on this. As you spend more time in the world of a cappella music, you'll find there are many occasions when you're not just writing for a group . . . or the context or format is different . . . or the group is a different configuration, and you're stuck with something that doesn't fit. We'll get you through all this.

Chapter 7, "Arranging for the Studio," examines the differences between writing for live performance and writing for the recording studio, and helps you unlock the potential the studio can offer. Even further, we also look at how to take an existing arrangement and make it "studio-ready."

Chapter 8, "Live Looping," looks at the fascinating and rapidly expanding world of live looping. At first glance, it seems to be a format that's all about the technology and doesn't require arranging in the same way. But a deeper look shows us that it's all about the arranging, making the most of the technology to serve a larger purpose: using the technology as a tool, rather than a novelty, to express ourselves artistically. Live looping is not just for solo artists, so we also demonstrate a number of ways how it can be used in the context of a larger ensemble.

Chapter 9, "Adapting Arrangements," is a practical guide for taking a chart for one type of group and writing it for another, such as reworking an SATB chart for SSAA. Though it's a common need for many ensembles or directors, no one else seems to have explained how it can be done, so we share our insiders' tips. We cover pretty much every scenario, from changing ensemble types, to "doing more with less," making a many-voiced chart work for fewer voices. Before you give up on that piece of music that you love, but don't have all the same voices to make it work, read this chapter.

For all the time we spend "making voices sound like instruments," there isn't a whole lot written about the subject: most of the time, the arranger is left to their own devices to figure this out. We love this self-exploratory method, but maybe you could use some help. Not all instruments are easy to translate vocally, and some instruments you may be unfamiliar with. You could be a seasoned choral arranger (or instrumental arranger, for that matter) suddenly thrust into this weird world of instrumental imitation that those of us deep in the contemporary a cappella world take for granted. Chapter 10, "Instrumental Imitation and Lyric-less Arrangements," takes a deep dive into this world, going beyond the "how to make that sound" and including detailed information on the particular instrumental idioms that define the instrument, and how they tend to function within the larger ensemble, orchestra, or band. We even discuss how to create lyric-less "vocal orchestral arrangements" where timbre and detail are even more important, with no lyrics to hold the listener's attention.

Grab your headphones, and let's start with a trip to the studio!

CHAPTER 7

Arranging for the Studio

Your group is about to make an album. Congratulations! Maybe you're an actively performing group, looking to record your tried-and-true audience favorites. The track list is complete, the arrangements have been sung countless times, and you're ready to go.

But will those arrangements translate onto a recording the way they do live, without the energy of an audience?

Or maybe you're looking to create new repertoire in the studio. You're ready to get creative, try new things, and enjoy all the bells and whistles the studio has to offer. You're going big, wild, and experimental.

But what happens when it's time to perform live? What do you do without all the "studio candy"? Can you even sing the chart live?

There's a lot to think about here. Studio recording offers a world of possibility beyond live performance: unlimited tracks and parts that can be recorded when each member is in perfect voice; unlimited flexibility; countless studio effects; more time to get every part just right; and the ability to edit, tune, and otherwise make something big, fanciful, and sonically perfect. The studio is an incredible tool, a powerful instrument for creativity, and it makes sense to use the studio to its full potential. On the other hand, you may want a "concert on a disc," a pure(ish) representation of your group's live soul. How do you make the best of both worlds?

The Big Picture

Before starting your recording project, it's helpful to start with the "big picture" and ask a few questions.

1. Are you planning to perform this album live? Most a cappella groups don't just exist in the studio: more than many other genres and instrumental styles, the human joy of a cappella singing comes from the intimacy and immediateness of a live performance in front of a live audience. But that's not the case

for all artists. Many famous artists, such as pianist Glenn Gould or even the Beatles, left the stage for good and focused on creating studio works of art, freeing themselves from the need to re-create their idealized, studio-perfect works in an unpredictable live setting.

But if you do plan to perform it live . . .

2. Do you have to perform every song from the album live? This doesn't have to be an "all or nothing" proposition. Many groups will have a core set of songs from their album that are still performed live, with a few outliers that exist only on recording. This allows for an artistic sweet spot where the group can please their audience onstage and still experiment artistically beyond the confines of live performability. It also gives the audience a bonus treat when they buy the album.

With these questions in mind, we can break down the process of arranging for the studio across a spectrum from "most live" to "most studio":

» "Live" arrangements that are meant to be replicated as-is
» "Live" arrangements that are augmented in the studio
» "Studio" arrangements that can be adapted for live performance
» "Studio" arrangements that have nothing to do with live performance

We'll examine each of these approaches and offer some strategies and specific techniques.

» *Dylan Says: When Cadence released our debut album,* Frost Free, *it made waves with its creative arrangements and years-ahead-of-its-time production values. But as we first started touring internationally, we were afraid the album production set the bar impossibly high, and our live performance would pale in comparison. It turns out the audience responded just as well to our (much-less-complex) live performance. You don't have to perfectly re-create your album onstage: engaging the audience is just as valid as a slick studio sound.*

» *Deke Says: Back in the early 1990s, we had a conundrum: the House Jacks were the first a cappella group with a designated vocal percussionist—the amazing Andrew Chaikin (now performing as Kid Beyond)—plus a variety of vocal-instrumental sounds and textures, and as a result, no one believed we weren't performing with tracks. However, in the studio we wanted to create recordings that pushed the boundaries and expectations of what a cappella could be. As a result, we decided to not use any effects at all when performing live—so we could proudly prove to the audience that everything they heard was coming from only our voices—but then, in the studio, we could use any effects we want to make the musical statements about what a cappella was and could be (if a guitar can have a distortion effect, why not a voice?).*

Listening with Your Eyes . . . and All Your Senses

You've probably heard the old phrase in cookbooks that we "eat with our eyes"; in live performance, we listen with our eyes as well. This is often interpreted to mean that the visual aspect of performance is the only other important factor, but it's far more than that. We have (at least) five senses, all of which are engaged in a live-performance experience. The look of performers onstage . . . but also the look of the theater, the lighting, the sight of your fellow audience members. The sound of a beautiful chord reflecting off the back of the theater, and moving around the room, mingled with the audience's murmurs of appreciation, the shuffle of programs, and the roar of applause. The smell of the venue, the snack you might be eating, the old wood of the concert hall, or the back kitchen of the club. Not to mention the human energy: the energy coming off the stage to you, as well as the collective energy of the audience, bouncing around the room and being sent back to the performers. It's a three-dimensional, multisensory experience, and the reason why nothing can beat a great live show.

In a studio recording, you have sound. That's it; that's all.

In a live performance, the musical/audio part may be the heart of the experience, but it's part of a larger whole. With a recording, the musical/audio performance is the whole. This is worth considering, especially when it comes to the live-performance arrangements you want to record.

To determine whether your live arrangements "make the cut" for the album, start by recording your group performing the arrangements, in a rehearsal space, with no audience. This can be a simple voice-memo recording on your phone: the "lo-fi" sound will represent the most-unvarnished, "before" representation of your potential album track. Later, give those recordings an honest listen—or better yet, have an unbiased friend listen—and see if the live-performance "wow" turns into a "ho-hum" when heard on its own, outside of a live setting.

"Live" Arrangements, Replicated As-Is

Before recording that live-in-one-take arrangement you've sung onstage for years, it's worth asking: Does this arrangement have everything you want in it?

There are some genres, such as barbershop, classical (European and non-European), and doo-wop, that benefit from a "pure" approach. Barbershop, for example, has a clear and traditional aesthetic: four voices aiming for the classic "lock and ring" of chords sung with perfect blend and intonation. With many European classical compositions, the aim is to replicate as faithfully as possible, note for note, the wishes of the composer. Often, these performance-based arrangements, especially if they're already being sung live, may have a natural ebb and flow and finely tuned phrasing that's hard to manufacture in the studio outside of a live approach. Adding more parts and textures may detract from the intent of the music. Or an arrangement may just stand on its own as a simple gem of a piece: it needs no embellishment, or it's designed to give the listener a breath of fresh air after hearing more musically dense tracks before and after. In all these cases, the original arrangement may be enough, and it needs nothing else to work in the studio.

This approach is not only effective in traditional musical forms. Pentatonix was formed for the live television show *The Sing-Off* and then followed up their season three victory with a series of YouTube videos in which they were singing current pop songs while sitting on a couch. In both cases, the arrangements were five-part: bass, VP, and three upper voices, usually one of them on lead. When they started making music videos of their arrangements, they continued to maintain this unadorned five-part sound, which was how they recorded their first album, and how they continue on through today. This is not to say they don't use any studio effects—they can double their parts for a warmer sound on a ballad, remove breaths and hold notes for impossible lengths, "split out" the vocal percussion sounds to create one vocal track that's just the kick drum and another that's just the snare, resulting in many VP tracks—but the aggregate sum is a shiny, polished, and carefully effected and mixed version of the same five-part arrangement they sing live. This is the sound they're known and loved for, and it makes sense they have chosen to stick with it on recordings even if they have the ability to add much more.

So, for our purposes here, let's say that "replicated as-is" means "the same parts you could/would sing onstage," not necessarily "only one voice per part in recording" or "five singers onstage means only five voices in the studio." To this end, it's worth our explicitly saying: background parts in an a cappella arrangement are often best when doubled, as it creates a warmth and fullness that single-tracked vocals don't have. Lead vocals can be doubled to give a specific characteristic sound that some professional vocalists use (like Peter Gabriel), but usually they're single tracked along with corresponding parallel duets and trios. Same goes for the bass line (unless it's a long, sustained note, along the line of something that would be bowed by an orchestral double bass) and vocal percussion. Simplest way to remember it: if in doubt, double your BGs; you can always use just one take if you don't like the sound.

"Live" Arrangements, Augmented

In the case of contemporary a cappella, the arrangement is usually an all-vocal rendition of a song originally including instruments. There are six strings to a guitar, eighty-eight keys to a piano, multiple instruments in the band . . . not to mention multiple overdubs of these instruments and, of course, the original lead and BG vocal parts. That's a lot of notes.

Chances are, in your four-to-eight voice group, you didn't cover every single note played on the original. Much of your arrangement work was a process of reduction or elimination: three guitar overdubs were amalgamated into something that two or three voices could handle, and many "superfluous" textures simply didn't make the cut.

It all works live, where a) the audience accepts that there's only a handful of singers onstage, and b) it takes delight in seeing how you manage to represent the song with the voices you have. But in the audio-only world of studio recording, it's possible that the arrangement sounds thin, and some of those textures the original artists saw fit to include in their version may have a place on your album. This, in many ways, is the easiest "win-win" situation. You already know you have a workable live arrangement: everything else you add for the studio version is just icing on the cake.

There are a few techniques you can use. First, start by retracing a few of the Ten Steps starting with Step Two: "Listen to the Original—Repeatedly." If you've been singing your live version for some time, you may have become so used to the sound of it that you've half-forgotten all the bits and pieces you had to leave out: have a few listens to the original to remind yourself of what's there and what you left on the cutting-room floor. Chances are, there will be a few moments when you say, "Oh yeah, that part. I totally forgot it was there, but I love it!" Make general notes on the parts and textures you like, but don't worry about notating them yet.

In addition, you'll likely find there's an overall fullness and/or warmth to the original studio recording that's different from your sparser a cappella version. That's likely the result of layers of sound you can barely hear, be it strings in the background or an additional layer of synth notes. In recording, this is called a "pad"—such as a synth pad, a keyboard pad, etc. This is not only easy to add to an existing a cappella arrangement, but it is an incredibly effective way to fill out the sonic space in your arrangement by creating a triad (in most cases, occasionally an open fifth or octave is better) of whole notes on a neutral vowel that will live quietly behind your busier live vocal parts. The listener may not really hear it, but they'll feel it.

Next, work out how to weave them into your existing arrangement: depending on what parts you're adding, and the structure of your existing arrangement, there are a few different ways to do this.

Adding New Material: Overdubbing

The simplest case is an added layer, such as another instrumental part/texture, that isn't represented anywhere in your live version. In this case, simply write the parts out, allocate your singers, and record. There's more on notational tips at the end of this chapter, but rather than grafting them onto an existing full score (or, worse yet, rewriting the full score), you can notate them separately in sketch form, save the sketch as "Song X_extra parts," and have the singers learn/read the bits and pieces as needed.

Here's an example of an original song Deke wrote for the House Jacks called "Quiet Moon."

Quiet Moon

Let's go down

Often when in the studio we would record our live parts and then just start to play, using our ears to tell us when and where we could and should add additional lines, but I would also sometimes write out specific parts when I knew what I wanted.

The live version featured myself on lead vocal, and I shifted to a vocal trumpet solo over the verse figure. The other band members were on two background parts—bass and vocal percussion—but this clearly wasn't enough (I love the lush bossa-nova orchestrations from the late 1960s), so I wrote out some vocal instrumental parts: a bank of strings, a flute section, and horns (all of which I tracked myself, so there was a consistency of phrasing and timbre). None were meant to be obtrusive, but rather they reflected the gentle, nuanced arranging of Claus Ogerman for Antonio Carlos Jobim.

Adding New Material: "Wild Tracks"

This is a technique used by groups such as The Nylons and other traditional doo-wop groups, but it can work with modern groups, too. It also works well for groups that learn/perform more by ear than with written music, and/or groups with singers who enjoy improvising.

In this case, the BGs may not be covering exact instrumental parts; instead, they are covering functional harmonies. Once the basic live arrangement is tracked, you can listen for any "thin spots" that could use extra textures. Or, if you are referring to an original artist/recording, you can listen with a "producer's ear" rather than a "transcriber's ear." What does that mean? Listen for additional parts, but pay less attention to what the part is (i.e., the instrument and its notes and rhythms) and more for what the part does (it adds drama to the chorus; it covers a transitional moment between sections; it thickens the sonic landscape; etc.).

Once you have a vague idea of where these spots are, and what you want in them, you can have a solo singer (or even a few) improvise lines and parts around the original arrangement. Record several takes: you may find they coalesce into several new parts, or you may find each take has something different to offer, and they can be "comped" (bits and pieces from different takes, compiled by the engineer) or layered into the arrangement in creative ways.

Adding New Material: "Reweaving"

So far, these techniques are all additive, leaving the original arrangement more or less intact, and adding layers. But it's possible you already cleverly interwove "hints" of the extra layers and parts you like into the basic parts. Adding more of the same may be redundant, or even sonically disruptive. This involves what we like to call "reweaving" the parts. Here's an example, from Dylan's arrangement of Michael Jackson's "Wanna Be Startin' Somethin'" for TTBB.

Wanna Be Startin' Somethin'

Michael Jackson

Here we have a live-performance arrangement, with two BGs doing not two, but three roles, over the course of just four bars: Rhodes, responsive BGs, and horns. It works live and covers a lot of sonic ground, but there's no reason for these vocal gymnastics in the studio: they sound better as separate layers. Instead, keep the Rhodes part going throughout and pull out the BGs and horns into their own parts, like this:

This has the added benefit of making things easier for the mix engineer, who would likely give the Rhodes part a different sonic treatment than ensemble vocals or brass. This also creates more sonic continuity between similar parts and more sonic variety to differentiate the different layers. This is also reflected in the different staff names: instead of T1 through bass—naming by singer—these are named after the instrument: the number of singers needed to cover the part is irrelevant.

"Studio" Arrangements, Adaptable for Live Performance

Very often, when recording a new album, you're also creating new performance repertoire. You're looking for an arrangement that takes full advantage of what the studio has to offer, but that can be adapted for live use, as well. It's a challenging needle to thread, but rewarding, too. Here are some general principles to make this possible.

A Modular Approach

This is similar to the "overdubbing" approach above, where we had a core live arrangement and added extra layers afterward. In this case, you're doing them semi-simultaneously. Imagine a six-voice group doing a contemporary pop song. In a live setting, that likely means one lead, one bass, and four BGs (or three BGs and one drummer). The lead, bass, and drum parts won't likely change much between the live and studio versions, so the main changes will occur with the BG parts. Start by writing your core live arrangement, using your three to four middle voices as you normally would.

Before you dig too deep into how you want to cover any extra instrumental layers and weave them into the live BG parts, start by keeping the inner BGs doing a similar part throughout, rather than switching roles. Take those extra layers, and write them on an extra staff: for example, one for an extra guitar part, and one for responsive BG vocals. As you write these extra layers, keep an eye (or ear) on how you would eventually fold these into the core BG parts for live performance. You don't have to do that yet—you're writing for the studio at the moment—but as long as it's front of mind, you can weave in the extra layers at a later time.

Here's another song Deke wrote for the House Jacks, called "Adventure Day."

Adventure Day

The song was written to be recorded in the studio, and so I thought about the structure less as a live arrangement and more as units, usually trios, that cover different functions from what instruments usually do.

Note that I didn't name the lines as instruments, as I didn't think of them as instruments, nor were they imitative in any way. Rather, they were distinct vocal units designed to fill different roles, the way horns, keyboards, and guitars do in a band arrangement (with the added bonus that they can sing lyrics when desired).

When designing the House Jacks, rather than looking for voices that were all similar, like most vocal ensembles of the twentieth century, I intentionally looked for very different vocal colors, more distinct than I'd ever heard in a vocal or a cappella group. My inspiration (here comes the nerdy part) was Schoenberg's *Pierrot Lunaire*, which later inspired the musical configuration known as the "Pierrot Ensemble": flute, violin, clarinet, cello, and piano (plus vocalist), where the flute would sometimes switch to piccolo, clarinet to bass clarinet, and all instruments would be used in different stackings and sonorities to create a wide range of sounds with just five instruments. To this end, I intentionally stacked our voices in different configurations. I'm "D," Garth was "G," and Austin was "A." By altering who was on the top of each stack, and knowing where each guy's voice shifted based on where the part landed in his range, I was painting with different colors, so the stacks would each have their own sound (generally Austin would provide a more gospel sound, Garth a more rock sound, and I'd sing the top part when we wanted a smoother falsetto or choral character).

Later I condensed all the notated sung parts into a singable live arrangement for just four voices plus VP:

Adventure Day

When you are doing so, your instinct will be to pack as much as you possibly can into the live version, but remember that you need to be reasonable—your singers need to breathe—and sometimes less is more. Introducing a figure that only gets sung for a half measure before being abandoned for another vocal part will likely just sound frenetic rather than full, or suffer from lack of sonic continuity. Also, you might wait until the studio version is mixed so you know for certain what the most important foreground elements are.

Expanding/Collapsing

This approach works well for arrangements (or sections therein) with homophonic and harmonically rich BG parts, such as Take 6 or Accent-style arrangements. In this example, imagine a four- or five-part group: bass, lead vocal, and two to three BGs. In the studio, expand your BGs by adding two more voices. You'll have a harmonic palette that is richer than the live ensemble, but that can easily be collapsible to two or three voices. Keep the eventual "live version" in your head as you write, and you'll be able to avoid any voicings that won't collapse well. Don't forget . . . in a live situation, your bass can temporarily pinch-hit as a baritone voice for a section of a bar, or the lead singer if they have any rests if you really want that extra voice!

Here's an example of Dylan's: "The Dry Cleaner from Des Moines," from the Cadence album *Twenty for One*. Cadence was a quartet, but many of the arrangements on the album were written for six parts, always with an eye to reducing them to four parts for live performance. The live versions work well, but the studio version gives the harmonic richness we wanted.

This chart was written for the studio first, and it looks like this (VP not notated):

The BGs start out as two voices: along with lead and bass, this is our four-part "core." To add dramatic effect, the voices build to five, then six, then back to five again. Since I knew I wanted this chart to be performable live, I made sure the extra two voices weren't always essential . . . and since the lead switches from myself to bass singer Kevin Fox, that leaves me free to pick up another part, and the three-part BGs stay intact:

When the time comes to collapse the chart for live use, see chapter 9, "Adapting Arrangements," for more detailed tips and techniques.

So far, these are fairly straightforward suggestions for creating an adaptable recording arrangement. The recording will sound like the live group, just richer and fuller, and the live adaptation will work equally well onstage. But what if you want something different, a larger "beyond the group" sound, but you still want to perform it live? It's a challenge, and it requires more work and technological help, but it's possible.

Live Looping

This is a bigger leap if you're not already using live looping in your live show, but if you're already looking to stretch that much artistically on record, you may be just as ready to do so onstage!

Live looping allows performers to layer their vocal parts in real time, similar to overdubbing in the studio. This can allow the addition of as many layers as you want to enrich the sound of the live arrangement. It works best with songs with a repetitive structure, or at least something that can be heard more than once. This can be as simple or complex as your technological and performance expertise allows. For example:

» A vocal percussion part is looped, freeing up a singer. Maybe more percussion parts are layered in as the piece expands.

Or:

» Song intro: the bass line is looped.
» Verse: the bass sings lead or adds their voice to the BGs to create a richer harmonic stack.

Or:

» Chorus 1: a basic live ensemble part is looped.
» Chorus 2: the basic ensemble part plays back, while the singers add a new layer live.

As long as the song isn't fully through-composed (i.e., no repeated parts from beginning to end), looping is a powerful tool to add depth to a live performance, and it may allow you to bring in some of the "studio candy" from your recorded arrangement.

For more detail on how to work with live looping, see chapter 8, "Live Looping."

» *Dylan Says: In my live-looping duo, FreePlay, we created a simple, intimate two-voice version of the Neil Young classic "Old Man." When it came time to record the album, we decided to go "full studio," and it became richly orchestrated. We fell in love with the new version . . . so we "reverse engineered" the studio version to create a new live-looping version for the stage that represented the studio version but was performable live.*

For both the studio and the live performance, Deke created a stack of live-looped parts to exist underneath DCappella's live performance of "Immortals" (by Fallout Boy in *Big Hero 6*). This song in particular needed more than six vocal parts. It needed a giant wall of sound, and the looper provided it:

Immortals

Backing Tracks

You can also abandon the pretense that your studio masterpiece can be replicated 100 percent live and use backing tracks to help. This works well for an ensemble of any size, but it may be more helpful for a smaller group that just doesn't have the number of live voices to cover all the studio parts.

Performing with backing tracks involves a certain "willing suspension of disbelief" from your audience: they don't want to feel like they are listening to a prerecorded track, even if they may be vaguely aware that they are hearing more notes than people onstage. You can help them enjoy your live-plus-tracks performance by keeping these principles in mind:

» Backing tracks should be just that: backing parts, not lead parts. Wherever possible, keep lead vocals, and maybe BGs with lyrics or any other "up-front parts," live.
» The more "instrumental" the part is, the less we notice it. Rhythm guitar–like parts, for example, work well as backing tracks.
» Repetitive parts work well: they "blend into the audio furniture," and while they may be essential to the structure of the song, we don't pay attention to them once we've heard the part a few times.
» Additional percussion layers (or even the whole VP track, if you need your drummer to sing) blend in well with live performances.
» Double-tracking of parts—even lead parts—can thicken the sound without drawing attention to the tracks.

Live ensemble parts can also be easily augmented with tracks. For example, if you have four BG voices in the studio, but only two live, the remaining two parts can be on tracks. You'll want to watch out that the tracks don't sound too different from the live singers: a studio track recorded to perfection on a ten-thousand-dollar microphone may not blend well with live singers moving around the stage singing on much cheaper, non-studio microphones.

To mitigate this, try creating a BG ensemble track like this:

» Part 1: sung live and on track, mixed at 50 percent
» Part 2: sung live and on track, at 50 percent
» Part 3: on track, double-tracked, at 100 percent
» Part 4: on track, double-tracked, at 100 percent

This gives a rich ensemble sound, represented "live" by two singers.

It helps to know in advance if you intend to sing the song live with tracks: you can arrange the studio recording with this in mind. When arranging and producing The Nylons album *Skin Tight*, the "live with tracks" version was baked into the studio version. To make this work, Dylan often arranged the album tracks as "double TTBB." One TTBB section represented what the singers would cover live; the other represented what would be covered by tracks. Here's an example: the classic superhero theme "Spider-Man."

Spider-Man

Paul Francis Webster
Bob Harris

You'll see that all the interesting content (the words/melody and the jazzy block-chord voicings) are in the top TTBB. The bottom TTBB, which would become the backing tracks in the show, have the neutral bass, percussion, and rhythm parts. They don't change much throughout the song, so they blend in, support the live singers, and stay in the background, where they belong.

"Backing Loops"

This is a clever trick for those who want to give the impression that they're creating the sound live, but who are actually using backing tracks. More and more, listeners understand concepts like live looping; they can perceive (even if they don't fully understand) that something was sung live, and now they hear it again even though the singers are doing something new. Some groups will "fake-loop" their parts: they sing a part as if they are looping it, but instead of being looped, the parts they just sang live are then represented by prerecorded tracks. This makes them blend more organically into the live performance. Regular live looping is unforgiving: if you sing incorrectly or out of tune, you hear it again, *ad infinitum*. Using backing tracks instead of actual loops is technologically simpler, and it avoids any live-performance risks. You could even use it to add more parts: if you "looped" three parts live and you hear five parts in the backing track, how many people would notice?

"Studio-Only" Arrangements

Up until now, we've presumed that the arrangement is going to be replicated live in some way. But it's not unusual to have a track or two where there's no thought of performing it live. Now the audio world is your oyster.

The first instinct will be, *More, more, more!* And why not? But you can channel this instinct into even more creative uses.

Think of the Beatles. Once they decided they didn't need to tour their albums, it opened up channels of creativity never before heard in popular music. If we're still recording a cappella, we've already got the "only voices" limitation, but there are plenty of techniques you could try that would be impossible in a live performance.

One Person per Instrument

We're used to the idea of having multiple voices covering a single instrument: it may take three or four voices to replicate a piano chord, or a strummed guitar part. The result is an ensemble sound that represents the part. With an instrument being represented by a multi-voice ensemble blend, and that same ensemble blend representing all the different instruments, you lose much of the individual character of each instrument: the multiple instrument characters can get lost in a homogeneous blend of voices. But what about having a single person per instrument . . . and only that instrument?

This is part of the Cadence arrangement of "Game," by the Norwegian acid-jazz artist Beady Belle. The instruments are: vibes, guitar, trombones, bass, and percussion. Cadence decided to experiment with true "instrumental separation" by allocating the instruments as:

» Dylan: lead vocal (one part, occasionally double tracked). To keep his sound "out of the instrument mix," he sings no instrument parts.
» Ross: electric guitar. His bright timbre works well for "bridge pickup" twang.
» Carl: trombones. His rich baritone lends itself naturally to lower brass.
» Kevin: bass and vibes. Kevin's smooth-but-bright tone easily replicated the pure-tone-plus-overtone sound of the metallic bars of a vibraphone, and the bass tone is muted and neutral.
» Drums: samples/loops by all members to avoid any "giveaway" vocal timbres from any individual member.

This was an interesting (and completely unperformable!) experiment, and it has a sound unlike the other tracks on the album *Twenty for One*.

Game

Beate Lech
Marius Reksjø

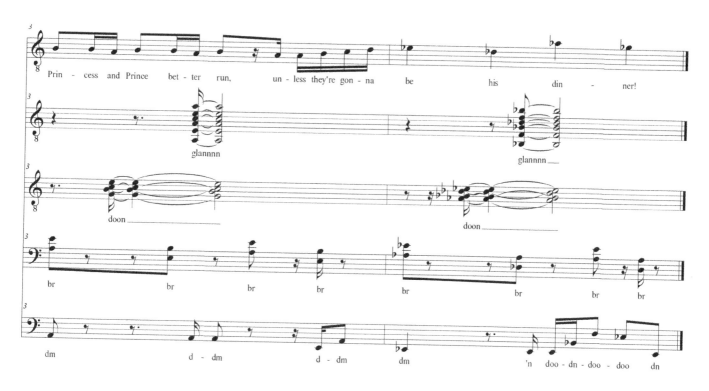

Another example of this is another song Deke wrote for the House Jacks, "After You." The song was designed for the studio; the group never even attempted to perform it live, as it was too layered, too nuanced, and just too much of a delicate studio-crafted arrangement to work well on the road. Perhaps it could have been performed in a completely different form, but not as it was envisioned in the studio, and Deke was fine with that.

After You

Not having to worry about what could be or would be done live was incredibly freeing during the arranging and recording of this song. Sometimes ballads are very fun to arrange, but making them work onstage after a frenetic, high-energy number (as many House Jacks songs were) means keeping a close eye on breaths, reasonable phrase lengths, and so on. Here it didn't matter, and that was a profound relief.

Mixed Double-Tracking

This is the polar opposite of the previous technique: instead of one person covering an instrumental section, we have multiple people covering the same part at the unison. Where same-person double-tracking gives a smooth, perfectly matched sound, mixed double-tracking offers a rich, complex, "fat" tone to the sound. The more difference between the vocal timbres, the more complex the sound.

A great example is the replication of a horn ensemble. Imagine the following combinations:

» Trumpet/trumpet: similar timbres, similar ranges
» Trumpet/alto sax: different timbres, similar ranges
» Trumpet/tenor sax: different timbres, different ranges
» Trombone/tenor sax: different timbres, similar ranges

You can create similar blends with voices.

» Soprano/soprano: similar timbres and ranges, similar voice types ("unchanged" voices). The timbres and ranges reinforce each other, but since no two voices are alike, the two singers will still give a consistent-but-complementary sound.
» Soprano/alto: different timbres and somewhat different points of range, similar voice types. Lower notes will be neutral/resonant in the alto, and low/light in the soprano. Higher notes will be clear/neutral in the soprano, and brighter/bolder in the alto. The differences complement each other.
» Alto/tenor: different timbres and somewhat different points of range, different voice types (changed and unchanged). Lower notes will be neutral/resonant in the tenor, and low/light in the alto. Higher notes will be clear/neutral in the alto, and brighter/bolder in the tenor. The differences complement each other.
» Soprano/tenor: different timbres and very different points of range, different voice types. Lower notes will be low/light in the soprano and medium-high in the tenor. Higher notes will be bright and clear in the soprano, and depending on the tenor and head-voice timbre, could be darker and resonant, or very bright and piercing. Either way, the differences can complement each other in different ways, over the common range of the two voices.
» Alto/bass: similar to soprano/tenor above, down a fourth or fifth.

» Tenor/bass: similar to soprano/alto above, down an octave.
» Soprano/bass: there's not as much common range here, but basses often have very resonant head-voices which can provide depth and support to complement the soprano's clarity.

For more information on mixed-voice ranges and blend, see chapter 4, "Vocal Ranges and Additional Techniques."

For a "fatter" sound, if the range of the part allows, a mixed-voice double track gives the most sonic variety.

In FreePlay's version of Miami Sound Machine's "Conga," Dylan and Suba were aiming for a broad, brash Cuban horn section sound. To do this, they each sang as many of the parts as their ranges would allow, with a different blend on each part. Here's how it was allocated, with the mixing balance of parts included in the notation.

Conga Horn Soli

You'll notice this notation is hardly "publisher-ready," and that leads us to . . .

Notation for the Studio

In our last book, we included a "Ten Commandments" of notational etiquette to ensure arrangements were considerate to the singers, as well as easy to read. In the studio, there's a lot more leeway.

Consider the purpose of standard notation. The premise is that, in rehearsal, the notation should allow for all singers to read their parts continuously from beginning to end, without any ambiguity as to which staff is theirs, or which note in a cluster is theirs, and with a clear form to follow. If the notation is too confusing to read in real time, much time is wasted explaining what parts to sing and when, and the rehearsal process falls apart. Our Ten Commandments were designed with these factors in mind.

Studio work is much different. In a typical contemporary a cappella recording process, singers are often recording either one at a time, or at most, a few singers singing similar parts together. The process involves singing a small section—as long as a verse, or as short as a couple of bars—many times until either the desired take is achieved or there are enough takes to comp together a useable take.

Taking this into consideration, continuity and clarity in notation is less essential. Instead, seeing the "function" of a part is more important for the singer, the producer, and the engineer. If a vocal guitar part consists of three-note chords, there's nothing wrong with notating them on the same staff: it may make things easier in the end for the engineer to see them together, to organize the tracks this way, and to edit and tune the parts. It may also make it easier for the producer to decide who tracks what parts, and when.

Here's an example of an untouched arrangement Deke brought into the studio with the House Jacks and Bill Hare (the sixth member for this album): "Unbroken" by Wes Carroll.

Unbroken

I heard his rough demo, a sketch of the lead vocal and strummed guitar, and in my mind I heard it blossoming into an industrial wall of sound over a slow grinding beat. Not only did I not bother writing out the melody, I didn't write in syllables. Or the form of the song (this figure was the intro/verse). I wasn't being sloppy, I was just providing the information needed for us to start on the journey to bringing the song to life, which we did, and, in fact, we named the album after it. Sometimes the best thing you can do in the studio is not overprescribe or over-intend, but rather start with some glimmers of ideas, then coax them to life in front of the microphone with your bandmates and engineer.

Similarly, since continuity isn't the key, it isn't always necessary for all layers and parts to be part of a master score. If you've got an idea for an extra gospel choir, scratch it out on a couple staves (or even one!) and just tell the singers which notes to sing and where to start. Go ahead—break a few rules. That's the magic of arranging for the studio!

CHAPTER 8

Live Looping

Question: What does live looping have to do with arranging? Answer: Plenty! Live looping has become increasingly common in contemporary a cappella practice. The most common format is the solo looper, performing as an a cappella "one person band" covering all vocal parts and drums (imagine a digital Dick Van Dyke in *Mary Poppins*, with an accordion in his hands and cymbals on his knees), or even focusing on a DJ-style hip-hop set of beatbox, grooves and hooks, and some singing. Much as the romantic ideal of a single person making all of the sounds themselves is compelling, live looping isn't just a dedicated solo art; it can be used in ensembles, as well. As live looping becomes stitched into the thread of modern a cappella practice, the associated arranging techniques deserve a special look. While it shares much in common with standard ensemble writing, there are plenty of differences and special applications of their own.

What Is Live Looping?

For those who are unfamiliar, live looping is the art of using technology—a loopstation*—to simultaneously record and perform musical phrases. The singer sings/records a phrase, and the loopstation plays it back as a continuously repeating loop. The singer can then layer other parts on top of this one to create multi-tracked parts. They can then sing live overtop (without recording or looping their live vocals), make different loops, switch between them, all combining to create some amazing textures. It's also possible to create full multipart songs approximating a full vocal ensemble all by yourself. It's a performance art all its own, and depending on the complexity of the arrangement and the performance, it can take years of practice to perfect.

---

* Loopstations are sometimes called "loopers"... but "loopers" can also refer to the artists who use live looping! For clarity, we'll use "loopstation" for the technology, and "looper" for the person.

Meet the Loopstations

The first "loops" were analogue tape loops constructed in the studio, sometimes several meters long, often running around the room and back into the tape recorder. They started out in the avant-garde world of *musique concrète* in the 1940s, and eventually they made their way into experimental pop music: the Beatles were early users of studio looping. Back then, there was no way to do this live. Nowadays, of course, the loopstations are digital and portable, and useable in live performance.

There are many different kinds of loopstations. They fall into two different categories, yet their functionality and application is largely the same.

Hardware Loopstations

These are dedicated physical looping machines that can be operated with foot pedals (useful for instrumentalists who have their hands full) or tabletop models with buttons and knobs operated by hand (more common for vocalists). Simple models may be a single pedal with only one loop, but most will have several, allowing for considerable freedom and creativity in building and manipulating the loops. Many have onboard effects that can be applied to the voice when recording or applied to the loops after recording.

Since they're designed specifically for this task, they work very well, with well-thought-out features. They tend to be intuitive, so you can get started fairly quickly after only a few hours of experimenting with the knobs and buttons. The downside to a hardware loopstation is that the features are largely fixed: for instance, if your machine has five loops, that's the maximum you can have with this station. You can't expand later since you're working with hardware, and perhaps someday (even if it's a long way away), you may find your creative ideas outgrow the limitations of the machine.

BOSS, one of the main loopstation manufacturers, has developed its loopstations with a cappella artists in mind! Newer models are typically created in consultation with a cappella looping artists, and each successive model is more "aca-friendly" than the last.

» *Deke Says: DCappella hit the road with a BOSS RC-505 on their first tour back in 2018, and they have brought it with them on major tours ever since. It allowed solo performances (such as "Step in Time" by only the alto—see below), as well as adding layers to complex arrangements, like their award-winning version of "Immortals."*

Software Loopstations

These vary considerably, from simple-but-powerful apps on your phone, to complex computer applications comparable to a DAW (digital audio workstation, such as ProTools, or Logic). In fact, sometimes DAWs themselves have looping capabilities built into them (such as Ableton Live), or they can be adapted to work as a loopstation (such as Reaper).

The main advantage to a software loopstation is power and flexibility. With a hardware loopstation, you have a maximum number of loops, functions, or effects. With the more advanced software loopstations, you are limited only by the processing abilities of the computer. Chances are, it can handle more loops than you can conceivably actively manage onstage. They are also practical: instead of another piece of equipment to carry around, it runs off your phone or laptop, something you likely carry with you anyways. However, all that power and flexibility comes at a cost: software loopstations tend to be more complicated to set up and use, they are more difficult to handle onstage, and though it's uncommon, the software is more likely to have glitches or even crash when contrasted with a solid state hardware loopstation.

>> *Dylan Says: When I started my a cappella live-looping duo, FreePlay, we started with a BOSS RC-50, a three-loop, foot-operated hardware loopstation. After a couple years of touring with it, we found that our creative ideas outgrew the features of the loopstation, and we eventually moved over to Ableton Live. As our creativity grows, the software grows with us!*

Basic Looping Principles

While this chapter won't delve deeply into the technical aspects of loopstations, it is important to understand the basic principles to conceptualize how to arrange for live looping. Both types of loopstations have the same general principles and abilities.

>> First, a loop is *recorded*. You can often preset how long the loop will be—e.g., four bars long—or it can be "free," meaning you start and stop it at will with the press of a button/pedal. If your loop is intended to be a specific musical length, you'll likely record it with the aid of the click track built into most loopstations.

>> Then you can *overdub* new layers onto this loop. You can usually overdub as many layers as you like: however, once they're recorded, they're generally "baked together," meaning they're essentially one thing. While you can generally "undo/redo" the last thing you overdubbed—for example, if you made a

mistake or weren't happy with your performance—you usually can't go back and remove a layer you added earlier.

» You can record other loops, doing the same process. You can even go back to another loop you recorded earlier, and overdub more parts.

» Once the loops are made, you can switch between them, or have them playing simultaneously.

You can think of the loops as "containers." Each container is separate, but the stuff in each container is all glued together.

Arranging by Instrument (A and B and C)

In contemporary a cappella ensemble arranging, we're used to the idea of one group of singers representing an instrument: for example, sopranos covering BGs, or altos and tenors representing a guitar. This approach lends itself well to loopstations. For example, you could arrange the pieces as follows:

» Loop A: drums and bass
» Loop B: guitars
» Loop C: BGs

With all elements of the same "instrument" on the same loop, it's easy to add/subtract instruments to create variety in the song performance.

Arranging by Form (A or B or C)

Or you could assign each loop to a section of the song, like this:

» Loop A: verse
» Loop B: chorus

Then alternate loops to create the form of the song.

"But wait!" you might say. "Only two loops for that? What about a bridge, or what if the verses aren't the same length?" We'll get to that in a moment.

Combination of Form/Instrument (A and [B or C])

Arranging by instrument or by form are both useful, but it's possible that you may want to combine both approaches. Most late-model loopstations (and all software loopstations) will allow this. That allows something like this:

» Loop A: drums (instrument)
» Loop B: verse (form)
» Loop C: chorus (form)

Then you can keep the drums going throughout while you alternate verses and choruses.

If your loopstation has mute buttons, you can also alternate song forms by toggling the mutes for the right loops, like this:

VERSE

» Loop A: drums
» Loop B: verse
» ~~Loop C: chorus~~ (muted)

CHORUS

» Loop A: drums
» ~~Loop B: verse~~ (muted)
» Loop C: chorus

This involves a little more dexterity with the buttons, though.

This cover the basic principles. Now let's talk about the actual arrangement process. For this purpose, we will imagine that you want to sing an actual song with layers and variation throughout, as opposed to laying down a single groove and jamming/rapping/DJ-effecting over it as they did in the days of early hip-hop in the 1970s and 1980s. And yet, even if you do want to replicate early hip-hop, many of the same considerations will apply, even if some will be simple and straightforward.

Arranging for Solo/Duo Looping

Let's use the Ten Step Method while considering arranging for loopstations, with specific attention to what we have to modify for live looping. But first, let's take a quick look at the two main inherent challenges of solo/duo live looping:

» *Layering takes time.* An ensemble can sing a four-bar chord progression in, well, four bars. For you, it's multiples of that. If there are four or more parts to layer, it takes four or more times as long (assuming you do everything perfectly without having to redo a section). All this means is that it can take some time to "build up" the start of your song; you may be a minute or two into the song before you've sung a single note or lyric of the lead vocal.

» *New sections mean rebuilding.* Once you've built up your verse, you're ready to launch into a big chorus, and . . . there's nothing. You have to build it up from scratch, just like you did with the verse, and this means a significant dip in energy and another length of time to get all the parts layered.

If these challenges aren't taken into consideration, your three-minute pop song becomes a meandering, seven-minute saga with lots of drops in the energy. Plus, if you're uncertain or confused, you'll be staring down at your loopstation instead of out at the audience. But fear not: for every challenge, there is a solution (or at the very least, a hack). We want your performance to be compelling and as cleverly condensed as possible. We'll show you how to structure your arrangement and jump the hurdles as we work through the steps.

Step One: Choose a Song

This is one of the biggest decisions and most important considerations when live looping. Looping is, by definition, cyclical, which gives us an important indication as to what kind of songs will work best. For your first loopstation arrangements, start with songs that fit any of these parameters:

» *Groove-based music,* such as R&B, funk/soul, hip-hop, or EDM (electronic dance music): The groove is a big part of the success of the song, so once you have a great-sounding, rhythmic texture, the other parts might not need to be as dense (a funky bass line and great lead vocal might be enough).
» *Simple, cyclical chord structures:* These don't have to be groove-based at all, or even have a rhythmic element. Think of folk songs, pop songs with repeated chords (like doo-wop), and the like. Some non-Western genres are built on this foundation, as well, especially if they harken to an aural tradition.
» *Ostinato or riff-driven:* An *ostinato* is a repeating musical loop, making it a natural fit. You could loop the ostinato, and "sing around it" for the rest of the song. Think "Another One Bites the Dust" by Queen, "Bittersweet Symphony" by the Verve, or "Superstition" by Stevie Wonder—a single musical idea/texture is a huge part of the song, with the melody varying over it. Pachelbel's Canon in D is a very well-known ostinato, and Maroon 5's "Memories" was effectively written atop it.
» *A small number of sections* (e.g., just verse and chorus): This means you have less to create, so there's less time building up to your full backing tracks.

Why is this important?

In theory, you could probably do just about any type of song, but consider that as a solo looper, you have to sing through any given loop a few times at least in order to get in all the parts. If the chord structure is longer (say, sixteen bars), that's thirty-two, forty-eight, or sixty-four bars just to complete that section of the song—and that's just laying down the parts, before you even start singing the melody.

Now imagine the song has several sections: a verse, a chorus, a verse with a slightly different length, and a bridge. Every time you have a new section, you'll have to create a new loop, again layering a few times before you have all the parts down. Not only does this take even more time, but since the new section has to start from scratch, your song will have that dip in energy every time you start a new section/loop.

One more consideration is the harmonic density of the song, which is another way of saying the complexity of the chords. A song with five chord factors in most chords, such as what you find in many songs by Steely Dan or in the jazz world, presents a similar problem to those mentioned above, as you will have to sing through the section five times as opposed to three for triads. This is a simplification, of course—a clever arranger can drop chord factors and come up with other ways to increase the apparent harmonic density (such as relying on the melodic notes)—but the challenge remains. Songs with long sections, many sections, and many harmonic notes all present the same challenge: they take more time to establish.

Step Two: Listen to the Original; and
Step Three: Look at/Listen to Other Versions

As you would when working on any arrangement, you'll want to listen to the original song over and over again not only to learn the melody, chord changes, and form, but also to absorb its soul, character, and emotion, while hearing through the obvious layers down to its little bells and whistles. Once you've spent enough time with the original, it's always valuable to listen to other versions of the song to see how others have approached the arrangements. As always: good artists borrow; great artists steal.

At this stage, if you're an experienced vocal arranger (as we assume you are, if you've picked up this book), you're probably starting to sort out a little of the who-does-what, be it as simple as mentally sorting the instruments into voices, or as significant as drastically transforming the song into something entirely new. In fact, if you're like us, you rarely hear a new song that you don't inadvertently start arranging in your head.

When arranging for a loopstation, you'll engage in this same process of absorbing, parsing, and recombining, but in a different way. You might listen to an instrumental part and consider how you'd distill it into a repetitive four-bar loop. Instead of thinking about your arrangement in terms of part allocation, you might be thinking of the musical "containers" you have (i.e., the number of loops you can/want to use), as well as how best to use them.

Step 4: Decide on a Form

This is quite different from standard arranging. We always say that "form is flexible": sections can be added/subtracted or moved around. In a standard arrangement, moving form around can happen for some creative purpose (or to keep the arrangement moving), but for looping, the main reasons are function and momentum.

We mentioned earlier the challenges of solo live looping. Creative use of form can help. For example:

If some sections have an uneven number of bars, see if they can be "rounded out" to a more standard four-bar form. For example, your chorus is ten bars long: a four-bar chorus structure done twice, plus a two-bar "break" before the next verse. Instead of a ten-bar loop to get through, cut out the break, and there's a good chance your eight-bar chorus can be done with a repeated four-bar loop instead.

If rebuilding the chorus disrupts the energy, consider starting your arrangement with the chorus instead of the intro or verse. Hearing the chorus being built can make for a compelling introduction, especially if you build the layers in an unexpected way. The audience's reaction: "What is that song . . . oh! Cool!"

If there are variations (say, one verse is longer than the other, or the choruses don't have exactly the same chords each time), consider some creative editing of the words/chords to make them the same. Then you can use the same loop for both verses or choruses. Sometimes a singer/songwriter adds pauses and variation for effect to emphasize lyrical moments (such as Harry Chapin's "Cat's in the Cradle"), and usually these can be rounded out effectively, at which point you can use other methods of focusing on specific lyrics (e.g., additional harmonies, or your emotional interpretation of the lyrics).

If there is a bridge, consider cutting it. Or if it is important, break it down to just drums and sing the bridge overtop the groove without spending much time establishing a new chord progression and/or texture. Not only will this save you the hassle of making yet another loop, but it provides a nice sonic break. A bridge is supposed to "take you away" from the song, then bring you back. The change in sonic texture can actually emphasize that, and a necessary hack becomes a cool, creative tool.

Also, deciding on form may not be the fourth step: more likely, it will be an "ongoing step" as you work through the various stages and discover the need for changes. You may need to spend some time figuring out what your layers will be before knowing how you'll build them, and once you have that order figured out, it may either inspire you or force your hand into a specific form. Either way, as is always the case with arranging, confident choices and performances put the audience at ease, and they'll never "see your work" and know that you felt you had no choice but to design the form in a specific order. Even if you only have one option, if it works, it works.

For experienced ensemble arrangers, much of the process of deciding on form is done inside your head: you know all the sections; you can move them around virtually and imagine what they sound like. Plus, the form of a song usually hews pretty closely to the original, with a couple trims here and there, so it's not an extremely complicated process. Since moving big sections around in notation can be messy, it's often better to work it out as much as possible in your head or on scratch paper before notating.

On the other hand, for live looping, the process is much more experiential: you need to go through the musical process, learning how long each part takes to develop as you'd like it to, and where the forward momentum is lost. Be prepared to work on individual sections—the chorus, the verse—then make changes once you hear what works and what doesn't.

Step 5: Prepare Your Materials

For arranging, this is all your scoring stuff: getting your notation software up and running, maybe mapping out your staves if you know the number of parts. For looping, this is getting your mic and loopstation up and running, and if you know some of the basics of your song already, preparing the loop parameters (such as loop length), setting a metronome and tempo, etc. Most loopstations allow you to store a song as a "patch," so set up the parameters, save them, and most importantly, name it! You don't want to scroll through a dozen "patch #X-es" later, wondering where your song went or, heaven forbid, overwriting it with another song.

It's also very helpful to have a pad of paper and a pen on hand. Many of your rough ideas will come quickly, and it's best to jot them down whenever they occur to you, then you can later address them fully once you're done with setup or whatever your current task is. Prepare before getting into the weeds with musical ideas, as the better you're set up, the better prepared you'll be when the ideas start flowing.

Steps 6 and 7: Write Out the Melody and Bass Line

These steps are less important to focus on and differentiate for a looping arrangement, but don't skip them entirely. Instead of writing out the melody, consider, as you would for an ensemble arrangement, how the melody and/or lyrics might inspire or factor into your arranging choices.

For the bass line, there are some functional considerations, particularly how the bass line fits with the different sections. If the bass line is continuous, you might want to put it on its own loop—or, if you want more loops free for other parts, you could put bass and drums on the same loop. If the chord structure changes from verse to chorus, you'll want to layer the bass line in as part of the loops for each verse/chorus.

One important consideration that affects both the melody and the bass line is vocal range, since a looped song is usually being performed by a solo singer.

Obviously you want as low and powerful a bass line as possible, and you want the lead vocal to sit in the singer's "sweet spot." Both may not be possible. Moreover, unless the singer is experienced in major tessatura shifts from measure to measure, it may be that singing at the bottom of their range and then immediately leaping up to a soaring melody is just too much to handle, even if both are possible on their own. If this is the case, consider building the song with much or all of the bass line first, then leaving the singer to focus on the melody. Many loopstations come with an octave effect: it can come in great use here.

Step 8: BGs

Like standard arranging, you'll spend much of your time on this, but again there are some considerations specific to looping.

On the positive side . . . much time is spent (especially in smaller groups with only one singer per part) creatively allocating parts to get the most out of the finite number of voices. In this case, live looping is akin to studio recording: you can keep layering parts to your heart's content. Keep in mind that layering parts takes time, but adding extra voices to a short loop doesn't take too long, and in fact, it can build energy and momentum. Also, you can't easily subtract individual parts once they're layered in, so maybe save the best for last.

Your method will be a little different from scoring a standard arrangement. First, you decide how you want to organize your loops. Depending on your loopstation, a good maximum number of loops is three to four (maybe five if you're experienced): any more than that, and it gets too hard to organize the starting/stopping/muting of loops as you go through the song. Consider what you need for the form of the song. If it has only one groove/chord progression, you've got lots of loops on which to put different instruments, and you can add many different textures to bring in and out as you go through the song. If there are verses and choruses, you'll need a separate loop for each of them. Remember: all the parts of one "instrument" (say, a guitar, or a horn section, or a set of BG vocalists) can go on the same loop.

Next, start jamming on your ideas to see if you like them. You can do this by instrument first; then, once you've got them sorted out, work section by section. Another way to think of this process is the variance between horizontal (moving through time/bars of music/sections) and vertical (layering parts in one section). Work on one until you hit a snag, then move to the other, back and forth, until you have a full song.

Step 9: The Final Touches

For live looping, we'd rename this step "assembly." This is how you work out the order in which you want to record the parts, and how you want to move between them, paying attention to factors like how long it takes to set up a loop and how to keep momentum going. If you have multiple choruses, for example, you don't have to build the loops up all at once: each time through the chorus, you can add something to it. You could even record the lead vocal first, then use subsequent choruses to add vocal harmonies or even instrumental-type parts. As mentioned earlier, you may only decide at this late stage what the final form will be.

This is also a good time to experiment. If you think of your arrangement as a finite set of building blocks, like the LEGO pieces in a small set, you can see what you have "left over," as well as what you need in the way of variation. You might try layering something on top you wouldn't have necessarily considered, but you only have so many building blocks, and your final chorus is in need of a "push over the cliff" (akin to Spinal Tap's amp that goes to eleven). Sometimes you stumble on unexpected cool combinations when "happy accidents" occur mid-song and you hit the wrong button; here in Step 9, you have an opportunity to see if you can stumble upon one. Most won't work, but that's okay, as you're looking for just a couple final touches.

Step 10: Perform and Learn

In your live-looping performance, this translates to "practice, make mistakes, practice again, make more mistakes, change something that doesn't work or is too hard to execute, practice, make a new set of mistakes, and eventually figure it out." This step is far more intense than a regular performance. We all know how to learn our part for a song: we've been doing it as long as we've been singing. But now, we're simultaneously learning all parts for a song, often for just a few bars at a time, and adding an extra layer of technological learning—something we haven't been doing forever.

It's important to remember: a loopstation is an instrument, not just a bunch of pedals or buttons. Learning and mastering a loopstation takes the same amount of repetitive practice and incremental progress that learning the guitar might take.

Moreover, in ensemble performance, once you make a mistake, it's gone, and chances are, you'll sing that part again in the next chorus and (hopefully) get it right. The rest of the ensemble has your back and will keep the song going. But the loopstation is unforgiving: make a mistake, and you'll hear it over . . . and over . . . and over again. Perfection (or something close) is the name of the game. And if you make a mistake with the buttons, you may not be able to recover from it. It's a lot to take on, but you will begin to get better at singing with precision, all while having enough bandwidth to remember the technological layers.

Be kind to yourself, recognize that you're learning and doing many things at once, and give it plenty of time to sink in. It's often said that you have to have made every mistake possible in rehearsal before you can properly perform a new live-looping song onstage.

>> *Deke Says: I'll be honest: many of the loopstation performances I've seen have been dreadfully boring as the performer is staring down at a hunk of metal instead of up at the audience, and the vocal performance has all the charismatic charm of a computer programmer trying to debug a confusing line of code. Remember that no one in the audience cares how technically difficult your process is; they just want to feel something, to be taken on an emotional journey. Look up and connect!*

We always recommend that an arrangement be considered "open-source software," open to tweaks and fixes as new issues get discovered in rehearsal. The same goes for a live-looping arrangement. You may not realize until several run-throughs that moving quickly from one vocal part or loop to another is just too difficult, similar to bad voice-leading in a written chart. If so, give yourself a little extra space and allow extra time through the loop before continuing. Remember that a good arrangement isn't one that only works in the most perfect of settings; it's one that works time and again, so if you're requiring something that can only be sung well 35 percent of the time, it's not a good live arrangement, and you're better off with a simpler choice. The audience will never know.

Finally, try to simulate your performance setting, or at least get used to different environments. We all know in regular live performance how different it feels and sounds onstage compared to in the rehearsal room: this goes double when you add a layer of technology. Maybe your loopstation is on a lower table and everything feels off, or your mic stand won't stay in place, or the lights are too low and you can't see the buttons well, or you always practice sitting at a desk and haven't tried it standing up.

>> *Dylan Says: I learned a few hard lessons about stage lighting while live-looping: on one stage, the lighting was such that the green "playback" light and the yellow "overdub" light were exactly the same color. I was totally lost. And try doing quick foot-pedal work in heels . . .*

Examples

"Fireflies" (Dylan)

FreePlay has a live-looping arrangement of "Fireflies," a pop song originally recorded by the UK synth-pop band Owl City. I loved this song, and it seemed like a good choice. I found a couple of challenges, though . . .

» The song has not one, but two choruses. They're very similar, but the ending lyrics are different, and the ending chord changes are slightly different.
» The drums toggle between softer and louder energy.
» It was a challenge to keep the momentum building through the song.
» There's a really cool breakdown to end . . . difficult to do when you can't "unlayer" parts!

This is how we solved those challenges and built our arrangement. A note is worth a thousand words, so we recommend listening along. The link can be found in Appendix C, "Music Links."

The song has four loops in total, set up like this:

» Loop A: light drums (4bb)
» Loop B: verse: bass line and synth part (4bb)
» Loop C: chorus instruments: bass, guitars, heavy drums, lead chorus vocals (8bb)
» Loop D: chorus BG vocals (8bb)

Here's what they look like in traditional notation. Keep referring to them as I describe the song. These represent the "end result" when all the parts are added in: we'll describe the order of the parts below. First, the verse loops (A and B):

Fireflies

Adam Young

Next, the chorus loops, C and D. Note that the chorus is actually an eight-bar loop, four bars of which are reprinted here:

The original song starts with a synth intro. But when we arrived at the first chorus, we didn't want to build it from scratch—a chorus is generally meant to have a rise in energy, not a lull as you build parts, so we started the song like this:

> » Record Loop A: drums (4bb). This will keep playing throughout the song.
> » Record Loop D: chorus melody (lower octave) + harmony (8bb).
> » Record Loop B: two synth parts ("Suba 1" and "Dylan 1"), then overdub a third synth part and bass ("Suba 2 and Dylan 2").

(You might be asking, "Why not record in order: Loop A, B, C, D?" See "Keeping Organized," later in the chapter.)

That whole buildup doesn't take too long, so the audience isn't bored waiting for the song to start. In fact, they're more curious to know what's going on: they see that you're building things, but they don't know what it will end up sounding like. Starting with the chorus words early on, rather than a minute of instrumental "doots" and "doos," gives them something to focus on and indicates where you're going.

> » Sing verse 1 live over Loops A and B. Suba sings the lead vocal, and I add a baritone harmony to the bass line.

Then we get to the chorus again . . . but instead of having two choruses, we simplified and used just one for the whole song:

> » Overdub Loop C: Chorus guitar parts ("Gtr" staff) while Loop A and Loop D (chorus melody) are playing back.

Normally the song goes into another verse right away, but after trying out the arrangement, we realized we needed a little more breathing room before launching into the next verse, so we added one extra round of the verse groove first:

> » Vocal interlude/string lines over Loops A and B (8bb).
> » Sing verse 2 live over Loops A and B. Dylan sings lead while Suba adds string lines, giving further variety to the song.

Now it's time to build up the second chorus. We already have melody and guitar parts, so now . . .

> » Chorus 2: add the chorus bass part (staff "Bass") and a doubling of the chorus (staff "Lead Vox") melody up the octave on Loop C, while Loops A and D play back.

Another two verses in a row:

> » Verses 3 and 4 over Loops A and B

Note there's no real buildup in the verses: we save that for the choruses. We've got two more to go, so how do we keep building? How about this:

» Chorus 3: overdub heavy drums (staff "Drums") and double up the high lead (staff "Lead Vox" again) while Loops A and D play back.
» Chorus 4: no more overdubs: rock out and improvise live over all the layers we've built.

. . . and now, time to end. The original ends with a breakdown . . . but we've built all this stuff up. What to do?

If you take a look back, you'll notice that at the beginning of the song, we recorded two vocal parts on Loop D . . . and we haven't added anything since to that loop. So . . .

» Stop playback on all loops except Loop D, sing live harmonies overtop.

. . . and there's your four-voice breakdown to end.

You'll notice that this was done with two singers. What if there's just one? It's still all possible: you'd just need to double each section you want to overdub. Or with a solo artist, you could add fewer parts as you go.

"Step in Time" (Deke)

When designing a set for the not-yet-formed DCappella, I knew I wanted to have the second act blow people's minds, and having one member perform with a loopstation would be a nice departure from the seven-member formula. I settled on the alto, who didn't have many solos throughout, but what should the song be? I needed something from the Disney canon, so much of which is harmonically complex and in some cases even through-composed, which is a nonstarter for looping.

Then I remembered the famous London rooftop scene where the chimneysweeps sang a song that sounded like it had been written for a British pub singalong: "Step in Time." With its frequent refrain, it was the perfect choice. However, creating a vibe for the audience is everything, and that song was designed to be a raucous dance party, which isn't easily reproduceable with just one person. So, I went the opposite direction, toward an ethereal, moody performance with a starry backdrop.

Rather than announce the song, we segued right into it, with everyone else leaving the stage and the lights dimming. I chose to leave the lyrics until later, and in place of vocal percussion, I started with some breaths: "ha, ho, ha," followed by a series of layers that didn't give away the song at all, but rather set the mood: a high descant on "ee," followed by a repeated figure "noo noo" and an offbeat "hoh." At this point, the audience had no idea what the song was, nor could they entirely tell where the downbeat lay. They were floating in sound:

Step In Time

This all not only set a mood, but it was clear the way these parts were performed that she'd make a sound, then step back from the loopstation and let the audience see that she'd recorded that part; it was now playing back. This "brought the audience along," so they didn't all of a sudden wonder where all the voices were coming from, or assume she was singing along with a recording. In this case, we needed to clearly show how looping worked without a boring tutorial, which this introductory sound-building did nicely.

At some point, we needed to build the refrain, but rather than have it all be laid out at once, I wanted to emphasize the word *time*, so over the loops above, the alto now just sang the word "time, time, hmm time"—middle part, then low part, then high part, and only after all three were recorded did she speak/sing "step in" in the gaps between:

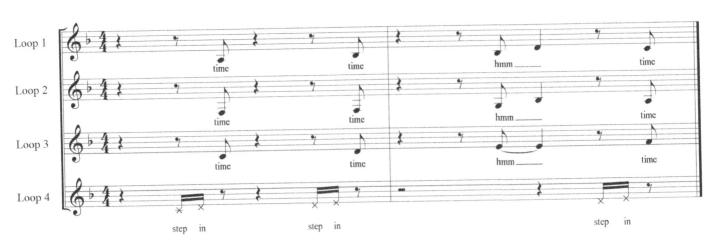

Now that we'd established how the loops were built, we could move more quickly, so she didn't wait to show the audience how these were recorded; she just sang these parts on top of one another in immediate succession. The result was that we started ethereal, and we were then building up steam. However, there's one more part of the song that we needed before we could go through the form in earnest:

Sung from the bottom note up, this four-part figure is necessary in the middle of the loop, and while recording it, everything else was muted, so it provided a bit of a break from everything that had been recorded thus far; more importantly, it felt momentous when it all came in at once together to create the complete unit:

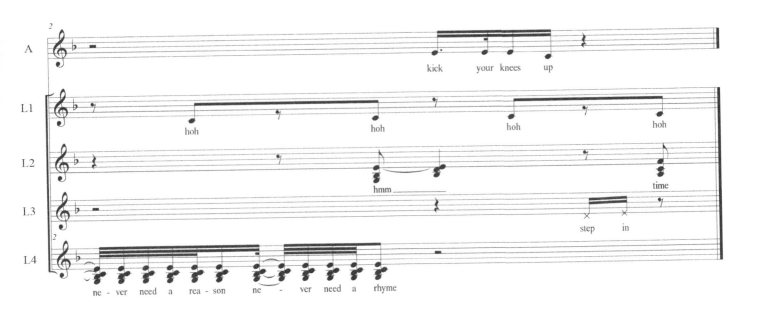

For many in the audience, it wasn't clear what the song was until this moment, and you could hear the gasps from the house as the core of the song started in earnest here. The beauty and charm of the situation at this point is that, like the original song, the lead vocalist can change the top line lyrics, and everything else remains the same ("round the chimney," "flap like a birdie," "up on the railing," etc.).

For the record, I initially arranged the song with the two-measure interlude between each loop, but upon rehearsing it, I quickly removed them. As is always the case in a cappella "trim the fat"—those two measures provided nothing, and the song flowed much more smoothly when one verse went right into another.

Now, you may be wondering why I waited to introduce vocal percussion. Two reasons: this song, while designed almost perfectly for a loopstation, has one drawback: it is unrelenting without a bridge or any other escape from the cycle—and we needed something to kick the energy up halfway through lest the audience get lulled into a somnambulant state (a little is a good thing, right after a high energy performance, but not too much, as we didn't want any snoring dads). Whereas most live looping relies heavily on the vocal percussion groove from the start to create glue that binds everything together, in this case I decided it was best to inject it halfway through, which we did, to the delight of the audience, many of whom had likely never seen a woman beatbox before.

Everything muted/froze, and she laid down layers, light "hardware" first (hi-hats and cymbals), then a full drop to the bottom of her range along with snare. Then, once established, the previous loops were reintroduced, and we were off to the back half of the song with a renewed energy and sound. We had everything we needed, and all that remained was how to end the song. Everything had been in place so long for so many loops I felt we needed something different at the end, to tie it up and give a sense of closure. Also, I wanted to return to the ethereal feel of the beginning, which was easier than finding a way to build even further with just one singer, who had pretty much spent the entirety of her beatboxing skills on the previous loops.

I took a line from the original "step in time you step in time" and removed the last word, so it became "step in time you step in . . . ," which was building toward something but didn't have a sense of closure. The alto mutes everything at the loopstation, sings the line three times (mid, low, then high, looping the others), and then brought back just the high "ee" and the last "hmm time"—so the line could end with the final word "time" we were all wanting, and the texture returned to what we had at the beginning.

You may notice the performance note "walk away from the board," which is not what I recommend you do while performing, but it did make for a cool moment as the song completed itself without her having to press any more buttons. Our sound engineer had to mute channels from the loopstation at the back of the house, but no one was thinking about that: it just gave us a great way to end the song with the loopstation alone.

Speaking of the sound engineer, having someone behind the soundboard allowed us to play with the EQ and placement of the various loops, which was an important part of creating the overall mood. The "Ha Ho Ha" was thrown in a delay, the "step in" was high-passed so it sounded like it was coming out of an old radio, and more importantly, it clearly was a different layer, and so on. When in a house with a stereo mix, our engineer could place the different loops in different parts of stereo space, from left to right, which underscored that the different loops were discrete units, reminding the audience of all the cool layers that had been built, "letting them into the process" a bit more, rather than just building a wall of sound that all blended together. I wanted the effect of having many altos coming from different places with different sounds, and having an engineer differentiate sounds helped this enormously. The BOSS RC-505 has six direct outputs (mix left and right, direct 1 left and right, and direct 2 left and right), so you can preassign what will be going through which channel in advance.

Keeping Organized

Trying to recall what loops are where, especially from song to song, can be challenging. It can help to have a system to organize your loops. There are a couple of options:

» *Chronological order:* A simple solution is to always record your loops A-B-C-D, regardless of what instruments they are, or what sections of the song they are. That makes it easy to get started, since building up the loops is where most of the critical button-pushing happens: moving A-B-C-D is nice and straightforward. But it might make it more difficult later on if you're starting/stopping loops. It's easier to toggle between a verse and a chorus, for example, if the loops are right beside each other. Also, there is no continuity from song to song; depending on what order you record your loops in, the guitars, bass, drums, and other parts may be in different places in each song.

» *Score/part/section order*: This can be a bit fuzzy, since not every song has the same parts or sections, but this is how I (Dylan) do it. Imagine a musical score (vocal or band) with the highest parts on top, and bass/drums on the bottom. I do something similar. In a song with few sections but lots of layers, drums (and bass, if it's on the drum loop) are always on Loop A. Next are rhythm-section parts on Loop B, then higher/more present parts such as horns or BGs in later loops. If the song has sections, I keep the drums on Loop A, then verses and choruses on Loops B and C. This makes it easier to switch sections, since the loops are side by side. An added bonus: if you start using effects (say, compression on drums or octaver on the bass), using the same loop positions from song to song makes it easier to copy effects from one song to another.

One system isn't necessarily better than another; it has more to do with what feels more natural and logical to you. But wherever possible, find a way to organize and stick with it.

Notation

Although we've provided notational examples here, we did this for the purpose of this book; we rarely notate live looping arrangements for our own use. Why? Consider the basic functions of Western-style music notation:

» Getting complicated combinations of notes down on paper so they can't be forgotten. Often these parts are too difficult to learn easily by ear.
» Transmitting that information efficiently to several people. Remember, in the days before recorded music, there were only two ways to transmit music: orally/aurally and written down. This was once for composers to give to musicians, and it meant their music could be reproduced anywhere in the world without them even being there.
» The information consists of pitches, rhythms, and musical performance instructions, such as tempo, dynamics, and aesthetics, meant to be passed from one person to another.

There's not much reason to write a full score unless you're arranging it for someone else to sing. However, there are many pieces to the puzzle: you'll definitely want something to keep it all together in your mind. Plus, there's a whole other level of less-familiar stuff—the technological side—that probably needs more notation than, for example, the rhythm of the guitar parts you came up with. You could write these looping instructions in a musical score, but they would be difficult to follow when combined with all the note information. Also, given that we've all had more experience in learning music than learning the looping technology, we're more likely to be able to memorize notes more easily than button-pushing instructions.

Many loopers will write a "script" that includes a line-by-line order, covering:

» What part of the song.
» What loops are being used, and what is being done with them (recording, overdubbing, starting/stopping, muting, etc.).
» A guide to what pitches to sing and when. You'll likely remember the general function of the parts themselves, but you might need a reminder of what order to sing them in (i.e., soprano, tenor, alto) and on what pitches they start.

Here's an example of a script Dylan made for a solo live-looping arrangement of the classic Ben E. King song "Stand by Me." Notes in [*italics* and brackets] are annotations/explanations; they're not in the script. To make the script make sense, here's what the parts look like in traditional notation:

Stand By Me

Stand By Me Script

> Loop 1: percussion/bass
> Loop 2: verse BGs
> Loop 3: chorus BGs
>
> 2–bar countin: 1, 2, 1-2-3
>
> ** L1: PRESS RECORD ON BEAT 3 [*for pickup*]
>
> L1 REC: bass (8bb)
>
> L2 REC: alto (starts on D, 8bb)
> [*I remember my part so I don't need to spell it all out*]
>
> L2 OVERDUB tenor (B♭); sop (F)
>
> L1 OVERDUB shaker/triangle ** OUT at m8
> [*the melody starts on a pickup: I have to leave a bar empty or the pickup gets recorded!*]
>
> 3 beats rest: Sing verse 1
>
> L2 MUTE
> L3 REC: chorus melody (start on downbeat)
>
> L3 OVERDUB: chorus lower harm ** OUT at m8
> [*why a double chorus at the beginning then the original song doesn't have one? Same "pickup problem" mentioned earlier. I need a full 8bb loop recorded first.*]
>
> L3/L2 SWAP [*my own lingo, meaning "mute L3 and unmute L2"*]
> Sing verse 2
>
> L2/L3 SWAP
> L3 OVERDUB: Chorus upper harm ** OUT at m8
> L3/L2 SWAP
>
> Scat solo (16bb)
> L2/L3 SWAP
>
> Improv/vocal stylin' over chorus 2X
>
> ALL MUTE/STOP
>
> Sing last bassline alone
>
> END

For the note-remembering part, especially if your arrangements are more dense or complex, you can always notate sketches in your notation software. I'd suggest a staff for each loop, if the loop has mostly similar parts (say, four-part BGs), or a staff for each separate instrument if the parts are very different (for example, a "verse loop" with bass, guitar, and some BGs might be notated over several staves). Put double bar lines around each loop and label them. This is for reference, not for sightreading, so don't worry if you put your four BG parts together, piano-chord-style on the same staff. You can break the rules of notational etiquette here!

By the time you've rehearsed the song a million times, you'll feel like you couldn't possibly ever forget it ... but many months and several songs later, there's a good chance you will! Along with the written-down notation methods, you can make a copy of your song patch on the loopstation with all the parts recorded, and label it differently—i.e., "Song X_sketch." You can reference it later, and having it in place on the loopstation gives you a more direct, visceral reminder of what goes where. Also, make a video of yourself with your phone performing the song: hearing and watching the song unfold in real time, and seeing yourself doing the button-pushing, is the most effective reminder.

If you're arranging for someone else, consider always keeping what they're singing live on the top line and then putting the looped parts on lower lines that correspond with the loop (A, B, C, etc.). This is the easiest way for a singer to visualize it all: the top part is sung, and the lower parts are buttons toggling the tracks on or off.

Live Looping with an Ensemble

Most of the previous information assumed you're working solo or duo. What about looping with an ensemble? At first look, you might ask why: if a loopstation allows a solo artist to sound like a group, and you've already got a group, what's the point of using a loopstation?

There are a few ways loopstations can work well with groups:

» *Freeing up a voice.* In smaller/one-per-part groups, vocal economy is always front of mind. With only a handful of voices/notes to choose from, you're always making decisions on what notes/parts to keep and what to leave out. Using a loopstation can ease some of the strain around this. For example, if a song has an unchanging drumbeat, instead of giving up one voice to keep it going, you could loop the vocal drums and free up that voice.

» *"Offloading" a repetitive part.* How many times, in a vocal ensemble, have you been stuck with an unending, repetitive part that you can't stand singing after a dozen repeats? If the song has an ostinato, riff, or other type of repeated part that's meant to just sit in the background, that's a great job for the loopstation. Your altos will thank you!

» *Creating textures.* Much of our looping talk thus far has been about time/groove-based loops, but loopstations are great for creating free, washy textures, as well. With a freely created loop and several unsynchronized, overlapping overdubs, you can create an atmospheric keyboard "pad" that might otherwise occupy many of your voices.
» *Looping whole sections of the group.* This is showing up in some groups with larger production capabilities. For this, you need the following:
  » A software-based looping/DAW program, such as Reaper
  » An engineer to run it from the sound booth
  » In-ear monitors, so the singers can hear a click track

Groups such as The Swingles use this in live-performance settings, and it allows for an impressive layering of sounds. Seven singers can become twenty or more, and it creates a whole new level of sound and arranging possibilities.

When using a loopstation with a group, there are a few considerations. First and foremost is audibility and staying in sync with the loopstation. Since the loopstation can't adjust to the group if they speed up/slow down, it's incumbent on the singers to listen and stay with the loopstation. The larger the group, the more challenging this is. There are a few solutions that can help:

» *Make your loops rhythm/drum-based.* Percussive sounds are overall easier to keep time to: that's why drummers, and not flautists, keep time in the band!
» *Have a "designated looper" with in-ears.* If your group is unamplified/semi-amplified, and if your group uses onstage monitors, it can help if the person creating the loops has very good monitoring: ideally in-ear monitors. This can allow them to focus on staying in time with the loopstation, and the rest of the group focuses on syncing with the designated looper. It helps if that person also has a percussive part that both complements the loop and is easy for other singers to latch onto, for example looping a drum part while the looper sings a bass part live along with it.

And lest we give away too much from the professional world of a cappella: many professional groups perform with a click reference in their ear, especially if they have to sync to any visuals, like a giant high-definition video screen (as DCappella does). If this is the case, it's very easy to keep in sync, as the vocal percussionist is already getting a click (and yes, DCappella's VP, Antonio, was the one to trigger the loopstation live on "Immortals").

The world of live looping is a fascinating and creative one, and once you get the hang of the arranging techniques (and, of course, the technical facility of operating the loopstation itself), it opens up all sorts of creative possibilities.

CHAPTER 9

Adapting Arrangements

As they say, the only constant in life is change. Groups change: they add members, lose members, members' voice ranges change . . . and if your arrangements were custom-made for your group, it's likely that those need to change, as well.

Perhaps you have a beautiful arrangement you want to try with a group with a different format altogether: for example, an SATB chart you want to try with an SSAA group. Or maybe you received an email from a group who loves your SSAA arrangement, but they're all lower voices and need it in TTBB format.

And it's not uncommon for a school group's membership to change from year to year, resulting in an imbalance of parts. Having your five altos "just sing quieter" than your lonely tenor just isn't cutting it.

Whatever the scenario, it's time to take your beautifully crafted arrangement and recraft it. We'll take a look at the most common scenarios and offer up some solutions.

Doing More with Less: "Part Math"

Example 1: From Eight to Seven

The most common situation might be a group that either loses a member or has a member who is frequently unavailable for gigs. You're left with a hole you need to fill. Let's imagine an eight-voice group, with one person per part, performing mostly contemporary music. Shall we dive into some deep score-study, searching like an auditor for doubled notes and other musical "savings"?

No! At least, not yet.

Most of us trust our ears more than our eyes, and what sounds good may not be the same thing as what looks good on a score. You've probably already discovered this in some of your own arrangements, where you got away with some voicing or techniques that "shouldn't" work, but somehow do. Therefore, before the score-study, have the group sing through the piece minus the missing person/part and record it casually in a simple format, such as a voice memo on your phone.

Then listen back and find the holes. You can do this alone—and you probably will, if you go back to redo the chart—but first, work together. The hivemind of your group is valuable here. You might find a particular section where all the notes are there, but one singer is left alone on a texture part and they don't like it. Or, you may have some hollow-sounding chords, but they go by quickly, and no one in the group seems to notice or care. If they don't, chances are your audience won't, either.

Once you find the holes, then you can look at how to fill them. Again, the hivemind is helpful. One person may find it easy to add a few extra missing notes to their part, or voice-lead down instead of up to cover a more important note. Maybe several parts "jump up" to fill that part. Maybe the lead vocalist has a few beats rest and can serve double-duty, swinging down to cover a responsive BG part in between lead phrases.

Working with the group is helpful for a few reasons. Not only do you have multiple sets of ears working together, but if they are part of the problem-solving, they are much more likely to be able to learn—and be invested in learning—any new parts or changes they have to make. Unlearning is much more difficult than relearning: if they're part of the "how and why" of any part changes, it will be that much easier for them.

》 *Dylan Says: My 1980s pop group Retrocity also included a member of another group, Cadence . . . and they were on tour enough that we often had to work without him. Instead of working up a sub, we wrote "redundancies and fail-safes" into our arrangements. His part was often a combination of doubling with another part, or a "luxury texture" we could live without . . . or when his part was essential, we made sure someone else's part was expendable at that moment and his part could be covered. Those charts sounded great with all eight singers . . . but they were designed to be fully functional with seven or fewer.*

》 *Deke Says: There were times on the road with the House Jacks when we'd be in the middle of a three-week tour in Europe and a member would get a bad cold or stomach bug. We had to reduce our two-hour show from five to four parts in a jiffy, something we didn't bother doing in advance, because depending on the person, different choices would be made ("he can cover bass on this song, but not that one . . ."). There were occasional open fifths and incomplete harmonies, but the audience never noticed. This is arranging "in the trenches," whereas reducing DCappella from seven to six members could be thoughtfully considered in advance with Finale open in front of me, a far easier and more forgiving task.*

A good amount of the filling-in can be done this way, but you might run into sections where it's too hard to work it out together, and it's best left to the arranger and the score. Here are a couple of factors to consider:

» *Lose the VP?* If the song has a dedicated VP (vocal percussion) part, is it necessary? Some people include a VP part by default, but if the song has a pretty basic backbeat, that could be covered another way. Depending of the nature of the bass line, the bassist may be able to "beat-bass" and cover the basic kick and snare of the drum part (see chapter 4, "Vocal Ranges and Additional Techniques," on how to do this). Or a backbeat can be built into a rhythm-section part, such as a guitar part. That can free up your VP to sing, and depending on their range versus the missing part, either they can cover it, or some part-shuffling can happen. Or if the song is a ballad or doesn't require the heavy impact of drums, it might sound great without percussion.

» *Remember your theory* . . . most pop chords contain only three chord factors, and sometimes a chord can be covered with only two parts in the BGs, especially when considering the melody and bass notes. Lose any doubled notes, and if you have to lose a chord tone, fifths are less essential than thirds, and the root of the chord is usually in the bass line on the downbeat.

» . . . *but voice-leading trumps theory.* Moving through a section of music, you've successfully covered all the necessary chord tones with minimal disruption of the other parts. You're pretty pleased with yourself . . . but one singer is paying for it. Their part is jumping around, frantically filling in the gaps. Not only is this cruel and unusual punishment, but you'll hear it: that jumping-around part will often stick out based on tessitura (where it lands in your singer's range), and it becomes its own texture—a separate, noticeable vocal line—in what's supposed to be a homophonic blend. If that's the case, sacrifice a note here and there for the sake of a reasonably smooth and singable part. Or, if necessary, make adjustments to more than one part to cover things smoothly and not draw unwanted attention.

» *Rewrite bars or phrases rather than individual notes.* This is not a theory-motivated suggestion, but a learning one. If a singer has only one note change, it may be hard to remember. A new phrase may be easier to unlearn/relearn than one note. By the way, if you only changed one note and the singer can't remember it (because they don't notice a difference or that anything's missing), maybe it wasn't that important anyways.

» *Try not to be precious!* We all love bits and pieces of our arrangements, and it can be hard to let them go, but sometimes with fewer parts, it's just easier to lose a particular chord voicing or extra flourish. Bells and whistles are fun, but they almost never have a significant impact on the audience's overall experience. Approach the adaptation with the same spirit you (hopefully) had when you brought the arrangement to the group in the first place. Think of it as open-source software that's meant to be tweaked and improved. More important than any specific moment is the simple fact that your arrangement just works.

Adaptation in Action
This is the chorus of my (Dylan's) original composition, "It's Not That I'm Lazy . . . ," along with my explanation of how I moved from eight voices to seven.

It's Not That I'm Lazy...

Dylan Bell

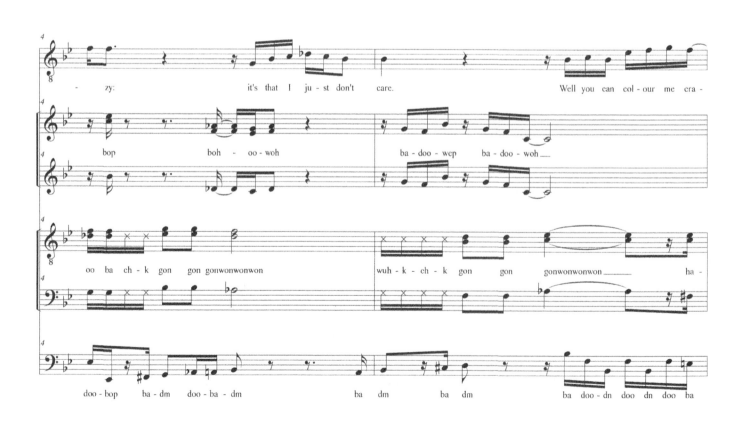

This is a downtempo funk piece in the style of Tower of Power or Earth Wind & Fire : a horn band with a rhythm section. As such, we have a lead vocal, a bass (doubling as drummer with kick and snare), and six BGs, divided 3+3: three horns and three parts I called "GuitaRhodes" since they function as a mix of guitar and electric piano. The two separate BG textures largely interlock rather than creating a large homophonic stack, so I had to start looking for "savings" in the parts. I started with a macro view: Of all the parts, which one was overall the most expendable? I decided the two top voices of the GuitaRhodes part could often be collapsed into one part: since they are functional and less front-and-center than the horn parts, as long as they cover the basic harmonies, two voices would do.

On the first sixteenth of measure two, all the BGs line up for a fat horn shot, meaning that for a moment, all parts line up for a nice E♭13 chord. My first thought was, since I was down a voice, to lose the thirteenth in the second horn part, and line up the BGs in an even tritone-plus-fourths stack (from top to bottom: E♭-B♭-F-D♭-G). That works, but ... I missed that thirteenth. Taking a closer look, I realized the lead voice is on the ninth ... the same note I'd given up in collapsing the two GuitaRhodes parts. I could have my hip note back again! I revoiced the chord back to its full complement: E♭-C-B♭-F (the lead)-D♭-G. Note that this means the lead voice has to be aware that they are, for that brief moment, part of the ensemble, and they must hold their note for the same length and phrase the same way for them to "sneak in" to the BG voice texture.

In the next bar, looking for savings, I realized I had all three horns in unison. I certainly don't need that, even to create the feeling of a unison horn line. So, I gave the top GuitaRhodes part to the bottom horn singer. Problem solved.

The last issue was the descending parallel cords in the final bar. It took me a few tries to find the right combination. Here's what the problem-solving process looked like:

» The horn 1 and bass are doubled, two octaves apart, and the first instinct is to remove any doubling. But there's a finality in having that line as both melody and bass note, and putting a different note on top seems to weaken that conclusion-feeling of the end of a chorus. I'd rather keep it.

» What about borrowing the lead singer like we did earlier? No, can't do that: they've got a pickup melody line, so they're already busy.

» We could try the tritone-plus-fourths idea we didn't use earlier. This gives a fat, familiar sound, suitable for the end of the chorus. But now that thirteenth sound is so woven into the sound of the chorus that it feels conspicuously absent.

» Of all the function tones and color tones, the one that's the least noticeable is the bottom horn part: the ninth. You could lose that part, and have the bottom horn sing the second horn part: the thirteenth.

» But that creates a problem. There's now a hole in the sound: the Guita-Rhodes parts are in dense thirds together, with a major seventh gap between the top GuitaRhodes and bottom horn. However, the great thing about the third-seventh shell voicing is that it can be easily inverted. So, looking at the first chord of the descending figure, we can go from D♭-B♭-C♭-F-D♭ to D♭-B♭-F-C♭-D♭. The largest gap, a seventh, is now between the bass and lowest BG, exactly where it belongs.

Example 2: From Six to Four

But what if your group is smaller? Each voice takes on a much larger role, and that much more is lost. Not all charts can be cut back that much without a full rewrite, but oftentimes it can work. In this case, we'll imagine a six-part jazz or jazz-pop group and look at ways of moving from six voices to four.

The nice thing about four-to-six-voice charts is that they usually follow a straightforward vocal allocation. For example, six voices give you a few combinations:

» Bass, lead, and four BGs
» Bass, VP, lead, and three BGs
» Bass, lead, 2x2 BGs (i.e., two pairs of BG singers doing different things)
» Bass plus five-part homophonic (like much Take 6 writing)
» Six parts homophonic

Four voices give you even more straightforward choices:

» Bass, lead, and two BGs
» Bass, VP, and two leads/two BGs (swapping)
» Bass and three-part block chords (melody in one part, other BGs parallel)
» Four parts homophonic

By and large, you can imagine the adaptation process as a sort of "conversion" to the equivalent format:

	Six-Part		**Four-Part**
1.	bass, lead, and four BGs	becomes	bass, lead, and two BGs
2.	bass, VP, lead, and three BGs	becomes	bass, VP, and two leads/two BGs
3.	bass, lead, 2x2 BGs	becomes	bass, lead, and two BGs
4.	bass plus five-part homophonic	becomes	bass plus three-part homophonic

Now let's get into some details. Keep in mind that an arrangement isn't necessarily written in only one of these formats; it may shift configurations, and you can move between conversions to follow it.

Bass, Lead, Four BGs to Bass, Lead, Two BGs

By and large, you can leave the bass and lead alone, working instead on turning four BGs into two. A six-part arrangement like this usually means some jazz chords with some juicy notes, and the challenge is to keep as much as of the color as possible. In a jazz chord, the function notes are usually the third and seventh, so start by giving most of those function-tones to the BGs. Conveniently, thirds and sevenths are a fourth or fifth (of varying quality) apart, which is a nice spread for those two voices. The harmonies will sound more sparse, but this is okay, like the difference between a Gene Puerling arrangement for the Singers Unlimited where they overdub and add additional chord tones whenever they want to become a block of six-part harmony, and a Gene Puerling arrangement for the Manhattan Transfer where he has to stick to just four parts (e.g., "A Nightingale Sang in Berkeley Square"). Both work very well. So far, so good.

But what if that's not enough?

Remember, you also have a lead singer. In your six-part arrangement, chances are the lead was left alone to do their own lead-thing, and all the harmony was covered by the four BGs. Now it might be time for the lead to pull some more weight. When they're singing something fast or scalar, you need them to stay with that part. But if they have some slower passages or held notes, they're not just melody: they're also harmony. Take a look at what those notes are and rewrite BGs to complement that. In effect, you're temporarily (even if only for a moment or two) imagining the lead as both lead and BG and writing them into what can now become a three-voice BG moment. It's important that the lead be aware of when and where their part is "harmonically functional" like this: they'll need to subtly blend with the other BGs so the voicing is heard as a unified entity. That means a small shift in timbre, vowel shape, and inflection/expression/vibrato to temporarily align with the BGs like this. It's not easy to shapeshift so quickly, and it takes great ears to do so, but the result is an aural "sleight-of-hand" where it momentarily sounds like more singers than you have onstage. The best professional groups can do this, and it's magical.

You can also temporarily change the function of the BGs and have them sing homophonically with the lead, temporarily creating a 1+3 bass/BGs combination instead of the 1+2+1 bass/BGs/lead configuration. This can strengthen the harmonic content and provide a great dynamic shift, as well. You can do this for short moments or even just a few beats to great effect, or you can change textures for several bars or even a whole section.

And let's not forget, you have a bass singer, as well. Not every chord has to have a root at all times. Sometimes the bass note can be inferred: the listener's ears will fill in the gap. This allows you to "borrow" the bass on occasion to fill out a harmony part, giving you a 3+1 BGs/lead combo, or even all four singers in temporary homophony. Again, a nice texture shift.

Here's an example: an excerpt of "Sunshine," written by Gillian Stecyk, arranged by Kevin Fox and recorded by Cadence on their album *Twenty for One*. It was originally written for six voices, but Cadence wanted to perform it live, so I (Dylan) took on the task of adapting it for four voices. This is the six-part version . . .

Sunshine

Gillian Stecyk

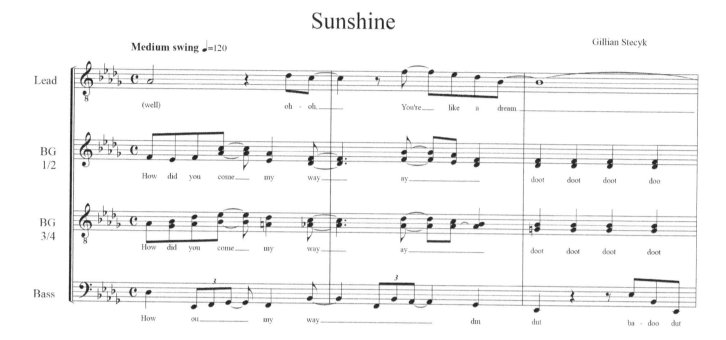

...and here it is, reduced to four parts.

The first thing I'm going to do is put our lead singer to work. In the first bar, the lead is resolving a line from the previous verse, taking their time to do so, and then there's a little filler before coming in for the next lead line. Instead, we'll ask them to resolve quickly, take away their little fill, and give them an inner part.

Next, I reimagined the bass part: instead of a responsive bass line for the first two bars, they'll now become a baritone part for a bar, then climb back down to bass territory.

For the next two bars, a four-part BG stack on the chord E♭9 is reduced to a third-seventh shell voicing. We lose the pretty ninth, but the lead is holding a melody note—the fifth—on top, right in between the shell voicing, thickening up the chord nicely. Even with that, hearing eight repeated tritones in a row with not much else going on can be a little grating, so instead, I gave the BGs a little melodic line in parallel thirds: if we can't fill up the space with thicker chords, we can give it some movement instead. The next few bars are a simple case of removing some doubling and leaning on functional notes.

Bass, VP, Lead, and Three BGs to Bass, VP, and Two Leads/Two BGs
This one is a little more context-dependent. This six-part format suggests that groove is as important as harmonically rich chords ... otherwise, you likely would have used that VP as a sixth voice. But with four voices, a two-person rhythm section only gives you two more parts to play with including the lead.

So, start by deciding for yourself, when you have to make choices, what's more important: the VP or the harmonies?

If you need the groove but it's a straightforward backbeat, as mentioned earlier, you could lose the dedicated VP and give most of the backbeat to the bass, or you could creatively distribute the drum elements among the bass and BGs together. Now you're looking at more of a situation similar to the first example, but even further ahead, as you're turning five notes into four, not six notes into four.

Or you could make a creative decision to bring the VP in and out. Maybe the bass takes more of the drum role in the verses, but when the chorus needs less harmony and more drive, you drop a BG and bring the VP back. Again, a nice texture change and a clever use of your four voices.

If you're dead-set on dedicated VP, that locks you in a bit, but strict parameters make for innovative choices and creative solutions.

This branch of the decision tree involves really putting your VP to work. Many dedicated VP/beatboxers revel in multilayered sound-making, and this can include vocalizing or humming while drumming. There's a good possibility your VP can hold long tones, or even some moving parts, while beatboxing: if so, they can sing something like long function-tones, "humdrumming" while the two remaining voices soar overtop. Or, depending on the bass line, your drummer might be able to "buzz-bass" (for a definition, see chapter 4, "Vocal Ranges and Additional Techniques") while drumming, and free up your bass as another BG voice.

If this isn't possible or doesn't suit your arrangement, you're essentially looking at "trio plus VP," and you can follow the guidelines for trio writing we suggest in our first book. In case you don't have it handy, here's what we said:

> It's not easy, but it can be done. We find it easiest just to think of the various combinations of voices:
>
> 3+0: three voices, singing in homophonic, triadic harmony
>
> 2+1: two voices singing lead/harmony, plus bass
>
> 1+2: one lead voice, two harmony voices

1+1+1: one lead, one BG, one bass. In this case, the BG has to be fairly agile as they may be "spelling out" chords in two-note chunks (i.e., bass sings roots, BG sings 3-5)

1+1+1: three melodic parts, in counterpoint

You won't likely want to use just one of these for a whole song: your arrangement will likely use a combination of these. I liken this to a palette with three different "colors" to choose from.

One advantage of three voices is that, because the human ear can focus on up to three things at once, the voices don't need to be stuck in one role. The parts are more fluid, allowing the singers/parts to "swim around" from one function to the next, and your listeners will still be able to keep up with what's happening.

Bass, Lead, 2x2 BGs to Bass, Lead, and Two BGs

This format is less common, but it is easy to "convert" to four voices. Most of the considerations we mentioned earlier when converting to bass/lead/two BGs apply, but the conversion is more straightforward. Your main choices are:

» Use just one of the two BG parts you wrote.
» Combine pieces of both BG parts into one.
» Have one voice per BG part instead of two. Working with only one voice per texture it will give a more contrapuntal feel . . . which could be quite interesting!

Bass plus Five-Part Homophonic to Bass and Three-Part Homophonic, and Six Parts Homophonic to Four Parts Homophonic

The techniques for these are similar, so we'll combine them. If your six-part chart has this much homophony, chances are it's also quite harmonically complex, and your mission is to save as much of that tasty harmony as possible.

This can be done in score-study mode, but we always prefer the experiential approach. Essentially, you always have two "holes" to fill, but they'll be easy to hear in a homophonic setting. We haven't specified that actual voicing, so we'll use the terms *parts one through six* to describe the parts in the chart, with one being the highest and six the lowest. We'll use SATB nomenclature to describe the four singers.

Like our first conversion example, most of the note changes will fall to the two middle parts. Read through the chart like this:

» SOPRANO sings Part 1.
» ALTO sings Part 2 or 3.
» TENOR sings Part 4 or 5.
» BASS sings Part 6.

If this is a chart you already know and sing, start with the parts you already sing, otherwise the tenor can start with Part 4, and the alto with Part 3.

Sing through the whole chart, passively noting how many holes there are. Then try it with the tenor on Part 5 (the alto still on Part 3), then with the alto on Part 2 (the tenor back on Part 4). Choose the combo with the fewest holes as your "default parts." Note that the middle parts are always no more than two parts apart; otherwise there will be too large a gap in your voicings. Note that if you need to have a gap, it's almost always best to have the gap between your bass and the upper voices, mimicking the spacing of the harmonic series. Low, dense harmonies will be muddy-sounding, whereas a chord spaced like the harmonic series will tune more easily and ring more consistently.

Work slowly through each section, recording each section as you go. Listen for the holes. When you find them, try a combination of experimentation and "micro-score study." When you find the holes, it may mean that . . .

» It's not really a six-note chord. Someone's doubling at the unison (say, Parts 1 and 2) or at the octave (say, Parts 2 and 5, or the melody and someone else).
» There's a function-tone (probably a third or a seventh) missing.
» There's a color tone missing that you really want to keep (usually a 2/9, sus4, 6 or 7).
» There's too wide a space between two of the parts.

The solution in all of these cases is the same: the alto or tenor "borrows" a note from the neighboring part—i.e., Part 4 borrows from Part 5, or Part 3 borrows from Part 2. Experiment until you find the switch that works best.

This may involve a lot of note switching. Make sure you don't miss the forest for the trees. It's really easy to get wrapped up in the minutiae of each single chord, at the expense of decent voice-leading and a sensible part. Where possible, try to lead into a "borrowed" note from the borrowed part so the voice-leading is sensible. In other words, swap a few notes or even a line, rather than jumping up/down for a single pitch.

When you're done, you likely have a mess of scribbled notes and arrows. If you can follow this, great. If not . . . don't be afraid to write the new part out again. If it's your chart, create new staves to represent the new "blended/reduced" parts, and delete the unused staves.

While most of the work falls to the middle voices, the soprano and bass can help out, too. As in earlier examples, the soprano, when not singing a melody that shouldn't be changed, could borrow notes from Part 2, and the bass could sing Part 5 and leave the root implied.

» *Dylan Says: One vocal jazz group I sing with, Hampton Avenue, started with ten singers, and over the years, it dwindled down to just four. It's hard to believe, but with a lot of clever reworking, we managed to reduce most of our six-voices-or-more arrangements to just four. The alto and I became so adept at the "part math" that we were able to do much of it on the fly.*

» *Deke Says: I'm asked periodically to re-voice existing arrangements, as someone will come across one of my published arrangements for which no version exists in the right configuration for their group. The next best/easiest option for them is to reach out to an arranger who has a version that simply needs to be re-voiced. I'm happy to send them a Finale file or XML so they can carve away as they'd like, but they usually prefer to have me play musical Sophie's Choice. Once you spend enough time reducing an arrangement, it becomes fairly easy, especially if you're not precious about anything other than the overarching emotional conveyance the song carries.*

Voice Reduction in Action: "Blues on Sunday"

Here's Dylan to demonstrate some of these techniques with part of his original composition "Blues on Sunday." This is the last verse and chorus.

Blues On Sunday

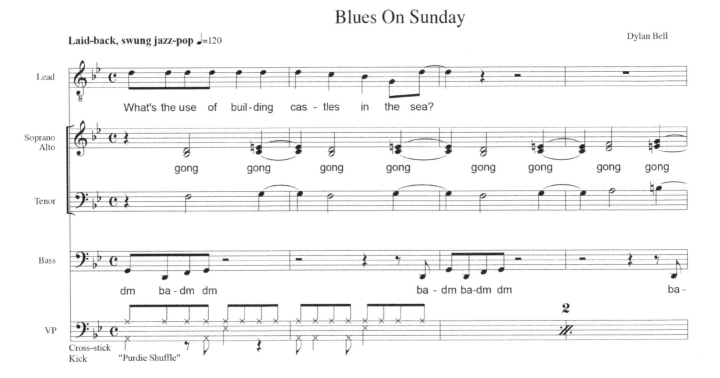

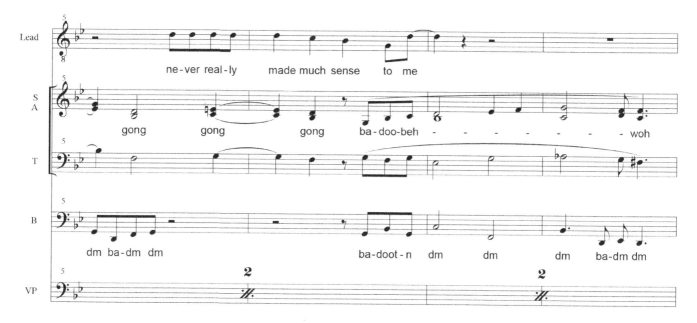

"gong" pronounced "gohng": dark electric piano sound

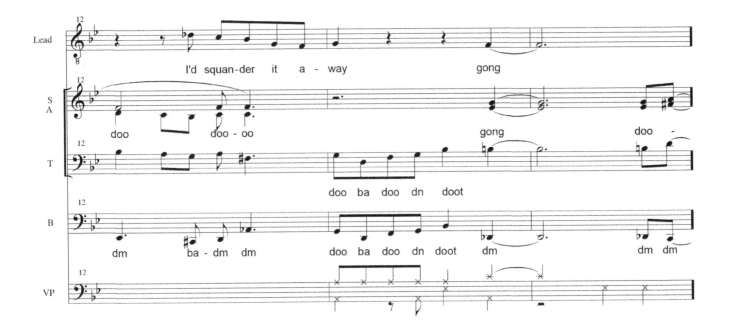

Lead: I'd squan-der it a - way   gong

S A: doo   doo - oo   gong   doo -

T: doo ba doo dn doot

B: dm   ba - dm dm   doo ba doo dn doot   dm   dm dm

G

Lead: I ne-ver thought that I'd get lost in the rain a - gain

S A: eh - oo-eh-oo   oo   doo dn dwa   doo dn dwa - oo

B: doot   ba - doon   doot   ba - doon   doot   ba - doon   doot   ba -

VP: to snare

2

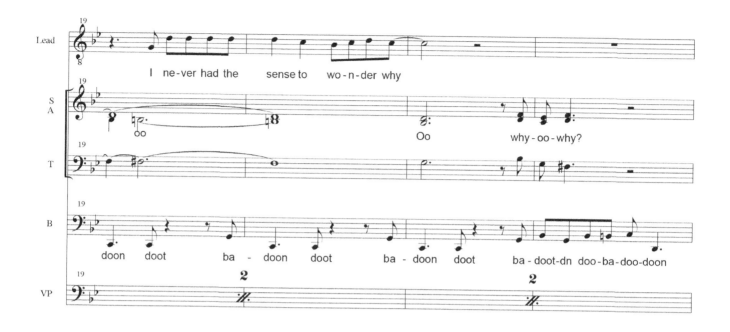

"Blues on Sunday" is a jazz-pop piece I wrote in the spirit of bands like Steely Dan: groovy and harmonically complex. It's built around a groove called the "Purdie Shuffle," a unique drum part created by the drummer Bernard Purdie. This groove is pretty central to the piece, so I decided to keep a dedicated VP, even though it was already a challenge to represent the jazzy chords with only three BGs. Now I was about to lose two voices, and I wasn't willing to give up the VP. Could it even be done? It was hard work, and it took a lot of experimentation and creative problem-solving, but I managed. I'll walk you through the process.

Since I insisted on keeping some sort of VP, the first major question was: Should I ask the bass to also cover drums, or ask the VP to cover a part? In this song, either could work: the bass line has enough space to sing a drum part underneath. But you may have a bass who isn't a strong drummer, or a VP with stronger multitasking skills, so I imagined this was the case here. Again, looking at the macro, I decided to reorganize the BGs as follows:

» Have the VP fill in notes where possible, usually the former tenor part.
» Have the lead fill in a bit here and there.
» The bass part is sparse in sections: it could take up the slack as well.

Here's what the four-part version looks like. You'll notice that I switched the position of the bass and VP staves: since the VP is also acting as tenor, it makes sense to see the parts from highest to lowest.

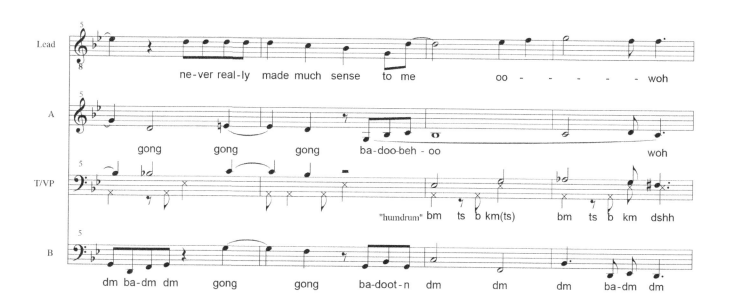

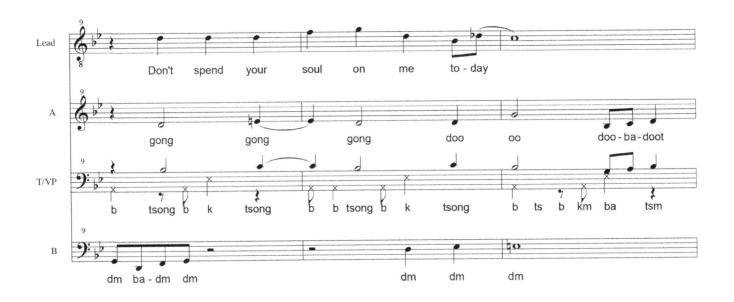

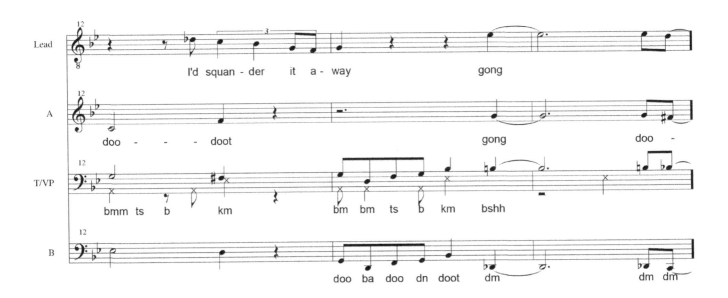

I ne-ver thought that I'd get lost in the rain a - gain dwa doo-dn dwa - oo

I ne-ver thought that I'd get lost in the rain a - gain dwa doo-dn dwa - oo

doot ba - doon doot ba - doon doot ba - doon doot ba -

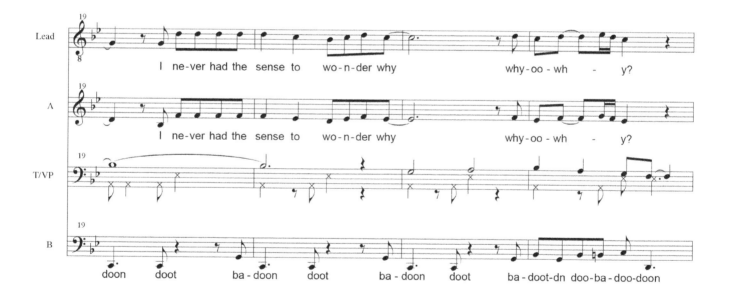

I ne-ver had the sense to wo - n-der why why-oo-wh - y?

I ne-ver had the sense to wo - n-der why why-oo-wh - y?

doon doot ba - doon doot ba - doon doot ba - doot-dn doo-ba - doo-doon

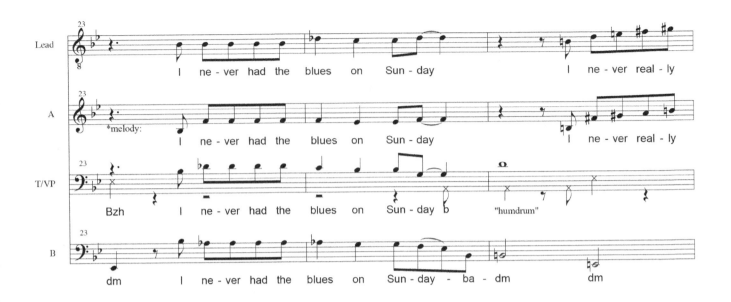

The first thing you'll notice is that the three-part "gong" comping (meant to approximate a Rhodes electric piano: I'll refer to it as "Rhodes" here) involves a little part switching. The VP takes over the tenor: since the part is on the offbeats, it doesn't get in the way of the kick/snare pattern. It lines up well with an offbeat hi-hat: put the two sounds together and "gong" becomes "tsong." It's worth mentioning at this point that, while I've notated some of the syllables in the VP part for illustration, and for you to try it out yourself, normally I wouldn't bother. VP is a highly individual art form, and each VP finds syllables and sounds their own way. Normally, I'd just give instructions: "Sing Rhodes with kick, snare, and hi-hats" and let them figure out how to "put it in their face," so to speak. The bass can easily sing the Rhodes in between lines: it's an octave away, not hard to find in the voice. At mm. 3–4, the lead takes over the Rhodes, and the bass adds an extra fill. Sometimes when you have fewer voices, you add more variety in texture to make up for the lack of thickness in the BGs: this is an example, and there are a few others that crop up as we go. At mm. 7–8, the VP "humdrums," covering some function tones, and the lead also pitches in for another moment of three BGs plus bass and VP.

Mm. 11–12 required a little bit of problem-solving. The harmony in the original is E7♯9♭5-E♭maj7-D7alt-A♭13: pretty chunky chords. I could barely cover those with three BGs: with only one BG it was going to be impossible. Instead of trying too many vocal gymnastics that probably wouldn't work, I sighed, let go, and simplified the harmony: The E7♯9♭5 became something closer to Em7♭5, and instead of the tritone-sub moment of D7alt to A♭13, I put a hard stop on the D7alt. Since I lost a little color, I decided to add a little texture, and at m. 11, I gave the alto and tenor/VP a little moving part in parallel thirds. Also, on the D7alt chord at m. 12, I made a subtle change in the rhythm of the lead vocal: instead of even (swung) eighths on the line "squander it away," the triplet figure makes it "squann-derr it away," emphasizing the interesting chord tones (seventh and flat thirteenth) to make the chord sit more solidly with fewer voices.

At m. 15, the chorus, I also made a fundamental change. The six-part version has the three BGs covering some nice color shifts in parallel triadic movement under the C minor-ish tonality. It's pretty hard to make triads with one singer, so I made the first half a duet with the lead and one remaining BG, with the VP humdrumming long-function tones (in this case, the m7) underneath. This is punctuated by the little filler phrases in between the lead lines, where we can have three voices together. Again, where we lose harmonic density, we can play with different textures to create variety.

At m. 23, we have the conclusion of the song: it's the end of the final chorus, and the first time we hear the actual song title in the lyrics. Originally this was a four-part block, plus bass and drums. I decided that, with the song title serving as a focal point, I wanted to keep the block voicing. I wrote a full stop on the downbeat, and we have a four-part block for the first time, with the VP singing a full part with lyrics. Once that focal point is established, I went back to the duet-plus-humdrum-plus-bass formula used in the beginning of the chorus. This part navigates some pretty tricky harmonic shifts, so the bass and VP cover the main harmonic support with the VP covering mostly thirds and sevenths against the bass roots, leaving the lead and BG to sing as a duet.

For the final bar, I decided once again to have all four voices in harmony for the final word "goodbye": the VP stops drumming and sings, and the bass temporarily becomes the bottom of a nice "So What" voicing* before adding a responsive line to land on the root, and thus to finish the song.

---

* Named after the prevalent chord in Miles Davis's jazz classic "So What?" this four-voice chord consists of two stacked fourths topped with a third. It's a very useful jazz voicing often used as a minor sus chord, or an implied major seven chord. In this case, it's an implied maj7♯11 chord.

Adapting Different Vocal Configurations

It's not uncommon to find or hear a chart you like, but it's written for an SATB group and your group has another configuration, such as TTBB. Assuming the same number of parts, adapting the arrangement is a fairly straightforward process. Adapting for a different number of voices is, in effect, a sort of rearrangement: practical applications are balanced against musical aesthetics, and decisions are made as to what to keep and what to let go. When changing configurations, you're not likely adding/subtracting/changing the notes themselves, just adjusting them to suit the ranges, and ideally the unique qualities, of the new configuration.

For this section, we'll stick with the most common four-part vocal configurations—SATB, TTBB, and SSAA—and figure out how to adapt them.

SATB to TTBB

SATB is the most common arranging configuration, and one we're likely all familiar with. It has an even balance of high and low vocal parts, each suited to their range. TTBB isn't that much different: it's overall lower in pitch, and slightly more constricted in range, but an accomplished first tenor can sing many of the notes an alto—or even soprano—can, and the overall vocal range from bass to highest tenor can still easily cross three octaves.

The first consideration is to look at the soprano and alto lines and see what is out of range or uncomfortable for the upper voices, then lower the overall key to get it in range. This may be as little as a second, but it could be as low as a fourth or fifth. But more often than not, if it's a contemporary a cappella arrangement, the song will work as-is. In modern pop music, it's common to keep female singers out of their head-voice, which is well within range of male falsetto.

Next, take a look at the bass part, and see if the lowering of key pushed anything out of their range. A bass in TTBB often sings lower than a bass in SATB, but you still have a low floor to deal with! You can compromise between keeping the bass and T1 happy, but overall, it's easier for a bass to sing a note or phrase up the octave than it is to mess with the melody if sung by the T1.

Not all TTBB arrangements put the melody in the T1: in barbershop writing, the traditional "lead" is actually T2, with T1 covering a higher harmony, often in head-voice/falsetto, "floating" above the melody without getting in its way. With this in mind, you can give T2 the soprano part, but down the octave, T1 the alto part at-pitch . . . and baritone sings the tenor. Like any triad, you can invert the parts and still have the sounds you want. Depending on the arrangement, you may want to experiment with different variations on the octave-transposition of a part or have it shift between sections of the music as required.

Goodnight, Sweetheart, Goodnight

This assumes the melody is in the soprano in the SATB chart. If the melody is in the alto, for example, perhaps T1 sings the alto at-pitch, and the soprano is sung down the octave by the baritone. Experiment, mix and match by section, and usually one combination will just "click." The overall goal is a) to keep each singer in their "sweet spot," and b) keep a relatively even distribution between parts, especially between the top three parts.

TTBB to SATB

TTBB to SATB is even more straightforward, since you're moving to a configuration with an overall wider range. Some TTBB arrangements can be sung "out of the box" by an SATB group with no changes at all. Some will work, but they may sound a little duller, as the soprano and alto are singing in a lower tessitura than usual, and the voices don't "shine" the way you like. If so, start by raising the key. Often as little as a tone will work, or a minor third.

White Christmas

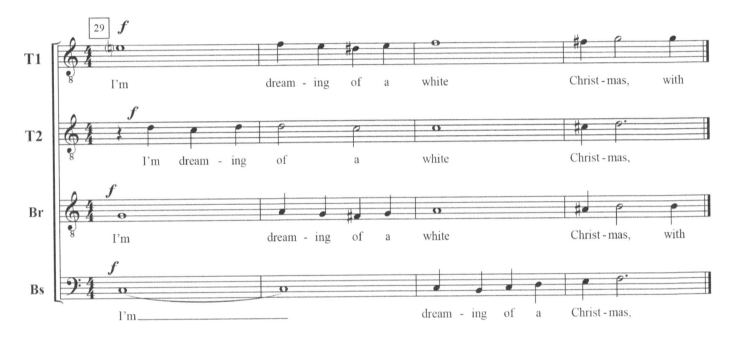

Note: this arrangement of "White Christmas" is published at the same pitch for TTBB and SATB, originally performed by the Gas House Gang—a legendary barbershop quartet—and sung each year by many SATB ensembles, such as the Los Angeles Master Chorale.

Once you get beyond a third, you'll want to check in on the lower voices, in particular the tenor: moving beyond a third may take some tenor notes out of reach. If the out-of-reach sections are just a few notes here and there, and you have tenors adept at singing in head-voice, you can allow them to do so where needed: at that range, evenness in tone and timbre is more important than full-on singing . . . and there are two voice parts above them to carry things along in those moments. If large sections of the tenor part are now out of reach, you may not be able to raise the key too much for risk of vocal strain and a brash, potentially unpleasant tone.

Don't forget your basses, though: again, a big key transposition can shift some higher bass parts too high, and you may lose some of the richness in the low end. In this case, you can possibly have the basses sing notes or phrases down (or up) the octave as needed.

If none of this works, you can try some part-swapping. Try this:

TTBB	SATB (transposed up)
T1	Alto
T2	Tenor
Bari	Soprano, up the octave
Bass	Bass

Since you're no longer stuck with the "tenor ceiling," and since basses can often take notes/phrases down the octave as needed, you may have more room to transpose upward. Transposing the tenor up the octave very often puts it in the "sweet spot" for sopranos. That said, we're hard-wired to hear the soprano as the primary voice in an SATB group: to bring out the alto melody, the sopranos will have to sing softer and blend into the sound.

SATB-SSAA

SSAA is a beautiful but different format to work with, and it has its own challenges and rewards. The overall available range is smaller than both SATB and TTBB. But in this range, voices can be closer together at any point in the range and still sound great, and exquisite cluster-chords can ring in a way you can't get with a TTBB or mixed formation. Imagine tenors and basses singing thirds or seconds low in their range: it's muddy. Now imagine the same with sopranos and altos: it shimmers.

Also, like TTBB, it's not uncommon for the melody to sit somewhere in the middle of the stack, with S2 or even A1 singing melody and the upper part(s) floating above in a light head-voice.

With all this said, there's a simple process that works pretty consistently as a starting point:

SATB	SSAA
Soprano	S2
Alto	A1
Tenor	S1, up the octave
Bass	A2, up the octave

In essence, by taking two of the parts up the octave (and redistributing the soprano parts), you're "collapsing" the SATB arrangement into a range that works for SSAA. Open voicings become close voicings: closer voicings become clusters. Most of the time, each part will be in their sweet spot, and often there's no need to change key at all. If it doesn't work for the entire piece, try a small transposition upward, and re-voice the occasional chord as needed.

It also may work, if the song is not voiced too high, to just bring the bass line up an octave when needed and leave the SAT parts at pitch for S1, S2, and A1.

When Will I Be Loved

SSAA-SATB

Like TTBB-SATB, you're moving to a configuration with a wider range, but depending on the style/genre, this one can be trickier. Of the three configurations we're discussing, SATB and SSAA (not SSAA and TTBB, as you'd think) are the most different: mixed voices versus similar voices, widest range versus narrowest. SSAA charts are written to take advantage of those unique characteristics we mentioned just a moment ago, and those may not translate as well to a mixed formation.

You can start by trying the opposite of the SATB-SSAA part-switching above, which gives us this:

SSAA	SATB
S1	Tenor, down the octave
S2	Soprano
A1	Alto
A2	Bass, down the octave

This, generally, will put all the notes in range. But there may be some other issues, including the following:

» *The bass*: if the SSAA chart is a more contemporary piece, there's a good chance the alto is singing bass lines. If so, no problem: they'll sound great down the octave, in traditional bass territory. But in more choral-type arrangements, the alto may sing less roots and functional bass tones and act more as the bottom note of a four-part voicing where the bass is either implied, or just not there: this is the magic of the floating, shimmering potential of an SSAA arrangement. Sung down the octave by a bass, these notes may sound muddy, or unfamiliar, or they may not translate as well overall as they did in alto range.

To illustrate: take a look at this Cmaj7 chord in SSAA, then re-voiced as we suggested for SATB.

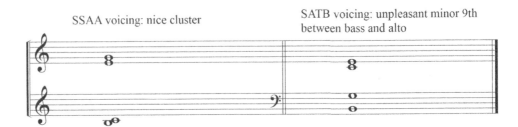

In SSAA, this is a nice clustery chord with that tasty minor second buzz between A2 and A1. In SATB, that nice minor second has become an unpleasant minor ninth. This might be fine in a brief passing moment leading to some resolution, but not a chord to spend any time on.

» *"Parts in wrong places"*: it's possible with this re-voicing that, while everyone's singing in an appropriate range, the parts just don't feel like they're in the right places. Imagine a living room with terrible *feng shui*: all the right pieces of furniture are there, but the layout just doesn't feel right. In this case, you may need to do more hands-on part-surgery, re-voicing sections, phrases, or notes differently to make it all fit. Unlike the "experiential method" we used earlier in the chapter, singing the pieces with the group to find the missing pieces, this one is probably best done score-study style by the arranger, alone.

However, it's also possible that, like in SATB-SSAA, the only factor that really needs tweaking is the bass line (which can be done by displacing the octave as needed).

Hit Me With Your Best Shot

TTBB-SSAA

This one's not too complicated: here we have two same-voice groups, though SSAA typically has a smaller overall range. To start with, simply transpose the chart upward by about a fourth or fifth. Like all transpositions, keep an eye on the parts moving toward their extreme ranges: in this case, the S1. If there's still room, go higher: this will help pull the middle-lower voices closer to their optimal range. If you're singing a more chorale-style or barbershop piece (or some close-harmony jazz), where the voicings tend to be closer together, this may be enough. Most SSAA barbershop arrangements are straight-up transpositions of their TTBB counterparts: a lot of effort is put into using certain specific voicings for that barbershop "lock and ring" effect, and re-voicing these would ruin that effect.

Depending on how low the original bass part is, you may find that A2 sits in an awkward spot: too low to be sung at pitch (even with the transposition), too high when moved up the octave. If so, try a compromise between the sweet spot for S1 and the lowest reasonable range for A2. Often, an A2 bass line can be sung in a higher register as long as there are a few low notes here and there (ideally, the tonic of the key or other important note such as the fifth) that the A2 can hit, just to ground the part and remind us that it's a "bass" part. If your SSAA group is singing pop, there's a good chance the A2 is using an octave pedal: in this case make the S1 happy, transpose as high as they like, and stomp on that pedal for the low notes.

Since U Been Gone

For the record, the arrangement of "Since U Been Gone" that serves as the audition song in *Pitch Perfect* was, indeed, originally an all-male arrangement for Deke's group the House Jacks.

SSAA-TTBB

This conversion has some of the issues mentioned earlier with SATB-SSAA, but not as much, since you're moving from two same-voice ensembles with less overall range than SATB. The main difference is register, and whether voicings in one register work in another.

In a TTBB ensemble, the T1 (and often T2) have significant range in their mix voice, and baritones and basses often have impressive head-voices. All this means that there may not be that many notes entirely out of reach. Start by transposing down until the T1 is happy: try a fourth or a fifth. Next, negotiate with the bass. Is their part too high to be comfortable? Do we lose that "bass magic" in that range? If the range is too high, keep going down until most of the part is in range.

Now sing through the chart. You'll notice that many of the unique characteristics of SSAA voicings are different, but they still work: what was a bright, shimmery chord in SSAA becomes warm and fuzzy in TTBB. No problem. Occasionally, you'll come across a voicing that's too muddy: if so, use the same technique we used in SATB-TTBB re-voicing: take one of the muddy parts—say, the baritone—and try it up the octave, crossing over the T1 part. If the baritone can do that smoothly, fine. If not, have T1 and the baritone swap that line if musically appropriate, or have everyone shuffle to another part temporarily to make it work. This could be done either experientially with the group or score-study style by the arranger.

As mentioned earlier, a big difference between SSAA and TTBB is the role of the lowest voice. If your lowest part isn't a bass part and most of it works, leave it as-is: you'll have a piece in your repertoire with a variety in bass texture. If there are lots of roots in the A2 part, try them down the octave to make the ensemble sound even richer. If you come across a note that doesn't work in the lowest voice, try part-swapping, or worst-case, rewrite that part.

Not every arrangement will work with any number of parts, or configurations. Maybe that arrangement needed all six voices to work, or that SSAA chart was meant to stay floaty and ethereal. That said, the techniques explained in this chapter will take you a long way toward making different arrangements work with your group.

CHAPTER 10

Instrumental Imitation and Lyric-less Arrangements

If you are primarily an instrumental arranger with less experience working with voices, this chapter is for you.

If you are an experienced vocal arranger but work primarily in the choral realm . . . this chapter is for you, too.

If you are already working in the contemporary a cappella field . . . don't skip this chapter just yet! Chances are, you have a vocabulary of "go-to" sounds and instruments, but you may come across new sounds and ideas here and widen your vocabulary.

One of the most notable elements of contemporary a cappella is the fact that voices are often used to mimic instruments, as well as being used in roles that were traditionally reserved for instruments. The most recognizable and informative element of this is vocal percussion, but that tradition runs far deeper—down to vocal bass—and wider, spanning a broad range of instruments, acoustic and electronic. These timbres are not brief quotes or novelty sound effects; they're deeply ingrained in the music, a central part of the sound.

The impetus for this was and is simply to replicate and reflect the complexity and sonic breadth of current and past popular music. As the rhythm section began to play a larger role in pop recordings, a cappella responded by moving from doowop bass vowels to timbres and phrasing that replicates everything from bass guitars to low synth lines, as well as imitating live drums and drum machines. As modern production techniques embrace a dizzying array of effects on an almost limitless number of tracks, a cappella has responded by building its own walls of sound—onstage as well as in the studio.

Let's start by addressing the most common and useful of these imitative instrument sounds, then we'll address how to use them in consort to weave together a powerful tapestry of modern sound. Before we do, the phrase "talking about music is like dancing about architecture" comes to mind, as we're going to try to explain how to make a variety of vocal instrumental sounds using text. The best way to learn is from another person, or through the internet (we both have videos on our respective YouTube channels), so you can see the process as it unfolds, and the words below can serve as a reminder and add additional insight on how to best create a number of new sounds.

Basic Principles

To help understand how to re-create instruments with voices, it can be helpful to break down the instrument's sound into a few categories:

» *Range*: is it high, low, in between, or all over? Here, we give rough approximations for the instrument's pitch range. It may seem obvious, but it helps with voice allocation. You won't likely write a flute part for your bass singer.
» *Timbre*: is it mellow, brash, somewhere in between, or capable of all of the above? This will help with choice of vowel.
» *Articulation*: much of the identifying feature of an instrument is its "attack phase," or the initial articulation. Is it soft, medium, percussive? Does the sound bloom (bwaaaaaaaaHHHHH), or is it percussive (dnk)? This helps determine the consonant(s) at the beginning.
» *Idiomatic Features*: what is particular or signature about the instrument in terms of what it can/can't do? This can have to do with the notes themselves (i.e., pianos can't bloom, or add vibrato; brass and winds don't have a very percussive attack) or stylistic and technical aspects (trumpets can't easily play wild intervallic leaps; saxophones have a wide variety of range and timbre; this instrument bends pitch well; that instrument has great dynamic capability).

Now is a good time to mention an important principle in vocal instrumental imitation: the need to stay away from "language vowels," especially diphthongs. Diphthongs are a clear indication that you're listening to a human and not an instrument, which doesn't typically have the ability to change internal shape the way our soft palate can lift and mouths morph, changing a variety of overtones. If this isn't clear, think of the word "mouth"—it's an "m" sound followed by an "ah," which changes to an "oo" before the final "th." That "ah" to "oo" shift while holding the pitch steady is part of what allows us to communicate vocally, but it also exposes the sound as human to a listener. How?

The human brain has different centers in which different information is processed: visual, mathematic, kinesthetic, linguistic, etc. When you hear someone singing "Happy birthday to you," your brain perceives both language (the lyrics) and melody (clearly defined pitches) and tells you, *That's a person singing*. The key to making these instrumental sounds work is that you want to trigger the musical center of the brain without triggering the linguistic center. Diphthongs are a dead giveaway.

Let's consider some simple bass syllables: "Dm" is a clean, clear instrumental tone. So is "thm." In both cases, you have an attack followed by a resonant sound. If you sing "dum" or "thum," you're likely to clue the listener in that the sound is vocal, as they sound much like the words "dumb" and "thumb," and that's what the listener will hear.

This gets to another important principle: try to stay away from syllable sounds that are actual words, as they'll register as words in people's ears/brains. Choosing syllables that are unusual are far more likely to come across as instrumental, or at least not clearly vocal, and if you need open vowels (as you often do when singing without amplification), you want to choose syllables that don't have diphthongs in them, for the reasons explained above.

While much of this applies to the translation of instrumental music to vocal, keep in mind that pure, literal sonic imitation may not be the only way to effectively represent instruments. While keeping sound in mind, also consider the instrument's function: what does it do, or what does it add, to the piece as a whole? This may be something timbral ("it adds shimmer" or "it thickens the texture"), or it might be more abstract or emotional ("it gives the moment gravitas" or "it signifies pathos and longing"). Aspects other than imitation might offer the same effect, and the voice may have an even more powerful way to express this than the original instrumental sound.

With all those fundamentals in mind, here's a rundown of many instruments, arranged roughly by instrumental group.

Brass and Woodwinds

Trumpet

» Range: high (B♭3-B♭5 average, F3-B♭6 extreme)
» Timbre: medium to bright
» Articulation: medium

The tradition of imitating a trumpet stretches back to the 1930s with the Mills Brothers, whose vocal trumpet solos were a trademark of their sound for decades, both when backed by a full band or a cappella. Of all vocal instrumental sounds, this is the most common (perhaps besides vocal percussion/beatboxing nowadays) and the most accessible. How is it done?

Start by producing a simple tone—"doo"—in your upper register (falsetto for men), as the pitch needs to be in the trumpet's register, which is on the high side of the human vocal range. Now change the attack from a "d" to a "b" and sing "boo." If you hold your lips too tightly together, you get a stunted sound, and if they're too loose, you get a "bbbbb" lip flap. The key is in the amount of pressure. This will be important shortly.

Next, close your mouth as much as possible so that after the "b" sound you have the smallest opening possible. It sounds almost like you're singing "br," but in fact, you're not making an "r" sound, which has your lips pursed; it's just a very tight-lipped "boo."

Note that this sound may come out of the front of your mouth, or one of the sides. Do whatever works best with your lips; there is no single correct way to make the sound. All that matters is that it sounds good, and that you're able to make the sound rather easily so you can start to play with it in a variety of styles once you start to become comfortable with it.

This "boo" sound is the core, but it's not possible to be very agile while singing it: try singing a scale up, 1-2-3-4-5, faster and faster, and you'll pretty quickly see that you're limited in how quickly you can reset your lips to the "b" sound to restrike each note. For a moment, abandon your "boo" sound and sing something very different: "tur," as in the beginning of the word "turtle." Once you're comfortable singing 1-2-3-4-5 on "tur," you now want to combine the two sounds—close your mouth as you did when you sang "boo"—with the "b" attack and close-lipped "oo" after, but inside your mouth you want to sing "tur."

This is a difficult approach to explain in text, but once you've got it, you'll never try a vocal trumpet another way, as it's far easier to restrike and sing faster passages. In addition, if you want to sing a very fast trumpet line (like "Flight of the Bumblebee" or a Dizzy Gillespie solo), you can do it by singing "tur-dle-ur-dle-ur-dle" and so on inside your mouth behind your "boo" embouchure. This allows you to sing/"play" very quickly. Trumpet players use a similar technique, called double-tonguing.

You have the tone, but that only gets you half of the way to your goal, as you now need to perfect the phrasing. Listen to Miles Davis, Chet Baker, and of course, the legendary Louis Armstrong. Listen to the attack, the sustain, the way they move between notes. Many young vocal trumpeters may have excellent tone, but their phrasing is a complete giveaway as they play the trumpet the way they sing, with portamenti and glissandi aplenty, sliding up to notes and adding vibrato where they would vocally. It is the case that the highest compliment many instrumentalists can be paid is that they "made their instrument sing." However, you're attempting the opposite: you want to sound like a person who is working within the parameters of their instrument, and sliding between notes on a trumpet isn't a common occurrence. Here are a few instrumental specifics for the trumpet:

» Trumpet lines are typically scaler, not angular. Due to the tightening and loosening of the embouchure required, it is difficult to execute wide leaps in rapid succession. Stick to stepwise motion. Arpeggios can work well, where trumpet players can move up and down the harmonic series with no changes in fingering, and only small changes in embouchure.
» Fast lines usually (but not always) descend, not ascend. Again, this is about embouchure: it's easier to relax the embouchure while playing than to tighten, especially quickly.
» Sustained vibrato isn't common outside of classical playing.
» Wide pitch slides aren't common, except for the "half-valve" slide, which usually only happens at the beginning of a phrase, or at the end (think of a Henry Mancini "horn splat" as an example).

There are all sorts of little fun "trumpetisms," such as shakes, doits, trills, and falls. Listen to big band charts to get a feel for some of these.

The best way to "get good" is to learn a few trumpet solos on songs you love: note for note, with every nuance in phrasing. This will start to teach you the vocabulary of a trumpet, and by learning solos by different trumpeters, you'll start to develop a language you can sing within and through. Obviously this isn't the most pressing of human pursuits, and yet it's a fun one—something you can do when you're walking or driving (preferably alone!), a harmless and completely free pastime that leaves you with a greater understanding both of an instrument and of your own voice.

Now let's look at how to use this vocal trumpet sound in an arrangement: Deke's version of "Caravan."

Caravan

My arrangement of "Caravan" predated my knowledge of the fantastic Mills Brothers version, and instead it builds on two trios (soprano, alto, and tenor) using a vocal trumpet sound as a stacked unit.

You'll notice I simply indicate that the sound should be a vocal trumpet, rather than writing the syllable under every note. I've found if I do that, people will often follow that too literally, and what I want is for them to abandon the concept of a lyric and instead focus on producing the trumpet sound with those notes.

You may find that some singers in your ensemble can't quite make the trumpet sound (it's one of the easiest, but everyone's different). If so, have them sing a tight-lipped "bur," which approximates the sound closely enough and will sound fine when stacked with other voices.

One thing you may notice is that the trumpet sound, when amplified, can be quite strong, but if you have a larger ensemble, such as a choir, and you're not close-micing their voices, you may find the sound doesn't carry as powerfully as you'd like (since it's a sound made with lips closed, which results in far less sound thrown than an open vowel). In that case, you can try putting half (or so) of your singers on a "ba" vowel and the other on the trumpet sound, and see if that gives you the best of both worlds, allowing you to blend in the trumpet sound for timbre and the open vowel for power.

Another way to use the trumpet sound is to interpolate in the middle of an otherwise lyrical phrase. Stevie Wonder's "I Wish" is a fantastic song that features horn hits between his lyrics in the chorus. Here's Deke's arrangement for the House Jacks.

I Wish

We tried having horn hits where the horns hit on the recording, but it didn't have the same impact we wanted, so instead we echoed the lyric in those places, and we saved the vocal trumpet horn hits for the end of the line.

A few things to point out:

» You don't need to use a horn exactly where it's used in the original song. Exact vocal translation/transcription is appropriate sometimes, but in the end, the effect is more important than the imitation. Audiences don't remember every nuance of an original recording when you're performing a song for them, nor do they care. They just want to be taken on a ride, and the lyrical echoes proved more powerful and effective for us than the trumpet sound in those spots.

» The "dj-v-n-v" is what I'd call a hybrid vocal-instrumental sound, not either but with elements of both. It was quasi-electric-guitar-like, but not precisely imitative. It didn't have vowels, but it still resonated when close-mic'd, and of course, it was deliberately quieter than the lyrics and horn hits. Syllables with vowels would have been too vocal, and we were driven by an overarching instrumental character in our background parts, so we came up with a vocabulary of sounds that worked well for us, and this was one of them.

» Note the careful and intentional inclusion of rests throughout. In fact, we had to breathe on the downbeat at the top of the chorus, a time when you might think you'd want all five voices to be hitting hard (there was a fifth member on vocal percussion, not notated), but in fact, that downbeat with the lead vocal wailing, the bass note hitting hard on the tonic, and a crash in the VP left us with a quick second to catch our breaths (and we did need it), but the same moment two measures later, that wasn't necessary, as we could breathe right before "why did those." Also there are breaths in the middle of the "ever have to go" immediately following, just before the horn hits. Why? Because we were usually running around the stage, singing full volume, and we needed the extra quick catch breaths. No time for longer breaths in this song at this tempo, wanting to keep the chorus busy, a full wall of sound.

» Note that there are no dynamics. It was the chorus of a rockin' Stevie Wonder showstopper, so forte was implied throughout.

» You don't know our voices, but yes, this had all three upper parts at the top of their chest voices by design. The melody is up there, classic Stevie, and to support and lend energy to the chorus, I kept the other two of us up in the stratosphere, as well. You could sing this in falsetto, but it would have a different effect, and at least in our case, it was more powerful in full volume high chest voice (all the more reason for the frequent breaths).

Here's Dylan's version of "I Wish," written for SSATBB, but also recorded in the same format by the TTBB quartet Cadence.

I Wish

Arr. Dylan Bell

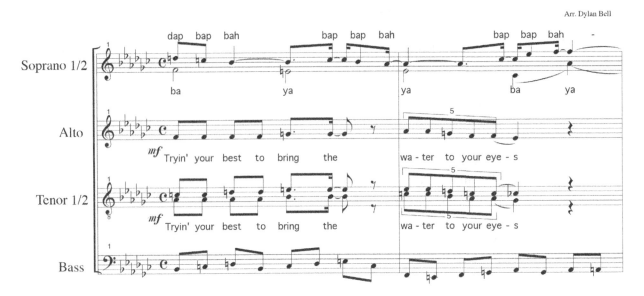

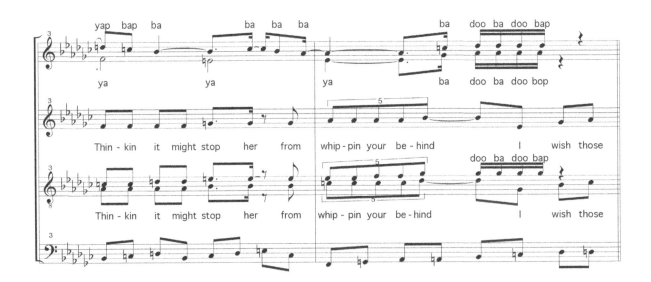

Here I have S1 and S2 singing trumpet parts over a three-part "lead stack" sung by alto, tenor, and baritone. Arranging horn lines doesn't always have to mean a literal imitation of the sound: often, more everyday vocal syllables will do the trick. If we think of the trumpet (in the context of a funk horn section, for example) as "high, bright, and loud," then a simple "ba-dap-bah" (articulated) or "ba-ya-ya" (legato/slurred) will actually function better than a more muted "brr brr brr" type of semi-occluded syllable. Balance-wise, since the "lead" is sung in three parts, there's plenty of dynamic room for S1 and S2 to sing open vowels in the middle of their range.

Now let's look at an arrangement that clearly was built on vocal trumpets, but it has swapped in other syllables in place of imitating trumpets: Deke's "Ring of Fire."

Ring of Fire

"Ring of Fire" by Johnny Cash starts with a classic mariachi-style trumpet figure, which absolutely wants to start any arrangement, especially a scholastic-level arrangement such as this. It is for that reason—I was publishing an arrangement for school groups to sing—that I decided to take the trumpets and render them in syllables that have, for decades, been used in place of trumpet parts. This arrangement is meant to be easily singable in high schools. However, you can easily take an arrangement you or someone else has done and reverse-engineer the vocal line back into a trumpet part by simply having your singers swap in the trumpet sound. Yes, it's that simple, and no, you don't need anyone's permission. Arrangements are road maps, not laws, and the goal is to make it sound great for your own ensemble.

There is so much more that can be done with vocal trumpets, from cool jazz to Afrobeat, funk, and Dixieland. Weave it into songs where it fits stylistically, and play with it as a new vocal color in arrangements farther afield.

Trombone

> » Range: medium-low (B♭2-G4 average, B♭1-F5 extreme)
> » Timbre: mellow to medium bright
> » Articulation: soft to medium

The core sound for a trombone is the same as a trumpet; the only difference is that it should be lower in your voice, and your phrasing will change somewhat. Most trombones use a slide rather than valves, allowing for more sliding into and between notes. Trombone is a far less common lead instrument, but you can hear some great performances from Glenn Miller, J. J. Johnson, and James Pankow from the band Chicago (to name a few).

Now's a good time to mention the importance of using your entire body in the production of instrumental sounds, most notably your hands and arms. You can play a vocal trombone by standing still, but you'll find your phrasing can improve when you move your hands as though you're moving the trombone slide, especially when singing vibrato at the end of a long-held note (which tends to be wider and slower than a vocal vibrato, as the slide needs to be moved up and down). Besides helping with your phrasing, moving your arms like a trombonist also clearly indicates to the audience the sound you're making, completing the illusion.

When it comes to arranging for trombone, you'll likely find the most common instance will be in a jazz horn trio: trumpet-sax-trombone. There's not much you need to do functionally within the arrangement other than indicate the instruments to be mimicked, as the little nuances of phrasing should be up to the singers. You can write in specific slides if you want them, of course, and anything else that's important about their phrasing—individually or as a unit.

The trombone is lower-pitched, which means it often works best with tenor and bass voices, with altos making a good trombone 1 in addition to a tenor's mix or head voice. A three- or four-part "trombone choir" can be a warmer, smoother alternative to a standard horn section, and this can often be found in Latin ensembles. In addition, the subtle bends into and out of notes can give the trombone ensemble a slinkier, sly sound, as well, much like the subtle note inflections in a contemporary lead vocal.

Here's an example of a trombone section in action: Dylan's original piece, "Gringo Samba," written for TTBB.

GRINGO SAMBA

In this samba-jazz piece, the trombones have a soli, typical of a Brazilian jazz ensemble, and I use standard block-voicing and other techniques described earlier in the book. Note that I also don't notate the syllables used, just the instruction "Tbn." However, I chose to notate the pitch inflections more specifically, as I had a specific phrasing and slyness I wanted to get across, and not everyone hears the inflections in trombone performance as easily. Also, while it's common to leave phrasing for singers to work out on their own, it's more common when writing for horns to tell them exactly what you want with articulations and phrase markings. I decided to follow that convention (somewhat) here.

Tuba

- » Range: low (B♭1-B♭3 average)
- » Timbre: mellow
- » Articulation: soft to medium

A tuba is a little different than the "trombone, but lower" sound you may expect. For one, as a valved instrument, it's not as slidey as a trombone. Second, it's almost all tone, with little articulation, just a little puff of breath to get the note going. A simple approximation is "hoh," with a soft, non-breathy "h" and a darker, non-diphthong "oh" sound (remember, a regular diphthong "o" is really more like "oh-oo . . ."—don't close the lips as you finish the vowel). Tuba works well for Dixieland-sounding ensembles or New Orleans bands.

Muted Trumpet/Trombone

For this sound, we're talking about the thin sound of a straight mute, or even more evocative, the silvery sound of a Harmon mute. Think classic Miles Davis, and you have the idea.

There's not only one way to make a convincing muted trumpet sound, as there's not only one muted trumpet sound. Bobby McFerrin's technique is built on a vowel that lands somewhere between an "e" and "uh" with an attack and phrasing like a trumpet. You can hear it across his work, perhaps most purely on the *Round Midnight* movie soundtrack as he sings the title track. Ultimately his beautiful timbre lives somewhere between vocal and instrumental.

Deke's personal approach to the muted trumpet is more challenging to initially achieve, but when you land it, you'll find it less obviously vocal and more instrumental in its raspy timbre:

When teaching the sound, the most effective method I've found is to start by having singers copy the speaking voice of Cartman, a character from the animated series *South Park*. When he gets angry, he goes up into his high falsetto range, and from there the sound can be shaped. Keep the back of your throat open while closing your mouth into a tight "oo" in the front and your tongue rolled tightly and partially blocking the opening. Attack the note with a raspy breath of air shaped similarly to "heh/huh" and imitate a trumpet's phrasing. I urge you to visit my YouTube channel ("dekesharon") for this instructional video in particular, as it's especially challenging to explain this technique via text.

Dylan's is similar, with a few subtle differences:

I think of the vowel sound as a very tight umlaut: "ü," such as you might find in German or Turkish. An "ü" is somewhere between "ee" and "oo," with mine closer to "ee." To get that tight, constrained sound (a Harmon mute effectively "squeezes" the tone), I raise the back of my tongue, squeezing the sound. To practice this, try singing a long "oo." Now try singing an "ee" vowel . . . but without moving your lips into the spread, smiling position you're familiar with. You'll feel the tongue pull back in toward your throat. This tight umlaut has a light, airy sound without needing to add breath to the tone. Despite the squeezed tone, it's surprisingly easy on the voice and can be done for some time without any vocal strain.

For muted trombone, simply move lower in your voice, and slide between notes more frequently.

This tone in particular is less useful as an ensemble element, as it's particularly rough and brittle: a chord of these tones would sound like a stack of icicles. (What did we say about "writing about music"?) Yet, it is quite effective when used in a vocal jazz solo, as the audience is amazed that such a non-traditional sound can be completely vocal. As always, work to keep your phrasing instrumental and avoid phrasing choices that give away that it's a voice instead of an instrument.

Harmon mute solos often sound nice with long, smooth tones and gentle bends/inflections into notes: the emphasis is more on the intriguing timbre than the quantity of notes, and it evokes the cool-jazz sound of 1950s Miles Davis. Here's an example of a Harmon mute trumpet solo by Dylan, taken from the Cadence recording of Joni Mitchell's "Dry Cleaner from Des Moines":

Harmon-Mute Trumpet Solo

from "The Dry Cleaner From Des Moines"
as performed by Cadence

Dylan Bell

Oo

bop!   Bah - oo-wahp

ba-doo way   ba doo-dn' doo-way bwanh   bwanh ba ba ba doo-dn bop!

Against a drum-and-bass background, with harmonically ambiguous pads behind, the solo is sparse and trippy.

Another common type of brass mute is the plunger, which is exactly what it sounds like: the original plunger-mute was the rubber end of a toilet plunger! It gives the nasal "wah-wah" sound often used in big band charts: if you're familiar with the old Charlie Brown television specials, the sound of the schoolteacher was made by a trombone with a plunger mute. This is one of those rare occasions where "human diphthong" vowels come in handy.

To sum up our tour of the brass section, here's a Dixieland-style snippet from Dylan's arrangement of "Hit That Jive, Jack," with straight-mute trumpet, clarinet, slide trombone, and tuba.

Dixieland Soli

from "Hit That Jive Jack"
as performed by Cadence

Saxophone

>> Range: wide (B♭2–F5 average (tenor sax), C2–B♭6 extreme, including baritone and soprano sax)
>> Timbre: wide; mellow to brash
>> Articulation: medium

A vocal saxophone is easier than muted trumpet, and the application can be either in a stack of horns or as a solo instrument. A nod to Richard "Robot" Steighner (of the Exchange, Freedom's Boombox, and now Fusion Music Academy in Melbourne, Australia), as his technique is truly superlative. Make a "duck face" (purse your lips and stick them out), then open them a bit and open your mouth a bit, resting your front teeth on your lower lip. The opening will be roughly a centimeter tall and wide, with your front teeth showing through. Now sing a schwa vowel, like a "huh," through your teeth, and it will buzz a little bit (but not as much as the kazoo/theremin/electric guitar sound mentioned later). Try to attack the note with a bit of a honk to replicate the reed engaging, and a little breath blown through your teeth before the pitch engages will give you a Dexter Gordon quality. Little bits of squeak here and there are also characteristic, and the sound moves well from chest voice through head and into falsetto. Just be careful not to give away too much of the characteristic vocal idiosyncrasies when shifting between.

Writing for vocal sax is as easy as writing for voice. Like the voice, the sax has a very wide range, can move easily from scalar to angular passages, and can shout, whisper, bark, and cry. It's arguably one of the most voice-like instruments, and perhaps this is why it is so universal.

Flute

>> Range: high (C4–C6 average, F3–C7 extreme, including bass flute)
>> Timbre: soft and mellow in low register, clear and transparent in high
>> Articulation: soft to medium

To get this sound, start with a clear "doo" sung high in your register (falsetto for lower voices), but instead of shifting to a "boo" for trumpet, attack the sound with a "th," making a "thoo" sound. Next close your mouth as much as possible, leaving a tiny opening, and sing the tone with far too much breath (think Marilyn Monroe), so much breath that it feels like you're half-singing and half-exhaling. Finally, for the vibrato, wiggle your lips. If you're having trouble wiggling them, try saying, "wuh wuh wuh wuh wuh" quickly, then go back to the sound and use the same muscles. *Voilà!* This is one of the easier sounds, and you should get it without too much trouble.

Deke used this sound not only as a soloistic instrument, but stacked for a specific sound in an original he wrote for the House Jacks called "All Away," where the texture is akin to the Mellotron flutes in the opening of the Beatles' "Strawberry Fields Forever."

All Away

Moving from direct imitation to function, a low-pitched whistle often does what a flute does. Often in orchestration, the flute doubles another melody or top-of-ensemble instrument, such as first violins. A whistle doubling a soprano line can add a similar, shimmering effect.

An interesting variation on the flute is the shakuhachi, or Japanese bamboo flute. It has a lower and richer sound than that of a Western flute: if you're familiar with Peter Gabriel's "Sledgehammer," the "flute" solo at the beginning is a (sampled) shakuhachi. Follow the same techniques above for the flute, with two changes. First, add a stronger attack, "ff." Second, add a little "r" to the sound, so that "oo" becomes "urr." Also, slow down the vibrato to a deep tremolo.

Clarinet

»   Range: medium (D3-C6 average, as low as B♭1 for bass clarinet)
»   Timbre: soft and mellow in low register, clear and transparent in high
»   Articulation: soft to medium

A flute has a pure sound with almost no overtones: the waveform looks like a smooth sine wave. A clarinet's conical bore emphasizes the odd-numbered overtones, and the waveform looks like a square. The result is a more "wooden" sound with a little more broadness and some clarity. To do this with the voice, start with your "oo" sound, but place the sound a little farther in the middle of the mouth (rather than forward), and stiffen your tongue a bit: this turns the mouth cavity into a more conical shape, and the result will be a more focused "oo" with a tiny bit of "r" in the sound, but not as much as the shakuhachi. For articulation, use a "silent h," engaging the diaphragm without adding breath to the "h."

Bass

> » Range: low (E1-C4 average, with the first octave usually sung up the octave to similar effect)
> » Timbre: mellow to medium bright
> » Articulation: usually percussive (except bowed acoustic bass)

Bass is the fundamental sound on which your ensemble is built, so you want to get this one right! Fortunately, it's one of the easiest to make. There are a number of subtle differences in tone and articulation, depending on what kind of bass you want to represent: acoustic, electric (fingerstyle, slap and pick), fretless, or synth bass. We'll give you some pointers on tone and style for all these variations.

Bass is all about function over flash, so a neutral tone is a great place to start. Try singing a gentle "hmmmm," medium-low in your register. Now behind that closed mouth, drop your jaw a bit so it's relaxed, and raise your soft palate a bit. The space inside your mouth should feel tall and open, and the tone shouldn't come from the back of your throat (which would fatigue you in the long run): rather, the "placement" (i.e., where you feel much of the resonance and vibration) should be right in the center of your mouth. This is your "center tone," useful for most bass sounds. Now, on to specifics.

Acoustic Bass

Most jazz, some classical, and early rock 'n' roll features the acoustic (sometimes called the "upright" or "double") bass. Its tone is smooth and round, and the articulation is gently percussive. All you have to do is close your lips, say "th" (a hard "th," with the tongue behind the teeth), followed directly with our center bass tone. In other words: "thm." Simple to sing; simple to spell out in your arrangements. Note that the "th" sound is hard and short, like "Thank you," rather than long, like "theater" or "theremin."

In jazz and jazz-flavored music, the bass often starts playing "in two," emphasizing the first and third beats, as in the classic "Fever."

Fever

This is complemented by the drummer, who is usually keeping time on the hi-hat on two and four. If you don't have a VP, the bass can easily handle this in between:

Razzle Dazzle

More often in jazz, an acoustic bass "walks," playing constant quarter notes, connecting each chord with mostly stepwise motion. You can keep the hi-hat backbeat going through this easily by singing "thm tm thm tm," or "thm tsm thm tsm" for a louder hi-hat.

Me And My Shadow

The bass can add a little rhythmic skip here and there for variety. Note that a quick eighth restrike is too fast for a full "thm," so a quick "b" will do nicely (without vowel—not "buh"); keep as closed a mouth as possible with the tiniest opening for the pitch. If the tempo is brisk and the walking bass line unrelenting, you might want to revert to a soft "dm" in place of "thm" (while maintaining the "tm" on offbeats):

Forget About the Boy

Electric and Synth Bass

On the surface, you might think "a bass is a bass . . . what would I do differently?" The differences are subtle, but worth exploring.

We describe the ideal bass sound as being somewhere between "dm" and "thm" with little to no vowel, and this is a good starting point for electric bass, as well. Electric bass has a more noticeable articulation with less "pull" on the string, so instead of "thm," we can get closer to "dm" for fingerstyle bass.

For classic R&B, soul, and earlier rock, the "P bass" (so named for the Fender Precision bass common at the time, and still the most universal bass sound) is your go-to sound. It's round and warm, like the upright, but with the tighter articulation of "dm." A big difference between acoustic and electric bass is the amount of extra percussion and groove that can be built into the bass line with different articulations, accents, and the use of "dead notes," articulations with little-to-no actual note attached. This is especially prevalent in funk bass lines where the bass is practically a one-person rhythm section.

Note the use of more articulations: d, b, bnk, and more accents through different vowels. Even more so than other instrument sounds, bass vowels will stay quite dark: instead of "doo-ba-doo," think "dm-beh-dm."

For a more modern bass sound, you can use all the techniques above and change your center sound slightly: close the jaw behind the "hum" just a little bit, activate the resonators in your nasal cavity more, and you'll hear more overtones show up in the sound.

Some songs use a bass played with a pick instead of the fingers. Everything else stays the same, but your articulating consonant will be more pronounced. Make your "dm" more articulated, closer to "tm" than "thm," or if you really want to hear the pick against the string, try "gm," like "gum" without the vowel.

Slap Bass

This is the same instrument, but a different playing technique: instead of plucking with fingers or a pick, the player hits their thumb sharply against the string, often alternating with a "pop" on a higher string, snapping the string with another finger. This "slap and pop" technique is bright and percussive, and it is exemplified by bassists such as Mark King from the 1980s band Level 42. For this sound, brighten up your tone and/or make it growly, sing "dm" for the slap, or "d-g-dm" for quick restrikes, and "benk!" for the pops. A great exemplar of this in a cappella is Alvin Chea's bass in the Take 6 song "I Believe":

Note the use of other syllables, as well, for the pops, such as "fa-um" for pops with hammer-ons. Unlike the "function over style" notes below, the bass is meant to be noticed here: more vowel variation helps with this.

Fretless Bass

This bass sound is probably the closest a bass guitar gets to singing. It's often used for more lyrical bass playing, though exponents such as Jaco Pastorius played fast, furious, and virtuosic fretless bass. For our purposes, we'll stick with the lyrical side.

The fretless tone has a softer attack and a "bloom" to the sound, and it has the ability to slide. For the tone itself, try singing "dwohnnn." Now say it behind closed lips. You'll feel and hear that subtle bloom in the sound, and the syllable will sound less like a word and more like a variation of tone. Try a gentle slide between notes for the sweet, slippery feel of the fretless. Here's an example of a fretless bass representation, from Paul Simon's "Diamonds on the Soles of Her Shoes."

Synth Bass

You might hear a synth bass in anything from old-school Stevie Wonder to modern pop and EDM music. The available tones for synth bass can vary wildly, but the most functional fall within more specific parameters.

Traditional synthesizers control their tone primarily through the use of the sound envelope (attack, decay, sustain, and release) and through the filter (cutoff and resonance). The envelope is typically set to represent something like a plucked string: a fast attack, quick decay, long sustain (although the notes are usually played short), and short release. The filter cutoff is usually fairly low, giving a dark sound, and the resonance is low to medium. The result is something like the word "own" said quickly, with the "n" clipped short. As always, rules are meant to be bent, and the use of a diphthong "Oh-oo" mimics the sound of the filter. A brighter filter and more resonance gives us something more nasal-sounding, like the Portuguese "ao" vowel sound. For the attack, make the "o" vowel glottal, or add a "b" or "d" consonant for articulation.

Particular idiomatic style aspects include the use of slides, long glissandi, quick vibrato, and quick pitch inflections and turns. Going back to Alvin Chea, in the last choruses of "I Believe" mentioned above, he trades his slap bass for a synth bass, and you can see and hear a difference in the phrasing:

Note that he still sneaks a "bnk" in there. This is a vocal bass: who says you can't mix techniques?

Acoustic and Electric Guitar

Like pianos and keyboards, the guitar is ubiquitous in many styles of music, and similarly, it's helpful to consider the function of the instrument as much as (or more than) the tone itself.

Acoustic Guitar

» Range: wide (E2-E6)
» Timbre: mellow to bright/transparent
» Articulation: percussive

Acoustic guitar can be either the primary accompaniment instrument (as in acoustic folk, or singer-songwriter genres) or an added "sparkly" texture in more layered or electric genres. In either case, the methods are similar:

» Articulation is percussive. It can be warm or bright: "d" works well for a softer articulation such as fingerpicking, and "j" works for the sound of a plectrum (pick).
» Vowel shape is in the middle ground.
» The sound decays gradually as the string sound slowly dies off.

Put these together and you get a few options: "dennn" or "dinnn" for something more mellow, such as a finger-picked guitar, or "jennn" and "jinnn" for a strummed guitar.

Acoustic guitar solos are somewhat uncommon in most contemporary genres, and they don't translate well vocally as a guitar. More often, you'll be writing for multipart BGs. They could be arpeggiated, or "strummed" together as guitar chords.

Electric Guitar

There are more tonal varieties and more roles to play for the electric guitar. The sound is more midrange-forward, and the vowel sounds change appropriately to overtone-rich "oh," "ah," and "eh" timbres. The sound of the pick is often more prevalent, and sometimes the "note-off" is audible as the strings are muted with either hand. This gives us a wealth of possibilities, starting with . . .

Guitar chords
» Long: "jennng," "johnnn," "jerrrrrnnnn"
» Short: "jenk," "denk"
» Muted: "jn"

You can get creative with these. A long, broad chord could be "krannnnnnnnng" or "gluuunnnng."

Lead/melody/solos

The "j" syllable works particularly well for chords and multiple strings played: for individual notes, "g" works well. A dark lead sound can work well with "gohn," "gowhn" gives a little more spice, and "gerwn" can add more brightness.

And don't forget the wah-pedal! Rhythm guitar can gives us "w-k-ch-k" and "gow-wow-wow-wown," and lead guitar "gwown-gwown-gown." These are a notable exception to our "avoid diphthong vowels" rule of thumb.

Here are some examples from Dylan's original, "Don't Fix What's Broken." In the song's intro, we have three-part strummed electric guitar. It's broad-sounding but not jangly, so we use "jon" (pronounce a little like the name "Joan"):

Don't Fix What's Broken

In the verse, there are two guitar parts: a muted, percussive rhythm part "jn" and an arpeggiated lead-ish part, "gohn." Add this to the electric bass part (our familiar "dm"), and you see three different articulations and vowel sounds, helping to separate the three parts. In addition, the vowel sounds aren't overly bright or brash, to make room for the lead vocal.

In the bridge, the arpeggiated, sustained guitar chords are given a tremolo effect to add movement.

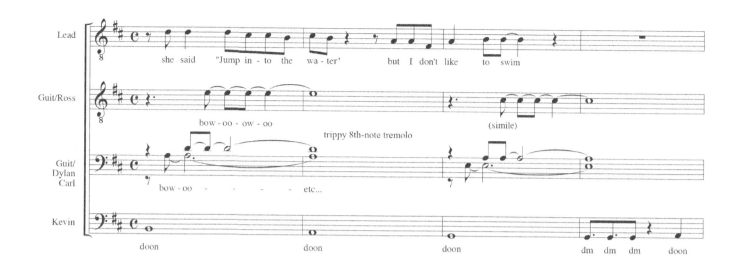

In short, the tonal possibilities for guitar are nearly endless! For the extra fuzz of a distorted guitar, see the "novelty" section below.

Harmonica

» Range: high (C4-G6)
» Timbre: thin, silvery to brash
» Articulation: slow and breathy

No, it's not part of the guitar family, but the harmonica's lead-guitar-like solo function and its place in rock and blues music makes this the best place to talk about it.

Like the muted trumpet, you need to start with a rather ugly, nontraditional vocal tone: start with a loud "ahhh," but a little darker, like the word "on." Or think of the French "on" as in "garçon": it's a little more nasal than the English "on," more like "ohn." Try singing it with a bit of a honk at the beginning of the sound and make it brash. Next, you'll want to cup your hands on both sides of your mouth, like you're about to yell to someone far away, and use your index fingers to block both of your nostrils, rendering your sound as if you have a head cold with congestion. Next, start the sound with both of your hands closed together, like your hands are cold and you're about to blow warm air into them to heat them up; then, once you start the sound, open them up quickly, all the time still pinching your nose. The result will be a "hwaa" sound, as your hands are basically playing the role of a second/external mouth that's closed and opening. You'll find if you try just singing "hwaa," the sound isn't as convincing.

Then, the *pièce-de-résistance*: for the signature sound of a harmonica's tremolo, you're going to close your hands completely and reopen them as quickly as possible, like someone cupping and playing a harmonica. You'll find that somewhat closing your hands is nowhere as effective as completely closing them, which is best achieved by holding one hand steady and moving your other hand away and back together quickly. This means you're un-pinching that nostril and re-pinching it over and over quickly. Be careful to not slam your hands together too quickly. You may find once you move to this vibrato, your moving hand moves to more of a flat position as your other hand remains cupped. Whatever it takes, make sure you're fully closing and reopening; start slowly and accelerate once you get the hang of it.

Like many of the sounds above, the harmonica is really best used soloistically, and it sounds great soaring over the top of a blues, folk, or rock song, perhaps interspersed between lead vocal lines, as so often happened in classic recordings. "Harmonica-centric"-playing techniques include the use of the above-mentioned tremolo and bluesy bending between notes.

Piano/Keyboards

Piano

> » Range: wide (A0-C8)
> » Timbre: mellow to bright
> » Articulation: percussive

Surprisingly, this one is quite difficult to represent literally: the pitch and timbral range is so wide and orchestral, and its application so universal, from European classical to rock to just about anything else, that it's difficult to pin down a specific sound to cover it. Even worse, the idiomatic aspects of the piano—the ability to play as many notes as you want, but lack of control over a note once it's played—are pretty much the opposite of what the human voice does well (one note at a time, but with infinite control throughout the note). Instead of worrying about the literal imitation of the sound and playable characteristics, look instead at the function of the piano in the piece you're looking to represent.

In most contemporary music, the piano acts as a harmonic and rhythmic underpinning. It's not just an interesting sound; it serves a function. Here's an example of the piano as a basic time- and chord-keeper, in the opening lines of "Killer Queen."

The piano is playing straight quarter notes in relatively staccato fashion, with no pedal. The timbre on the original is bright and jangly: a combination of a grand piano and toy piano. For this arrangement, the relatively neutral syllable "dohn" is used. Why not something more literal, like "jink" or "thnk"? Any of these would work well, but the arranger chose to mimic the main function of the piano, to provide a warm vowel for fuller chord tones, and keep the focus on the lead singer.

Electric piano, such as the Fender Rhodes, has a warmer tone than a piano, with fewer overtones, and the sound of metallic tines added in for a little sparkle on the articulation. A decent equivalent is "gonng" (pronounced "gohng," not "gong" like the giant metal cymbal).

Synthesizer

There are as many synthesizer sounds as there are orchestral instruments. In fact, there are very many more, as a synthesizer can replicate any traditional instrument, as well as create banks of sounds that have never before been heard. Rather than teach you a specific technique to get every synth sound, we're instead going to give you some parameters to help you create new vocal sounds that play the same role.

As mentioned earlier in the synth-bass section, many synth sounds are defined by the envelope (attack, decay, sustain, and release) and the filter (cutoff and resonance). In more human terms, "filter cutoff and resonance" are really just different vowel shapes, from dark and muted ("oo") to bright ("ah") and resonant ("eh" and "ee"). Think of the sound as a combination of a beginning, middle, and end. Usually the beginning and end can have some kind of consonant character, but they may also be a morphing sound that is replicated best by a diphthong. For the middle sound, rather than thinking specifically of the closest vowel, look for resonant open-mouth tones that most closely replicate what you're hearing. What's the best way to do this? By singing along, of course. Don't get frustrated because you can't precisely replicate the sound; instead look for a non-linguistic (so it doesn't sound like words, as mentioned earlier) tone that you can then somehow convey through words, or simply teach by ear.

You may find that the sound is perpetually changing. For instance, some synth sounds, rather than constantly repeating the same sound, are morphing, perhaps because of a flanging effect across the tone or a sweeping movement of the filter. Therefore something like "mo-mo-ma-ma-meh-meh-mi-mi" (and so on) may represent the sound most effectively (like the synth at the beginning of the Who's "Won't Get Fooled Again"). You can write out the entire set of syllables if the part will be sung by a group of people, or you can start it off to give your solo singer a sense of the character, then let them improvise the sound as you've established it.

Strings

» Range: wide (E1-E8)
» Timbre: mellow to bright
» Articulation: slow to percussive

When we think "strings," what comes to mind is the orchestral string section of violin, viola, cello, and bass. Though the human range ends with the cello's lowest range, and most sopranos can't compete with a violin's extreme high range, strings are often voiced similarly to SATB, making an easy transition.

When aiming for a string-ensemble sound, the main "identifiers" are the longer attack phase of a bow, the rich sustain (perfect for the voice), and the use of vibrato. Vowel sounds can range from a soft, muted "nn" to a dark "ee" (with the sound closer to "ih"). No initial consonant is needed for bowed strings.

For more specialized techniques beyond legato bowing, try the following:

» *Staccato/spiccato*: "hn" with a strong, guttural "h" for the bow sound, or "vn."
» *Pizzicato*: "thn" works nicely; "plm" gives a nice string-pluck sound, but it can be a little more challenging to sing accurately.
» *Solo string*: a solo string instrument is nearly analogous to a solo voice. Use all the ideas above, and feel free to enrich the vibrato. It almost sounds like wordless classical singing. Keep the vowel sound dark and neutral (and of course, no diphthongs!) to avoid any "vocal giveaway."

For a unique, "rosin-y" bowed sound, see the "novelty" section below, along with the notes on mixing and matching the neutral ensemble sounds above with the rosin-sounds.

Drums and Percussion

We covered drums and percussion in some detail in our previous book, so we'll include some of that here, with some additions and more detail.

Many people classify different vocal styles such as vocal percussion, vocal drumming, beatboxing, etc. For our purposes, we'll used the general term *vocal percussion/vocal percussionist*, shortened to VP.

VP is a newer practice, a highly individual art form, with its best practitioners each bringing a unique set of skills to the table. As a result, there isn't an established, academic-sounding common vocabulary of techniques. That said, there are enough common sounds to start building a library of useable sounds, achievable by just about anyone.

Basic VP Vocabulary

Here's a basic building block of sounds you can write for a VP part. These are based on the common elements of a drum kit, with a few extra basic percussion elements. For the kick and snare, we offer two options: "voiced" and "unvoiced." The voiced sound utilizes the vocal cords, and this is the best option if the VP is acoustic, or not mic'd individually, as the sound projects farther. The voiced version is also easier for less-experienced "drummers" to make: you can use this if you don't have a VP specialist. The unvoiced version relies on the proximity and power of the mic, and it works best if the VP has their own mic, held close enough to the mouth to the point of touching.

» *Kick drum, voiced*—"dm." Short and powerful, with strong support from the diaphragm. The tone of the drum is low in the vocal register, usually back in the throat.
» *Kick drum, unvoiced*—"p." This is a short "plosive," or a quick puff of air directly into the mic. Close the lips, put some backpressure behind the lips/teeth, and let it out in one short burst. Note that this does not require any support from the diaphragm: the little air pocket and plosive comes from the front of the face. To practice this, hold your palm about two inches from your mouth. You should feel a strong puff of air against your hand as you create the sound.
» *Snare drum, voiced*—"keh," or "dzh." "Keh" works well for a lighter, bright snare sound. Imagine the short "huh!" sound you might associate with a martial-arts move: short, intense, and from the diaphragm. Try that feeling with "keh," and you pretty much have it. The "dzh" is a great option for a heavy, gated snare sound, as you might find in 1980s pop. It feels similar to the voiced kick "dm," but it has a longer decay: the "zh" sound imitates the snares. You can "tune" the snare lower or higher with the pitch of your voice behind the sound.
» *Snare drum, unvoiced*—"pf." This is similar to the unvoiced kick. It involves a similar quick outburst of air, but with two major differences. First, instead of

an open puff of air, it gets squeezed through the "snares." To make this with your face, rest your top teeth over your bottom lip, as you would to make the sound "fffff." But instead of pushing air out from the diaphragm, as with the letter "f," you'll squeeze that little puff of air through the f-shape. Second, the puff of air is much tighter. With the kick drum, the lips are loosely pursed, giving a deep plosive. With the snare, the lips are pursed tightly, similar to a brass player's embouchure, and the sound that emerges is higher and tighter. To practice this, hold your palm in front of your mouth as you did with the kick. This time, the sound should be louder, but the puff of air is not as strong as with the kick. With practice, the snare can be "tuned" with the embouchure. A loose snare is good for 1970s and 1980s music; a tighter snare sounds good for drum-and-bass and other similar genres. The kick and snare is the "heartbeat and backbeat" of the drum groove, and all else is secondary. It's worth taking time to work on these! Moving on . . .

» *Cross-stick*—the "click" of the stick against the rim, instead of the snare drum sound, "kh." Like the unvoiced kick/snare, this does not use the diaphragm.

» *Toms*—"dng," or "gng" for a brighter articulation to cut through the mix. Toms usually come in sets of two (high and low) or three (high, medium, and low), and they are typically tuned about a fifth or sixth apart (for two toms) or about a fourth apart (three toms). Tom fills are almost always played "high to low."

» *Hi-hats*—"ts" (closed), and "tsss" (open). Note that an open hi-hat can be done as an in-breath as well as an out-breath: an in-breath open hi-hat is a great way to breathe while keeping the groove going.

» *Crash cymbal*—"kssssh," "pshhhh." Drummers use crash cymbals as musical "signposts," signaling the end of one section/beginning of another, and they usually fall on a downbeat. Pay attention to the decay of the sound: a smooth decay will mimic the gradual dulling of the nonharmonic overtones as the cymbal sound dies away. Cymbals are often combined with a kick, giving "bshhhhh." A real crash cymbal may last ten seconds or more, but yours won't be nearly this long. With a single VP, your crash will be as short as a single beat: you'll need to hit that next snare on beat two!

» *Ride cymbal*—a whispered "kinnggg." Where a crash cymbal is brash and is played once as an accent, the ride cymbal has a drier sound and is often played in eighth notes similar to a hi-hat. Or, in jazz, the ride keeps the main swing beat. For the ride, whisper the word "king," but make it much longer: "kiiinnnnnnnng," letting the long "ng" decay as a cymbal would. The whisper gives the dry metallic "hash" sound of the cymbal. You can tune this cymbal with the vowel shape: brighter "king" or darker "keng."

» *Shakers*—shakers usually outline a sixteenth-note pattern. To imitate the natural accents of a shaker, try "CH-sh-ch-k CH-sh-ch-k." The "sh" is the softest sound. These can also be "tuned" high or low, from a little egg-shaker to a big maraca or shekere (gourd shaker). For a higher sound, smile while making the sound for a more sibilant tone: for a lower sound, purse your lips. You can even "filter" the sound from high to low by moving the mouth shape for an interesting effect.

» *Congas*—these come in sets of two to four or more, but most conga patterns can be covered with three tones: high and low, pitched about a fourth apart, and the harmonic slap, about an octave higher. The high and low congas can be sung as "bng" (or "dng" or "gng," depending on how prevalent you want the attack) and the slap with "bok!" sung in head-voice/falsetto.

» *Tambourine*—Do you know what a "lateral lisp" is? A normal "s" sound comes from over the top/center of the tongue, but with a lateral lisp, the sound comes from the sides of the tongue and has a sound somewhere between "ss" and "sh." This sound works well for the metallic jingle of a tambourine: try "ksh" with a lateral lisp, and you've got it. Bonus: for jingle bells, try the same lateral lisp with a push from the diaphragm and no "k," like this: "SHHhh-shh-shh-shh."

No matter how the VP approaches these, you should be able to get the sounds you want within these parameters.

Extra/Novelty Sounds

Kazoo/Bowed Strings/Theremin/Electronic Guitar

This multipurpose sound is thin and buzzy, and it can be used to approximate a few different instruments. It's a bit like whistling in that it will take some time to master, but once you have it, you'll always have it. What we're going to do is create a sound that makes your entire mouth vibrate and buzz the way a kazoo cone does, and it takes a little time to properly set up and explain.

Let's start with the letter "n." When you're saying "nnn," it's a bit like humming, but your mouth is open. If you were to pull your tongue away from the roof of your mouth (which we're going to do—more on this in a second), you'll find you move to a basic schwa sound—"nnn-uhh-nnn-uhh"—as you take your tongue away from the roof of your mouth and return it, etc. This will provide the core sound that will make things vibrate.

Next let's create the cone: you want to take your front teeth and gently rest them on your lower lip, like you're about to say a word that starts with the letter "f," but you're not going to blow any air and make that sound; just rest them there. Next you want to make sure you have a complete seal, and there's no space or opening on either side of your teeth. To do this you need to make a face a bit like a bunny rabbit with buck teeth: your mouth will have somewhat of a square-shaped opening with just your front teeth showing. The pressure wants to be just the right amount—too little, and air passes by and you don't get a buzz; too tight, and the buzz is blocked off. Aim for a gentle seal, then sing that "nn" sound . . . and pull your tongue away from the roof of your mouth. *Voilà*: you should get the buzzing sound.

Do not despair if it does not happen right away: like whistling, it takes a little time to get the mechanics just right. When you first hear this sound, you may think you're listening to someone singing the letter "v" but you're not. The letter "v" requires much more air blown across the lips, whereas this sound, like a hum, requires very little effort and is much easier to make quietly. If you're a beatboxer, you may know this sound referred to as the "siren," which is often how it's used in a beatboxing routine. However, since we're focused more on pitched instruments, we're going to harness it in different ways.

First off, we can use this sound as an alternate for a bowed string instrument, from violin down through cello to string bass. Rather than just create a straight tone, like a string player, you should introduce vibrato (by varying the pitch with your voice), and phrase each note the way string players would (such as attacking the note gently and crescendoing into it). This sound is easily swapped into any long-held note, and it can work if only some of the singers can make this buzzing sound, with others simply singing "nn" (with the requisite string vibrato and phrasing).

Instrument number two is the first-ever electronic instrument: the theremin. If you haven't seen one, your left hand, waving in space near the device, controls the volume, and your right hand controls the pitch. Playing a theremin precisely is quite difficult as there are not only no frets, but you're moving your hand in three-dimensional space, so as a result there's a lot of sliding between notes and heavy vibrato (such as in the song "Good Vibrations" or the original theme to *Star Trek*). This might not be the most common or useful application, but the next one is.

Take that perfect seal you have with your teeth on your lower lip and introduce a little bit of saliva. Once you do you'll hear a crackling, distorted sound, which is what you want. Lean into that, especially on long-held notes, and put some attitude into your singing, and you have a distorted electric guitar. Needless to say, this (and the theremin) are best used as solo instruments. As with all instruments, the tone is only half of creating the audio illusion; the other is phrasing that matches the specific instrument's character and parameters.

Mandolin/Xylophone/Steel Drum

Although all three of these instruments are quite different, the best way to vocally replicate them is similar (with the differences being in phrasing and application): you want to create a tremolo by moving your tongue up and down across the opening in your mouth, an opening that's just large enough to accommodate your tongue so that it brushes the sides of your mouth as it comes in and out. Start by saying the word "blung" and notice how your tongue moves from the "l" to the "u" part of the word. Now try to reverse it, returning your tongue to the roof of your mouth, with your mouth opening tight so you can feel your tongue returning. Then out again, and back in, over and over and faster, until you're making a sound that at half speed would be best represented by typing "luh-ll-luh-ll-luh-ll," and so on, and then once you get it going quickly enough, it just sounds like a tremolo.

This tremolo is the core of the sound of a mandolinist repeatedly quickly plucking the same string up and down, a xylophonist repeatedly hitting the same wooden bar with a pair of mallets, or the same action happening on a specific gong (section) of a steel pan or other steel drum instrument. You may argue that this sound is rather vague and not particularly timbrally specific, which it is not, but it's also almost impossibly rare to hear a voice used this way, so you have a new texture to play with that can be applied to anything from Eastern European folk music to Caribbean pop. For quick single note hits, start with "blung" as a straightforward, neutral single version of the longer tremolo sound, and modify as needed to match the character of the song.

Related to this is the strummed banjo: instead of "blung" we have "flunk." A rapidly strummed banjo can give us something like "flunky-dunk-flunk, ga-flunky-da-flunk-fldldldldl." It's fun and works surprisingly well.

Bagpipes

This one is just for fun. Start with your lowest singers (basses) singing a note that's close to the bottom of their vocal range on a buzzy, obnoxious vowel "reeee," repeating from time to time. Then have your higher voices sing a fifth and octave above it, matching the tone and repetition. This creates the drone. Finally, once this is established, you can sing a traditional Scottish or other folk song on the vowel "reeee," with the addition that every time you restrike a note, you gently tap your larynx with your thumb, index, and middle finger joined together, causing the note to jump. Precise singing is not required. This is less meant for any kind of practical application and more offered as a way to get an entire room of singers to burst into laughter. You're welcome.

A great reference from days of old for all kinds of sound effects, including instruments and drums, is a book entitled *Mouth Sounds* by Fred Newman (you may know him from *Between the Lions* and other 1990s shows on Nickelodeon), which is available on the Internet Archive for free (one hour "checkout" at a time, find the link on our website). The book came with a removeable floppy vinyl disc that included some of the sounds; alas, that's not included on the Internet Archive. You'll find his way of teaching some of the sounds above is different from ours, which is quite useful and informative; there is not only one way to skin a cat, as they say, but they should more accurately say there's not only one way to make a vocal instrumental sound, especially since there's no specific place where these techniques are taught, and certainly nothing has been codified. If you find your own technique or best practice, we urge you to make a video and upload it online so others may benefit (and if you see us in person, please teach us too!).

Now let's look at how these instrumental and percussive elements can be used in arrangements.

Lyric-less Arranging

Deke's had plenty of experience creating lyric-less arrangements, so we'll hand this section over to him.

Orchestral Arranging

When asked to arrange a song based on a full orchestral score, you have both to consider how to condense the many parts into fewer, and what vocal tones/syllables/vocal instruments you want to incorporate. Doing a strict one-to-one vocal imitation of all instruments won't work in almost every case, for many reasons including vocal range and the number of singers you have available to sing their own unique line. There are forty-four instruments in a typical orchestra, and whereas there are many doublings, such as in the strings, there are easily twenty different sounds being produced, and that's not counting that some instruments are creating many pitches at once, like a piano.

"The Glory Days"

For this reason, it's important to take a larger, wholistic approach to the translation: What's the overall effect of a passage, and how can the voices you're using best replicate the overall effect of the piece since you're not going to mimic it. When asked to create a vocal version of "The Glory Days," the theme to Disney's *The Incredibles*, for DCappella, the first step was to take a look at the score:

1m2 Rev - "The Incredibles"

Composer-Michael Giacchino
Orchestrator-Tim Simonec

If you're not used to looking at scores, your first impression will leave you overwhelmed. There are so many staves compared to vocal scores, and some of them are transposed and/or different clefs. However, after a moment to digest it all, you'll start to notice that there are some similarities. For example, both tenor and bari sax, as well as all four French horns and four trombones, are playing in unison, as are the flute and piccolo along with the first and second violins, as well as a percussionist playing bells. And there's a third part in octaves played by the violas, as well as cellos and basses, reinforced by timpani. The overall effect is a huge sound, but the actual number of parts isn't many . . . three, in fact. If you think of the opening of Beethoven's Fifth Symphony, that, too, has a huge sound, and a lot of instruments playing one line in octaves. Orchestras can explode into a symphony of sound (pun intended), such as in the works of Ravel, but in many cases, it's likely less complicated than you assume.

So, how will we reduce this down to just six vocal parts (setting aside the vocal percussion)? Let's start with the fact that we need those three lines covered by at least one voice. Our bass singer needs to cover that driving cello/bass riff, and the part played by the horns definitely is the predominant line, so let's give it to the soprano . . . or is the flute line higher? Seeing as how we're not going to have that flute line ride up to a high C, it needs to be down the octave in the middle of the female range, so let's give the horn line to our soprano so it rings out on top and we have a chance of that E being powerful—in a high, belted chest voice when in the studio, or at least a mixed voice when live.

This is a good moment to mention that this piece could have been moved into any key. Why didn't I? Because there was no good reason to. If the goal was to reflect the original version, which it was, I prefer to keep pieces in their original keys as well as original tempo (with the caveat that a cappella pieces tend to feel a few BPM slower when at the same tempo, so speeding them up two to three BPM usually makes them feel the same). Some people hear a song in a specific key and it feels "right"; others have perfect pitch; still others like to "A/B" the two recordings and compare what you've done. If there's no good reason, and it ain't broke, keep it where it is.

Back to the first measure: we still have a third line that can go to the mezzo. It could go to the alto, as well, but why did I choose not to do this? Because I decided I wanted that horn line to be sung by the other members—it wants to be big and brassy and doubled more than the other lines—and I wanted to have the first E, rather than be a big unison, explode into a chord. Why? Voices when doubled, tripled, or sung by an entire choir don't necessarily get significantly larger the way a variety of instruments do. Much as we all have different vocal timbres to our voices, the timbre doesn't vary all that much—not as much as a tenor sax and French horn, for instance—so the overtones that are cast, especially if everyone's vowel is aligned, are largely reinforcing instead of expansive. You'll get a warm, rich tone, not the bright, brassy buzz you get when several different kinds of horns are aligned. So, I decided to explode out the chord to several notes, which results in more overtones, a larger sound, and more buzz.

The Glory Days

Now let's talk syllables. This wasn't a time for direct instrumental imitation, fun as that might be. Why? Because a vocal trumpet sound, while sounding far more like an instrument than a voice on an open vowel, is essentially a closed-mouth endeavor. Great sound, but not a big sound. In fact, in the studio, I've often had singers double their vocal trumpet sounds with another layer of the same voices on the same notes, but singing "ba," which I then mix in. The two combined give both the timbre and the punch/ring I'm often looking for.

So, if "ba" is big and bright, why did I use "buh"? Well, the overall color of the opening measures of the original recording isn't as bright as if it were trumpets. This was obviously a conscious choice by the original orchestrator—Tim Simonec—as trumpets seem like they'd have been the obvious choice. The character and tone is more ominous while still being powerful, like a James Bond score, whereas bright trumpets ringing feels more celebratory, like at the end of the first *Star Wars* film during the awards ceremony. The feeling is "something's wrong, something's happening," which the sound of trumpets might belie. To that end, a slightly darkened vowel—"buh"—struck me as more appropriate, as it's still big and bright and loud, but not celebratory. I went with a "duh" in the bass line for the same reason—"da" felt too bright. As for the mezzo line, the imitation of a flute wouldn't work as it would get swamped by all the brassiness, and a strictly flutelike "thoo" would be difficult to restrike at this tempo, so I went with a simpler "hoo" as the initial tone, but that's also too hard to repeat quickly, so I put in a quick-tongued syllable between the "oo" vowels, the same way Celtic *puirt à beul* ("mouth music") uses nonsense syllables like "hi-dl-ee di-dl-ee."

Let's look at a couple moments later in this piece, as it features passages with different tempi and tone colors.

There's a passage in which everything becomes quiet, almost like the characters are tiptoeing carefully while in danger. The flute and piccolo play a melody quietly, which is then punctuated by a staccato, ascending arpeggiated line in the violins and clarinet. I wanted the line to be high, yet controlled, and a different tone color than the soprano, so I went with mezzo (it might get a little high in an alto's range, necessitating a shift to head-voice, and I wanted it smooth), and an "oo" vowel, which I use when I want my singers quiet. An "n" at the top guarantees a soft attack, even softer than just "oo" itself, which requires a glottal approach. One other reason to use the mezzo here is that in the exact next passage this melody is restated forte, and the mezzo is in perfect range for a big, brassy jazz shake on the same phrase. Sometimes these choices are about not only what's happening, but what's to come.

As for the other voices, I leaned into the sound of the pizzicato strings with "thm" and a different person on each note. Why? Well, frankly, it feels more right and . . . fun. Each person has their own sound and personality, and with each one singing only one note, it has more of that tiptoe character. It's difficult to explain precisely in words, but the different voices each taking one quick short note feels more to me like . . . the characters in a *Scooby-Doo* cartoon whispering quietly to each other when in danger or scared. As for the fun part of the equation, I didn't just want this arrangement to be impressive and reflect the original powerfully with voices; I also wanted it to be playful and enjoyable to sing and listen to. This was Disney, after all.

One more thing I did to give this passage a different character: I decided to add another layer of sound to that quiet mezzo line: the same melody whistled. I recalled the playful character of some of Antonio Carlos Jobim's recordings in which he whistles a melody along with the piano, and the two together have a certain character. The overtones are different, and the whistle is more like a piccolo than any other instrument, so the sonority aligns. Plus, again, it's fun.

One more passage from this one to consider:

This piece isn't long, around ninety seconds, and yet I'm always thinking of the listener experience, be it recorded or live. By this point in a piece of music, after a minute or so, people's focus tends to wander if there's not clear foreground (which, in a cappella, is almost invariably the most compelling foreground possible: a lead singer). This piece doesn't have that, and I feared as *The Incredibles* theme progressed, and the different passages continued to shift, listeners would likely recognize less and less of it. I never want to lose an audience, so I wondered, *What can I introduce here that will keep people focused on the music for another thirty seconds?* It occurred to me, *If only the song had lyrics . . .*—and I realized I would never be allowed to write a bunch of lyrics and have this released on an official Disney soundtrack—but what if I simply introduced the character names here? Try to match up their names (Jack-Jack, Dash, Violet, Elastigirl, and Mr. Incredible) with the rhythms of the various melodic lines, ideally ones that match their superpowers and personalities? I got clearance from Disney, and *voilà!*

First of all, this passage is driven by a *Mission Impossible*–esque three-note line I felt was best represented by a "deer neer" syllable, which is a playful quasi-guitar sound that's suitably nasal and appropriate to the kind of guitars used in late-1960s spy films, such as the James Bond theme. The melody, which is presented in parallel harmony, twists and turns, and it felt especially suitable to Elastigirl. The end result was beyond my expectation, as when the singers sang it, they exaggerated the character, sliding and bending between notes to reinforce the character's special ability. This is exactly what I want when creating something a cappella: the end result should hopefully engage the singer's personalities so they give each passage something human that instruments just can't reproduce.

For the record, distilling down this passage of the piece was more difficult, as it meant dropping some chord factors in the middle of some wild and wonderful complex chords. If you find yourself in this situation, just remember your music theory: drop the fifth if it's not needed, look at what notes are covered in concurrent parts, and I'll add a third consideration: if a melodic line is moving around in parallel harmony, don't worry about hitting every chord factor in every chord voicing, especially if it's moving pretty quickly. Keep the overall shape of the melody and distance between the parallel parts, and use the movement from note to note as a chance to tag down on previously unheard chord factors as you move along. The aggregate will reproduce the entire harmonic structure in people's ears, just as an arpeggiation does.

There's a third element to this passage—the eighth notes with rests between them that arrest and replace the driving spy guitar line. Rather than just continue on with the same syllables, I decided to paint with a more vibrant color, always wanting this arrangement to be a kaleidoscope of vocal timbres, and I went with "wow," which, if not directly intended to reflect the sound of a synth, gives a quick vocal flange—from "oo" to "ah" and back to "oo" in the length of an eighth note. The change in syllable draws attention to the part, intentionally so, just as the melody lands on a long-held note. This is intentionally a "lots of bells and whistles, keep the audience experiencing something new" arrangement.

Now, you may be looking at all of this and thinking, *How am I supposed to know all these things? I've never arranged like this before.* The answer is that you're not. Do not expect every answer to be a clear one, and every problem you approach will not have an obvious solution. Sometimes good is good enough, and most of all, you might have a choice you like but not know why. That's fine. Your taste and instinct are why you're arranging, and you have a lifetime of listening to and analyzing music of all kinds, both consciously and subconsciously. You understand the grammar and syntax, and you know what you like and what you feel works. Now that you're creating something new, your instincts may offer you new solutions you don't understand. Try them. A little voice inside your head is offering up something you know, even while you don't realize you know it. At some point, you'll be able to go back and understand why.

The Three Little Pigs

When creating DCappella, one of my very first ideas came from the initial concept for the group (which I pitched to other professional ensembles first): if orchestras are selling out symphonic halls playing the score to famous movies as they're projected on a huge screen, wouldn't it be amazing for an a cappella group to do the same? I wanted to take one of the scenes from *Fantasia*, or a *Silly Symphony*, and do the entire thing with nothing but voices—instruments, vocals, Foley, everything.

My first choice was the short film that launched Disney's first big hit song back in 1933: *The Three Little Pigs*, featuring the song "Who's Afraid of the Big Bad Wolf?" But was it even possible?

An orchestral score no longer exists, so I had to arrange by ear. Also, the score is constant and very much in the "cartoon music" realm, which means the tempo is ever-changing, with lots of fast runs up and down the scale. Not entirely conducive to a vocal ensemble as a stand-alone piece, but when sung with projection (and singing with an ever-changing click track in their ear to keep them in sync with the screen while not facing it), it became perhaps the biggest hit of the opening tour.

Three Little Pigs

This first passage is pretty straightforward, save for a couple items that bear mentioning. First of all, you'll notice that the tenor is replicating the Second Pig's violin. Each of the three women—soprano, mezzo, and alto—voiced one of the pigs with their high voices, and our bass was, of course, the wolf, but any vocal part could be sung by anyone. The tessitura was perfect for our tenor, and he was a great vocal instrumental mimic.

Why did I choose "blum" as the background syllable? Throughout this piece, I used a variety of syllables to capture the character of the often-jaunty cartoon orchestra, and "blum" strikes me as a bouncy, playful syllable. It's not something I've used often, perhaps never before, but it just felt right, like a sound you might sing to yourself while strolling on a sunny spring day.

Another question you may have is, "What's going on in the baritone line?" Well, it takes some context. There was so much going on in the original recording that I could have used all the voices just to cover the various sounds, but I realized it would be fantastic to have one voice commenting on the proceedings and making some of the sound effects (along with our vocal percussionist, who was a wizard at sound effects). This task fell to our baritone, who, like the members of *Mystery Science Theater 3000*, would comment in gaps and at various moments about what was going on. This kept the overall audience experience at a high peak, as there was never a down moment, plus we could draw attention to various elements through these comments. At this particular moment, the baritone is replicating the sound of the ladder, which is bending rather alarmingly as the Second Pig plays violin while effectively bouncing on an upper rung.

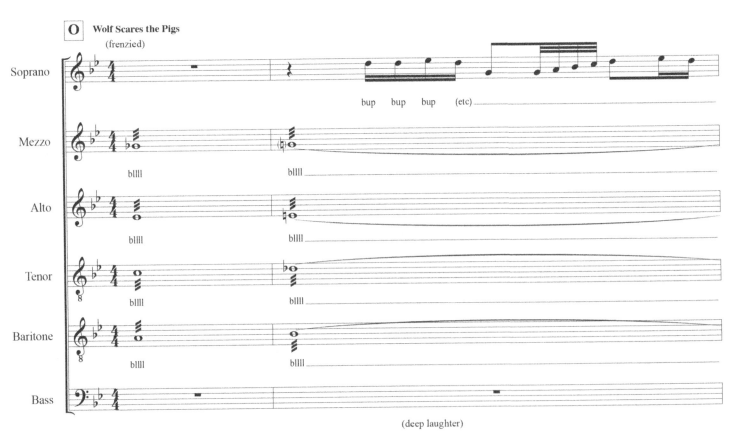

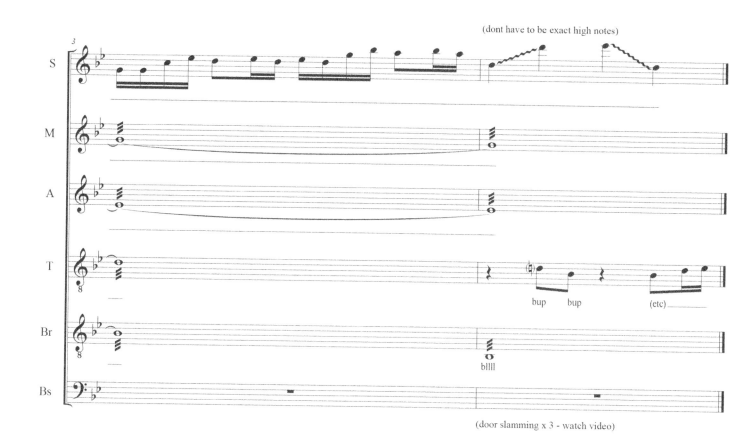

(dont have to be exact high notes)

(door slamming x 3 - watch video)

When it was time to introduce the wolf, the timbre changed considerably: The orchestra leaned into a string tremolo, for which I used the mandolin/xylophone/steel drum sound with a strong "b" attack: "bllll." The wolf was laughing—out of time—which accounted for our bass singer, and one of the challenging vocal lines in this case was assigned to our soprano, who, on "bup" (which felt to me like an old black-and-white movie chase scene syllable), did her best to hit all the notes in this passage. Was she ever perfect? Probably not. Did it matter? Not a bit; the audience loved it. It was more about melodic shape than precision.

One more passage, just to show that not everything needed to be instrumental in nature and practice. At times I wove lyrics into the parts, in this case "danger," "what's he gonna do?" and "climbing on the roof" (which, of course, was so high that the soprano's vowels, like just about everything sung by a coloratura soprano up there, reverted to an "ah"). Again, no one was listening for or caring about technical precision from the soprano; it was more about a rapidly ascending musical line to the top of her range to punctuate the drama. In this moment, the instruments, by commenting on the action, increased the drama as they sung in exaggeratedly emotional voices, like a silent movie star cowering in fear. The baritone line was left wide open for the sung commentary, save for a line I wrote in to capture the overall feeling: "uh-oh!" which happened in/around another of the wolf's laughs.

Fully accepting how hard it was to learn this piece (singers needed to rehearse with a slowed-down version of the music and cartoon), it was worth every minute, and once the tour got underway, the cast may have tired of other songs, but never this one. It was different every night—different inflections, different snarky comments, and just so many moving parts that it remained engaging through closing night. All this, and the fact is the Disney producers wanted me to pull the song at dress rehearsal, convinced it wouldn't work. I convinced them it needed an audience, and if they didn't like it after opening night, it would be cut. They laughingly apologized after the audience's roar of approval at the end. I say this to remind you as an arranger: never, ever let anything get in the way of your remembering that the audience experience is paramount, and as much as we musicians like to get technical, persnickety, detail-oriented, and judgmental, the fact is that most people experiencing music do not hear it as we do. Remember that, and while you never want a song to be sloppy or unprepared, ultimately there are times when precision is less important than the overall experience. Arrange with this in mind.

"The Simpsons Theme"
Continuing with the cartoon theme, this amazing, frantic theme song by Danny Elfman is known the world over. Opening on a tritone, it takes off and never lets up. The original, in a way, is a great example of a theme and variations, as the same simple motif is repeated over and over in different keys and orchestral combinations, resulting in an array of colors and flavors throughout. How do you make this work with voices?

The Simpsons

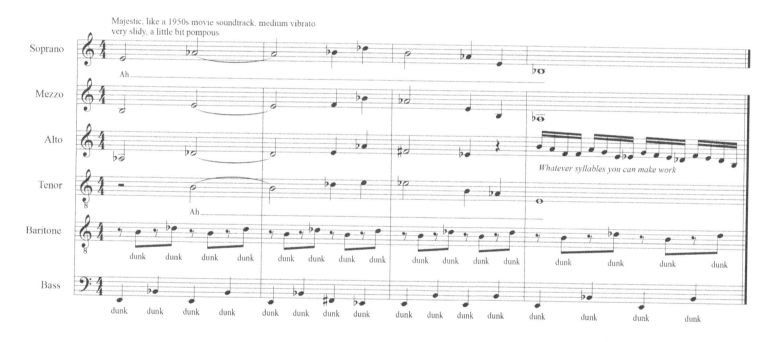

The vowel I wanted in the upper voices here was simply "ah," but if you think about it, there are dozens, if not perhaps hundreds, of different ways to sing it. So, instead of trying to come up with a way to express this in the syllable itself, I wrote a performance note that goes further than any score markings could toward getting the broad, sweeping, over-the-top character I was looking for in this piece. Other passages have the text "like a school band, somewhat instrumental in sound, very loud and excited but not so in time," "intense, like a John Williams action film score," "fun, playful, childlike, like a calliope in a carousel," "like kids on a playground singing," and so on (each with their own syllables, of course).

You'll also likely notice my lack of a syllable choice in the last measure. Sometimes something is so fast or otherwise extreme/challenging, you can't really know what a person is able to do, and if you're not asking an entire section to create a unified sound, you can leave it to them to figure it out. I wouldn't do it often, but sometimes it works.

Vocal-Instrumental Hybrids

There are times when you don't want something that's heavily imitatively instrumental in nature, nor do you want to arrange something with standard syllables. In these cases, there's a third path (if you will): a series of syllables that are reminiscent of instruments, especially if they're leaned into as such, but not fully instrumental. Some of these have been introduced above; let's look at an arrangement that is based around them.

"Sing, Sing, Sing"

This song is a classic, and this arrangement is designed to work not for professional ensembles alone, but for scholastic groups, as well. To that end, having the arrangement based on imitative instrumental timbres that must first be taught is unreasonable and almost a guarantee of misunderstanding and confusion, so instead I went for a number of syllables that lived somewhere between vocal and instrumental.

Sing Sing Sing

Let's start with the obvious question: What's "bahnp"? I'm going for a vowel that's the same as the classic line "I caaaaan't staaand him" from the beloved movie *Singin' in the Rain*. Lina Lamont, the former silent movie actress, had a harsh New York accent, and I wanted that same flat, wide vowel. Written syllables can be difficult to convey: a note at the bottom of the page is helpful, and something non-standard helps alert singers in the first place. Also, when performing this with choirs myself, I have them cup their hands around their mouths and pinch their noses, as we do when making a harmonica sound, with the effect that it becomes more nasal and sounds a bit like the sound is coming through an old gramophone belled horn. The "beh dep" is a different vowel, in the tenor line, but similarly nontraditional, and the basses are singing the "thm-tm" we discussed above, resulting in the off-beat hi-hat, especially useful if there's not a vocal percussionist.

It's worth noting that the "ba da ba" at the end of the fourth measure here was the beginning of a passage of "ba" syllables, for which I'd have the singers remove their hands from their noses. The sound in this first section would go back and forth between the old-timey gramophone and modern horns, with the B section, usually played on clarinets, leaning on a "hoo-dl-oo" vowel for a woodier tone.

This passage is based on a piano figure, and piano figures can be some of the most difficult to directly replicate in voices, as mentioned earlier. So, rather than go for a specifically imitative hybrid tone, I went with a series of syllables somewhat reminiscent of a honkytonk saloon piano. The line starts with a bright "ding" and moves through "deng" to "dung," intentionally darkening as the line descends. The brief "g" syllable between each—brief because this song is swung so these syllables were each roughly half the length of the "ding/deng/dung"—is a natural reset for the "ding" vowel, akin to a fast reading of the line "ring-a-ding-a-ding" in which each "a" is closed off and closer to a schwa. If "g" becomes "guh" in some voices, it's not a big deal, although once the song is sung up to tempo, there's not much time for the vowel to ring out (pun again intended).

Remember that "don't make your syllables sound like real words" rule? Time to break it. The bass line is a cartoonish "thum," which is an exaggerated "thm" with a vowel sound, made more cartoonish by the turnaround at the end of this phrase—"rub-a-dub-a-wub-a-nub-a"—which basses love to sing. It's silly, playful, and the opposite of the boring, repeated syllables they often are saddled with. Together it sounds like it belongs in an animated Halloween cartoon, someone exaggeratedly trying to tiptoe, but in fact, it's more lumbering than delicate. As for the tenors, I always teach this line to be as raspy, harsh, buzzy, and gritty as they can possibly make it, like a burlesque trumpet blasting over the rest of the band. Again, this is about character, having the singers enjoy themselves, and engaging the audience while hearing a song that's about a century old without the focused aid of a lead singer.

Here's a look at the final four measures, in which everyone's in full fortissimo mode, horns blaring. The "w"-focused syllables are playing on the sound of horns with plungers, opening them at the top of the sound for that "oo" to "ah" expansion. I wrote "wa nop" because although "wa nap" looks cleaner, the second syllable would likely end up sounding like a baby's afternoon activity. You'll see I went with "nap" as the final syllable, hoping to brighten their syllable, and expecting that once they're at the end of this whole passage, they'll not change the vowel entirely (some of this is just experience with singer psychology and/or laziness).

The sound "hwah" was chosen because I wanted a harder-blown breath attack, a bit of the honk as discussed when making a saxophone sound. Same honk goes for the "why ya" in the tenor line. The basses again have a silly set of syllables, "dow thow" being something they've likely never sung, nor ever will again. Again, some silly, playful vocal fun.

"Cantina Song"
I can't say you'll be asked anytime soon to arrange a piece from a long time ago and a galaxy far, far away, but considering the range of sounds coming out of modern synthesizers nowadays, you may find yourself working on something that sounds otherworldly. Or, in other words, not specifically instrumental, and certainly not vocal.

Star Wars Cantina

"Womp," "wah" . . . wait, you're probably thinking this all seems a lot like a big band piece, and you're right. I'm convinced John Williams based this song on "Sing, Sing, Sing" and other classic 1940s swing-era classics. The instruments sound a bit strange, but that's largely because when we hear them, we're looking at large, bald creatures playing space instruments. Just listen and you can hear clarinets, a steel drum, and the like. All definitely terrestrial. However, that won't keep us from having fun.

These syllables are intended to be reminiscent of—are you ready for it?—W. C. Fields. If you can imagine the song in his voice, you're very close to what I was aiming for. Or Jimmy Durante, or any gangster in a 1930s–1940s movie. It's a muted/plunger horn in a speakeasy. If the horn players could be playing with a cigar hanging out of one side of their mouth and gambling with a free hand, they would be.

At this point, I'm way off the map. I'm not trying to replicate instruments with "heh-det"; it just had the correct, angular, nonlinguistic, semi-glottal character that felt right to me (the "hoo-dl-oo" is definitely a space clarinet). I wanted a sound that was sharp and hit hard, but the attack to be breath ("h"), and a tight exit ("t"). There may not be a limitless number of combinations of consonants and vowels, but most have not been explored, especially those with less pure and wide vowel sounds like "eh," as they're not popular in classical choral idioms ("eh" would be sung with a wide-open mouth, transforming it to a tall vowel, as in the word "every"). By getting away from the usual vowel choices, you're working with different colors, leaning into different overtones.

All this is to say, you're painting images with sound, so lean into the images you see in your head when you hear it, mess around with your own voice, and try your best to reflect that on the page, ideally following up by communicating with the singers directly.

"Axel F"
And sometimes you have an instrumental song that you just want to keep simple. Sometimes classic syllables are classics for a reason.

Axel F

Whatever syllables you choose, however you decide to orchestrate your voices and motivate them with various performance notes, the cat is out of the bag, and Pandora's box is open; there's no going back to the days when a cappella groups sang only lyrics and a few standard syllables. Nowadays, there are no rules or expectations. Whatever works!

Arranging "In the Style Of . . ."

You've fallen in love with a particular vocal group, and you want to emulate their arranging style with your own group. Perhaps someone has commissioned you to write an arrangement "in the style of" a certain group, or has given you a reference recording and said "do it like them." Or maybe you're just curious as to "what makes that group/arranger unique." Whatever it is, we've got you covered: in this section, we'll analyze samples of some of the greatest groups and arrangers who have influenced the contemporary a cappella world as a whole, take a good look under the hood, and see what makes those arrangements run.

All arrangers and groups stand on the shoulders of those who have come before them. This section, while not a full "history of a cappella arranging," is presented in four chapters:

» Chapter 11, "The Foundation: The Persuasions, The Nylons, The Bobs," covers groups from the 1960s to the 1980s that led to the current sound of a cappella.
» Chapter 12, "The Contemporary Sound: Boyz II Men, Straight No Chaser, Pentatonix," covers contemporary groups from the 1990s, when a cappella music really took off, to today.
» Chapter 13, "Lush Jazz Harmonies: The Four Freshmen, the Singers Unlimited, Take 6," highlights the groups that influenced the world of vocal jazz.
» Chapter 14, "Around the World: Vocal Sampling, The Swingles, Rajaton, Ladysmith Black Mambazo," features innovative groups and arranging styles from outside the United States.

Before we jump in, a few caveats and qualifications.

1. *This is not a "genre guide."* In our first book, we covered most contemporary a cappella styles, from barbershop to doo-wop to gospel. If you're more interested in learning how to write in a particular musical genre, we suggest you look there.
2. *This is not a comprehensive "how-to" guide.* That would be another book of its own! The work of any group/arranger cannot be boiled down to a few measures and paragraphs, and we won't pretend that it's possible. Instead, we'll

offer a general summation of each group/arranger's style, as well as where it came from, then take a look at a few particular techniques that help define their "quintessential sound."

3. *We can't cover everyone!* This is an incomplete shortlist that hopefully covers at least a decent sampling of the most influential groups and arrangers to date. If you're looking for the sound of a particular group, genre, or era that is not presented here, look at the nearest equivalent that we've analyzed. It will likely cover about 80 percent of what you're looking for, and you can likely extrapolate the remaining 20 percent on your own. In addition to the works we analyze, we'll reference other related groups, as well. This will give you, at the very least, a springboard to do your own discovery, as well as a methodology by which to explore other works yourself.

4. *It's largely culture-specific.* We can only write from what we know, and what we know best is Western contemporary a cappella music. For every genre and group we reference, there is a whole world of influential a cappella music that we know of, but that we may not be well-versed enough to discuss in its entirety. There are a few international groups that became household names even for contemporary Western a cappella listeners, and we would be remiss in not including them as much as we can. For examples from non-Western cultures, we can offer a musical analysis . . . but remember, there are often deep cultural roots and meanings to the music, and we are not qualified to cover this. Out of respect, we will present any such analysis as "this is what happens musically," rather than "this is how you can imitate it." For a deeper understanding of any such music, we suggest learning directly from an expert in that style of music so the transmission of knowledge is both accurate and appropriate. If there are parts of the world we've left out, it is not for lack of significance; it is simply that it may be beyond our ability to give the music its due.

With all that said, let's begin.

CHAPTER 11

The Foundation
The Persuasions, The Nylons, The Bobs

A cappella music starts with the dawn of the human voice, but we won't start that far back. Our previous book, *A Cappella Arranging*, gives something of a history of a cappella music, so we'll pick up the story where contemporary music—rock and roll, R&B, and pop—really took off, in the late 1950s to the early 1960s.

"Contemporary a cappella" at this time really meant doo-wop. Many of the groups at this time started as "streetcorner a cappella," performing in ad-hoc groups outdoors, often young singers in or just out of high school. The arrangements were worked out by ear, and more often than not, when they were recorded, they were backed by a rhythm section. For a prime example of an a cappella doo-wop group, we'll start in the 1960s with the Persuasions.

The Persuasions

The Persuasions started out as high school singers in 1962, and they received their first big break when Frank Zappa, a lover of doo-wop music, signed them to his label, where they recorded their debut album, simply known as *A Cappella*. In 1979, they were featured by Joni Mitchell on her *Shadows and Light* tour.

When looking at the twentieth century, the 1970s were perhaps the nadir of popular a cappella singing, both professional and amateur. The Persuasions were the beloved standard-bearers during this decade, and continuing on for several more, as they bridged the gap between doo-wop and the modern sound paving the way for contemporary a cappella.

The success of the Persuasions as a commercial group can be attributed in significant part to the creative input and sensational lead vocals of Jerry Lawson. Their sound and arranging style is focused on underscoring his flexible, soulful leads, with Jimmy Hayes's rhythmic bass line providing the majority of the momentum, and backing vocals floating above by Jayotis Washington and "Sweet" Joe Russell, as well as a fifth harmony by Herbert "Toubo" Rhoad, until his untimely passing in 1988. This format—strong, fluid lead vocal; moving bass line; and block two- or three-part harmonies that sometimes echo the lead vocal in call-and-response format—is the basis of the Persuasions' signature sound.

Harmonic complexity was not the focus of their by-ear arranging style, as their repertoire was drawn almost exclusively from pop, R&B, and gospel. The emphasis, perhaps more than most a cappella groups, was passion and soul. As such, in listening back to their classic recordings, there's a "looseness" that stands in contrast to the careful precision of barbershop and vocal jazz in the tradition of the Singers Unlimited—one that is more representative of the popular music of the time. Moreover, if you saw them live, you might have noticed that they didn't use a pitch pipe; Jerry would just start singing where it felt right, and the others joined in. If this seems antithetical to a cappella, remember that for most of human history (and all of prehistory) people sang without worrying about A440.

"Good Old A Cappella" was a signature song for the group, both thematically and sonically. Written in 1973, it postdates doo-wop, yet it lives very much in that vein stylistically and nostalgically. Harmonically, the song is very simple—just I, IV, and V chords—without a chromatic note or even a seventh to be found anywhere in the song. In this way, it captures and reflects a style of a cappella that was aural as opposed to written.

Looking at the first verse, we see on paper clearly what we hear: Jerry's predominant lead vocal; Jimmy's (very) low bouncing bass line on chord factors with occasional passing notes and a rounded, resonant vowel. Having heard this song sung several times live, I can attest to the fact that Jerry's lead vocal wasn't always delivered the same way, and neither was Jimmy's bass line, so notating these parts feels more like capturing a snapshot than recording the single, definitive version. In fact, when transcribing, it's clear the key of their recording (from their album of the same name) lives somewhere between G and A♭.

Filling in the BGs, Jayotis and Joe are singing "ooh" in parallel harmonies. No doubt, these parts started as whole notes in their first rehearsals, and then as they played with their parts, they added ornamentation in the form of passing notes and suspensions, to create more motion and interest while outlining the simple, repetitive chord progression. When this was a five-part arrangement, with Toubo, they added the D under Joe's part—a third parallel harmony.

Good Old Acapella

When we come to the chorus, we lock into one of the classic elements of traditional popular a cappella, found everywhere from traditional barbershop to gospel: the call and response. The lead (Jerry) sings, "Soul to soul," and the backs repeat it, on their chord factors, then "Brother to brother" in the same form, and as you can see, "a cappella" . . .

And then the backing vocals lock back into their "oo"s as Jerry completes the line, with Jimmy continuing his bouncing bass line throughout, playing the role of rhythm section as he provides both the roots of chords as well as rhythmic drive. It's a simple, yet very effective element in vocal harmony, especially when music is created and taught by ear, be it in the classroom or on the street corner, where doo-wop came to life. If you look back at our more fundamental arranging techniques in *A Cappella Arranging*, you'll see that the Persuasions represent a perfect exemplar of the "bass, lead, and two BGs" format used by just about every four-part a cappella group out there.

Although much of this book focuses on a variety of complex techniques, it's important to remember that simplicity is sometimes the best choice. The Persuasions were perhaps the most-beloved a cappella group of the latter half of the twentieth century, and it wasn't because of complex chords and shimmering overtones; it was because they arranged music in a way that connected with audiences, and they always sang from the heart.

The Nylons

The Nylons was formed as a quartet by four Canadian actors in 1978, something that can be heard in their dramatically captivating performances, both live and recorded. They lived on the precipice of the modern a cappella sound, having created a pivotal sound by adding a drum machine—a very typical sound in 1980s popular music—to the tried-tested-and-true style of four-part doo-wop singing. This led them to worldwide acclaim, as well as the first Billboard pop hit for an a cappella group ("Kiss Him Goodbye," #12 in December 1987).

The Nylons' sound can be described as an energetic, emotionally driven lead vocal, a doo-wop-styled moving bass line (with plenty of playful, diphthong-heavy syllables), and two-part harmonies covering the remaining chord factors on lyrics or standard vowels ("ba," "ooh," etc.). With the drum machine driving the sound and filling most every eighth note, the background parts were free to be a bit less rhythmic and focus on lyrics and harmonic function. Their repertoire started out as doo-wop and vocal harmony standards, but as they gained international acclaim, they moved toward more recent popular music and originals.

Looking at the first verse of "Kiss Him Goodbye," we could be forgiven if we mistook it for a Persuasions arrangement. In fact, the "mouthier" syllables in the bass line are a direct descendant of doo-wop, definitely more so than the Persuasions, who predated this group by over a decade and a half (1962 versus 1978). Doo-wop bass lines with lots of syllables (think "Blue Moon" by the Marcels: "ba b b ba . . . dang a dang . . . ding a dong . . . ," etc.) were a trademark of the doo-wop sound, even when so many a cappella songs were taken off the street corners and recorded in a studio with a bass guitar (and other instruments) supporting them. In essence, The Nylons were more of a doo-wop group than the Persuasions, relying more on those syllables and idioms, but by singing with a drum machine supporting them, they had a "retro-meets-modern" aesthetic.

Na Na Hey Hey Kiss Him Goodbye

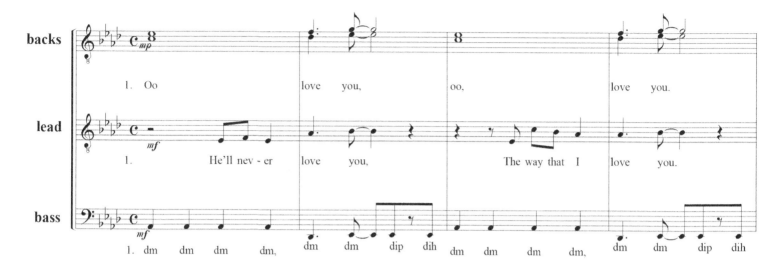

The arrangement continues in this mode, with things getting even simpler: when the "na na na na" refrain first comes, the four Nylons sing it in octaves before breaking into parallel harmonies. And then in the bridge, we get an arpeggiated passage reminiscent of the Chordettes ("Mr. Sandman"/"Mr. Santa"):

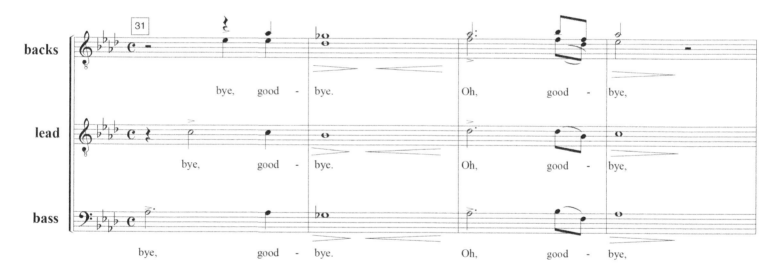

It's important to point out that this simplification of layers, having everyone in the group lock into a single unit during an up-tempo pop song, was made possible by having the driving beat beneath them. This was a key step toward the current contemporary a cappella sound, underpinned by vocal percussion, as it let everyone know that if you wanted to keep pace with modern popular music, vocal harmonies and moving bass lines weren't enough.

The lead vocal over bass line with backing harmonies moving between simple syllables and lyrics is The Nylons' sound, and to replicate it today, you'd be best served by singing over a drum machine or otherwise programmed electronic drum loop—ideally one that's very "tight" in its rhythm, without human "feel," as the early drum machines were robotic in their precision.

They also had some great ballads, including a remake of the 1962 hit "Up on the Roof."

Up on the Roof

Here, their layers are considerably simplified, with no drum machine and no separated bass line. Instead, you could consider this almost barbershop in that there are parallel harmonies, a homophonic texture around the lead vocal, followed by a passage in which the BGs sing a pattern of "doo doo"s. Unlike barbershop, there's no careful voicing in which the melody is in the second-from-top part, and through this song, the lead vocal is much freer, sometimes singing higher than all the parts, over a bed of "oo"s, and sometimes dipping down below the backing harmonies. All the while, the lead vocal is expressive and rubato, singing with a soulful passion and fluidity.

In short, The Nylons found a sound that was informed by both doo-wop and barbershop, yet with the drum machine driving their up-tempo songs, and lead vocalists who were as much actors as singers (and, therefore, able to deliver impassioned, emotionally compelling lead vocals), they moved a cappella from the street corners onto the airwaves and set the stage for the modern a cappella revolution. Groups such as Rockappella and the House Jacks owe much of their sound to fundamentals exemplified by the Persuasions and The Nylons.

The Bobs

If The Nylons introduced the world to the sound of a cappella with modern rhythms, The Bobs introduced the world to a cappella with modern textures and timbres. Formed in 1980 by members of the Western Onion Singing Telegraph Company in the San Francisco Bay Area, The Bobs took convention and turned it on its head, creating a sound and style that was inimitably unique, often funny or quirky, and very much an essential step toward the modern sound.

Let's start by looking at the opening passage to "Bus Plunge," an original song about a bus driver worried about driving off the road. No, not a common topic for a pop song, and the texture was not at all common either:

Bus Plunge

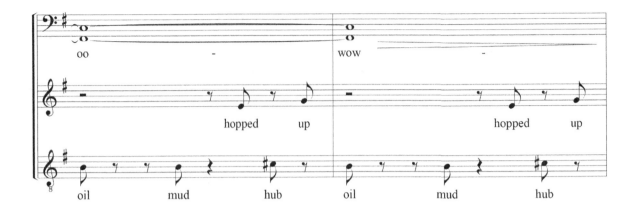

There was no vocal percussion, and these pointillistic, staccato lyrics aren't heard so much as words as varying sounds. It should be noted that their vocal technique favored very flat (as opposed to round) vowels with rare ornamentation (vibrato, portamento, etc.). At times, the sound was almost like shape-note singing or the Bulgarian vocal tradition: straight tones that almost buzz in their unrelenting brightness.

What do we see when we look at the harmonic language? It's essentially impossible to tell what key this song is in at this point due to the chromaticism and lack of bass line, and the downbeat isn't even certain. The effect is disorienting and hypnotic, exactly the effect they were trying to have before launching into the first verse.

"Through the Wall" is another original song, this one about a guy obsessed with the woman who lives next door. This excerpt is taken from the middle of the song:

Through the Wall

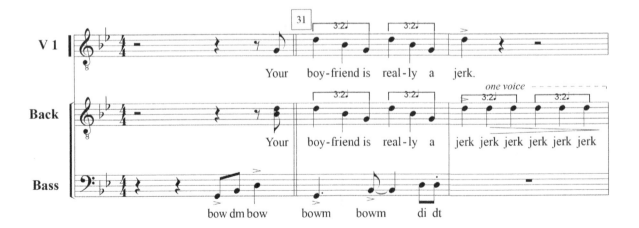

The key is somewhat clear, but when we get to the "will he ever learn" passage, we're looking at quite an unusual chord voicing. Mistake? Certainly not, as Richard Greene was an instrumentalist, and Gunnar Madsen graduated from the University of California, Berkeley with a music theory degree. An F7 chord with the seventh in the bass isn't unheard of, but with the bass note striking first and the A in the melody on top, the tritone is predominant, creating a very unsettling feel.

And before that, note the use of parallel unisons, pulling back to a single voice echoing on the word "jerk." The Bobs were not afraid of silence, as well as "unbalanced" chords, and a variety of other choices that flew in the face of traditional music theory and four-part harmonic writing.

Background syllables weren't always lyrics, but when they weren't, they were often something unexpected:

Trash

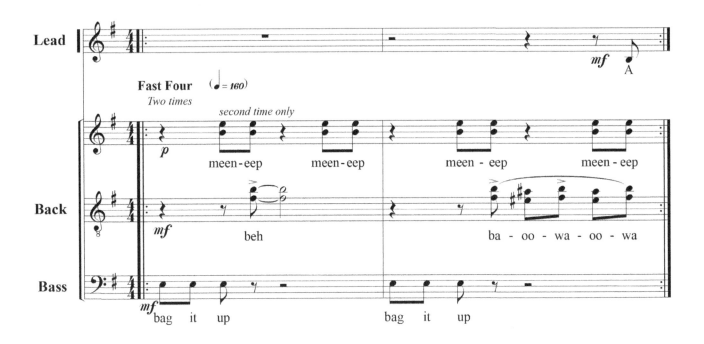

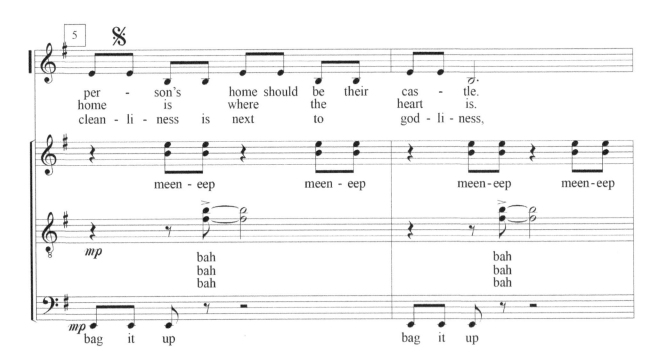

"Bag it up" certainly fits the theme of a song called "Trash," and it is typical in that Richard Greene liked to play with lyrics in his bass lines. "Bah" is very standard, and "ba-oo-wa-oo-wa" is reminiscent of doo-wop, if a bit unusual when being sung while dipping a half step, but the real standouts are the "meen-eep"s up top, which sound like a digital alarm or other device. The song is clearly in

E minor, but the timbre sends it in an unusual direction, like some kind of robot reggae.

The Bobs' use of humor, unusual syllables, and original material continues a thread that starts with the Comedian Harmonists from Germany in the 1930s, and influenced later a cappella groups such as Da Vinci's Notebook and Germany's Maybebop. If you have not heard The Bobs, we cannot urge you strongly enough to take the time to listen, as printed arrangements only capture a percentage of their quirky charm and unusual sonorities. They changed a cappella by showing the world how many vocal colors, textures, and timbres we were missing out on by relying so heavily on block chords and standard syllables. The modern sound of a cappella owes them an enormous debt—a group that never had a single radio hit, yet that brought wonderful, unique, original all-vocal music to life for decades.

CHAPTER 12

The Contemporary Sound
Boyz II Men, Straight No Chaser, Pentatonix

The 1990s represent the first big "a cappella explosion," the decade when many of today's contemporary a cappella techniques were being developed. The success of groups like the Persuasions and The Nylons paved the way. Bobby McFerrin's breakout hit "Don't Worry Be Happy" shortly followed, and Spike Lee's 1990 PBS documentary *Do It A Cappella* gave the genre even more attention.

Collegiate a cappella groups also came into their own: the glee clubs modernized, and with the rapid rise of the internet and global communication, likeminded groups could perform with, and learn from, each other. A cappella organizations such as CASA (the Contemporary A Cappella Society of America) connected groups and a cappella enthusiasts together, and a cappella artists as a whole created, innovated, and shared ideas. Vocal percussion, once an effect or a sideshow novelty, became embedded in the sound, and the true "vocal band" was born.

A cappella music was still being influenced by vocal harmony groups with instrumental backing, which leads us to our first group: Boyz II Men.

Boyz II Men

Although they're not specifically an a cappella group, Boyz II Men is one of the bestselling vocal harmony groups of all time, with fifty total weeks of number-one hits (the sixth most in history), as well as the only group to have two a cappella hits on the charts. Wanyá Morris, Nathan Morris, and Shawn Stockman continued on as a trio when bass Michael McCarey had to leave the group for medical reasons, and they're still going strong today. There are few non–a cappella ensembles who have had more of an impact on modern a cappella.

Even when their songs weren't a cappella, they often had a cappella breakdowns, such as this classic moment in their first single, "Motownphilly":

Motownphilly

This is a classic a cappella arpeggiation harkening back to "Mr. Sandman," and yet several elements are different: rather than spelling back down the chord, the voices hit an arpeggiated "da da," and then repeat the pattern, but a beat before the downbeat, so it's all syncopated, followed by a parallel flourish, and finishing off with a descending figure that's far more R&B in phrasing and vowel (an "oh" that cheats toward a schwa). In sum total, it's fun, it's playful, and it shows off their harmony chops on something far more complex than a series of whole notes. And yet, it's a series of whole notes that anchored their second single and brought them a number-two hit in America.

It's so Hard to Say Goodbye to Yesterday

"It's So Hard to Say Goodbye to Yesterday" was a huge hit, cementing the group as balladeers—most of their hits from this point forward would be slow love songs. It couldn't be much more simple: a lead vocal with three BGs, all on a loose "oo" vowel (as opposed to a tight, careful classical vowel), and a chain of descending notes with occasional R&B ornamentation. The only percussive element is a snap on two and four. The result is a song that's a very clear support for an emotional, powerful lead vocal, with a sound very reminiscent of street-corner singing. The chorus is hardly more complex: the major change is that the BGs join the lead when declaring the lyrics in the song's title.

Much of the a cappella music on the airwaves in this period was a throwback to the classic streetcorner sound of the 1950s and 1960s, and Boyz II Men's other a cappella hit was, in fact, a remake of "In the Still of the Nite," originally a hit for the Five Satins back in 1956.

One other song of theirs that made a big impact on the a cappella community was "Thank You," from their second album, *II*, in large part because it was anchored by a new jack swing beatbox groove at a time when vocal percussion was just beginning to spread among collegiate and professional ensembles.

Thank You

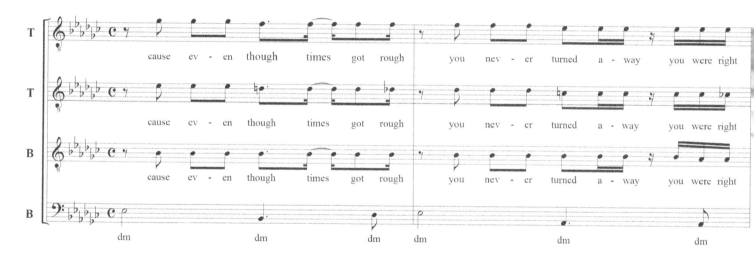

The bass line is simpler than you'd expect, certainly less busy than a typical bass line in many an a cappella ensemble today, but they were letting the beatboxer do the rhythmic work, leaving the bass line to lay down clean tonic notes over which it's much easier to tune. (Remember, this was before Auto-Tune and Melodyne, so there was no pitch correction in the mix.) The upper three voices are singing parallel harmonies and lyrics in a descending pattern, reminiscent of barbershop, but with much cooler/relaxed vowels and an R&B sensibility. The final "thank you" is sung in octaves, making it pop.

Straight No Chaser

If you had to pinpoint the epicenter of the SNC sound, especially in the early days, it would be the mid-1990s, when the group was originally formed at the University of Indiana as a collegiate ensemble, shortly before vocal percussion and other elements of instrumental imitation swept through the genre and became the norm. For that reason, their core sound has relied more on traditional vowels (such as "ooh" and "ah") and using lyrics frequently in background parts. In a way, this makes them one of the more traditional-sounding contemporary a cappella ensembles as they continue into the 2020s, at least timbrally. However, their high-energy performance, frequent use of comedy, and layers of sound make their performances and recordings some of the most compelling, which is why they remain one of the most popular a cappella groups today.

Straight No Chaser broke the mold of the professional touring a cappella group, in that they were ten members (now nine) when most ensembles are in the four- to six-member range. This allows them to stack vocal layers live as if they're in the recording studio. The format typically includes a bass line, vocal percussion, lead vocal, and two separate vocal units, a trio and a quartet (or two trios and a "floater" who can sing ad libs, duet lines with the lead, etc.). This format isn't a rule, and there are many times when they compress into four-part harmony, with each vocal line doubled/tripled, for a more traditional male choral/close harmony sound.

Although it was their version of "The 12 Days of Christmas" that made them a viral sensation on YouTube, they quickly established themselves as a significant player in the a cappella community with denser arrangements and more voices on a professional level, and a sound that is informed by their collegiate roots, but not anchored to it.

During the COVID-19 pandemic, they recorded a version of Counting Crows' "A Long December." While originally not a holiday song *per se*, the effects of pandemic isolation made it a poignant holiday song in contrast to their often-zany earlier releases.

A Long December

The format is clear: lead vocal, bass line, and two sets of backing triads (in addition to a vocal percussionist). This many voices and parts is a luxury that's afforded only to larger ensembles, or small a cappella groups when they're over-dubbing in the studio. You'll notice the backing syllables are rather traditional—"dum," "duh," etc.—befitting their sound and style that was born in the 1990s, before vocal percussion and instrumental idioms began to dominate the sound of collegiate a cappella.

In this case, one backing trio is providing the role of a rhythm instrument without imitating it, singing "duh" on chords that could be played on a keyboard or strummed on a guitar. The other trio is interpolating between singing a more traditional backing part—"ah"—followed by brief quotes of Christmas carols, in this case "God Rest Ye Merry Gentlemen" followed by "O Holy Night" (there are more than a dozen woven throughout the song, a way to further nudge this pop tune toward a holiday song). The voicing is close, and the male vocal range is used, from low bass through falsetto.

Later in the song, there's a post-chorus, where the lead vocalist sings a quasi-improvised "la la" passage.

The formula holds steady, as we hear the upper trio quote "Deck the Halls" before locking into parallel harmonies with the lead. The lower trio continues their role on supporting harmonies, and the bass is simple, with the vocal percussion doing more of the complex rhythmic work.

Here's one more example: "Don't Dream It's Over," from their album *With a Twist*. The twist for this song is that it's got an island reggae feel (vocal percussion not notated):

Don't Dream It's Over

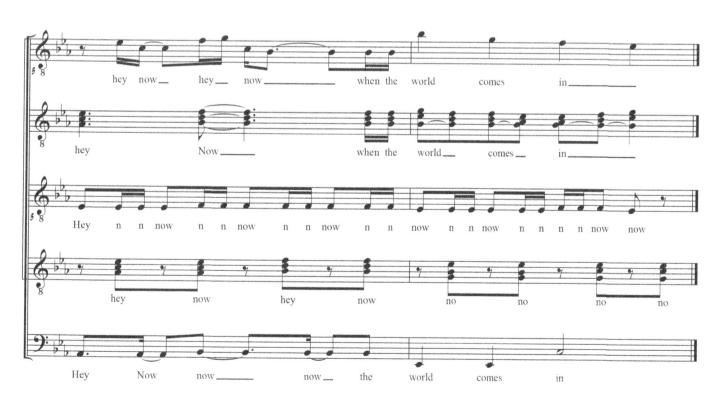

The "two backing trios" formula is in this arrangement, as well, along with a driving ostinato rhythmic backing line. What's notable about this texture is that it's built almost entirely of lyrics instead of syllables. When working with multiple layers, overlapping and repeating a couple of key lyrics doesn't draw attention; instead, they fade into sounding like a more standard texture, albeit one built upon the consonants and vowels in the melody. It's a form of painting with the same sonic colors—in this case, a lot of the "eh" of "hey" and "ow" of "now." It all comes together smoothly without drawing attention, the way a series of changing vowels would.

In general, Straight No Chaser has performed songs in different styles, but they all revolve around pop idioms. They don't avoid chromatics and complex chords, but they don't lean into them either, generally keeping the harmonic language of an arrangement similar to that of the original recording, even if they're flipping the style into something else.

Note: their entire arrangement of "We Three Kings" can be found in the appendix of *A Cappella Arranging*, with comments about it throughout the book.

Pentatonix

Pentatonix is arguably the most famous a cappella band in the world today, a household name for people, even for those who know next to nothing about a cappella music. As far as brand-new innovation goes, Pentatonix hasn't really done anything that other a cappella groups before them didn't do: it's just that they do it so very well—in tune, with personality and panache—and they had the blessing of having been launched on a television show (*The Sing-Off*) when three of them had just graduated high school, making them one of the youngest professional a cappella ensembles in recent history. They took every advantage, and through incredibly hard work and artistry, they now fill stadiums and have more followers on YouTube than Beyoncé.

The core of Pentatonix's sound is consistent: a rhythm section underpinning three voices that interpolate between a lead vocal and two-part backing harmonies, and a three-part homophonic "group lead."

During the rise of Pentatonix, their bass, Avi Kaplan, was one of the lowest and most resonant basses in a cappella. His bass lines were clean, and not particularly busy, which wasn't a problem since Kevin, the vocal percussionist, is one of the busiest in the business, often filling patterns with a rapid-fire array of thirty-second notes. Furthermore, although his role is very much that of a vocal percussionist, his battery of sounds takes more from the beatboxing world, most notably his use of a "k" snare, which sounds more sampled/electronic than the more traditional "pf" rock kit snare.

When looking at the upper three voices, their vocal stylings lean mostly toward pop, with a healthy dose of R&B in their runs and vowels. Most often, Scott sings lead, which is unusual as he's a baritone, and lead vocals in pop music usually feature tenors singing in the top of their range. When PTX is looking for a high tenor sound, they go to Mitch, who has a remarkably clear tone that pops seamlessly into his falsetto. On the top of the vocal stack most often is Kirstie.

Usually an a cappella ensemble has either a balanced number of male and female voices, or is single gender, but for Pentatonix, their sound came naturally as Scott, Mitch, and Kirstie were high school friends, developing a tight vocal sound before ever contemplating singing professionally. When it comes to a tight vocal blend, there is no substitute for time spent singing together (except "family blend," but of course, siblings often have a lifetime of singing together on top of their similar genetics).

Pentatonix's arranging style is unique among a cappella groups, in that they often arrange using a combination of by-ear and notated music, with the involvement of their frequent collaborator and music director, Ben Bram. For their two Best Arrangement Grammys, all five members of the group plus Ben are credited as arrangers, a testament to their collaborative approach.

First, let's look at a piece of the song that won them their first Grammy and has garnered 371 million views to date: their Daft Punk medley.

Daft Punk Medley

What's notable about this is that it's actually not that complex. Though there's not anything new here, the pieces are cleverly assembled to maximize their sound and impact: the upper three-voice trio is placed where Kirstie's voice can get up to the top of the powerful part of her voice, while Mitch on the second line is in his soaring falsetto, a characteristic element of their sound, and Scott gets up to the upper-chest range of his high baritone. In short, each is in their sweet spot as they rise in this musical figure, and the composite is glorious, three close high school friends who learned how to phrase lines exactly alike, almost like a family group.

Underneath them, Avi has an extremely syncopated bass line, which is reinforced by Kevin's busy percussion line with many sixteenths between their aligned hits filled in. Soaring three-part parallel harmonies over a driving rhythm section: the signature sound of Pentatonix.

Now let's look at a ballad, one in which Kevin sings and they're locked together in five-part close harmony. Here's the penultimate phrase from the classic Elvis Presley song "Can't Help Falling in Love":

Can't Help Falling In Love

Much of this arrangement is aligned in clear, tight-voiced block chords, but by this point in the song, they open up and show some of what makes them unique: Avi drops down to his bass register (although he has far lower range when he wants to use it), and Mitch soars above Kirstie in a rare moment that pulls his falsetto into the foreground. Kevin's on the middle voice, and Scott is pedaling an A as the other voices move around him. There are a few passing notes for color, but otherwise this arrangement leans heavily on the combination of their vocal tone and phrasing.

Looking at a more recent arrangement, we see more of the characteristics they're known for:

Can You Feel The Love Tonight

Matt is not as low a bass as Avi was, but he is very comfortable up high, which is where he's placed here. Scott, who has more leads than anyone else in the group, is in his element in high baritone range. Later in the song, Kevin shifts to vocal percussion, but here he's singing an inner voice, starting on the add9 of the chord, a common added chord tone in their (and Ben Bram's) slower arrangements. In this case, it's Kirstie with the pedal note, an E, so that everyone starts the passage within the space of a perfect fifth, but by the end, they're spread out, with Mitch again rising above Kirstie. It's a fast arpeggiation on sixteenth notes, which drives the song forward, and it would be too difficult to execute for many other groups, yet PTX makes it sound easy.

These are but three examples of the many choices that Pentatonix makes when arranging songs. They're capable of a wide range of pop idioms, generally hewing close to current popular music with occasional classics tossed in their repertoire, as well as an album of original music and several holiday albums that are already classics. Whatever they sing, they have a legion of fans worldwide ready to hear their signature sound.

CHAPTER 13

Lush Jazz Harmonies
The Four Freshmen, the Singers Unlimited, Take 6

We promised this wouldn't be a simple linear "history of a cappella" section, and this next chapter proves it. We'll take a step back in time to where we started the pre-contemporary chapter—the late 1950s and early 1960s—and look at a parallel evolution in a cappella music: vocal jazz.

Prior to the rise of rock and roll, jazz was the popular music of its day, with early doo-wop, jazz, and even barbershop music existing in close proximity. But as each of these genres grew unto themselves, they also grew apart. While still occasionally borrowing from each other, they each developed a more specific vocabulary and writing style, and the same can be said of the a cappella genres that mirrored instrumental music developments.

Yet, to identify these two evolutionary branches as entirely separate would be an oversimplification: much of the time, vocal jazz and contemporary a cappella often influence each other to this day. Contemporary arranging frequently borrows from the harmonic complexity of jazz, and vocal jazz groups often borrow "vocal band" instrumental imitation from contemporary groups. But for the sake of analysis, we'll treat them as separate streams. We'll start where they really begin to diverge—in the early 1950s.

The Four Freshmen

Any meaningful discussion of contemporary pop-jazz vocal writing would be remiss if it didn't include the Four Freshmen. In the 1950s, at a time when there were few a cappella vocal groups outside of barbershop and classical music, the complex harmonies and tight blend of the Four Freshman would blaze a trail from which all vocal pop-jazz groups would follow.

The Four Freshman started out as a barbershop group, and this is evident in many aspects of their writing, including the TTBB format in general, with the focus on a tight timbral blend and the use of close-harmony voicings. However, the Freshmen were listening to vocal groups that worked with big bands, such as the Modernaires and Mel Torme and the Mel-Tones. These groups were blurring the lines between instrumental big band sectional writing and vocal harmony, with complex sax section–like block voicings being represented by voices to become another "section" of a big band. However, with the exception of occasional stand-alone sections within a larger song, these were not yet a cappella: there was almost always a band behind them. The Freshman were not an a cappella band *per se*—they typically accompanied themselves on instruments—but they also started fusing these big band jazz techniques with their familiar barbershop self-contained harmonizing to create an advanced, brand-new sound to a cappella music.

The Freshmen started with barbershop-style writing, and they expanded the harmonic palette. Where barbershop frequently used major six, dominant seventh, and diminished chords (the latter usually only in passing), the Freshmen extended the harmonies to include major and dominant sevenths, with ninths, elevenths, and thirteenths added and altered, and diminished major seventh chords. These allowed for a much richer sense of consonance and dissonance, harmonic tension and release. They frequently used jazz reharmonization of ii-V chord progressions, tritone substitutions, and chromatic voice movement not yet found in typical vocal music.* Here are examples from their a cappella version of Bobby Troupe's "Their Hearts Were Full of Spring" from 1960:

Their Hearts Were Full of Spring

as performed by the Four Freshmen

---

* For more information on the reharmonization vocabulary that follows, see chapter 6, "Harmonic Principles and Techniques."

In the first two bars alone, the Freshmen are already expanding beyond their barbershop roots. One beat per chord, we have:

» A♭maj7.
» Adim(maj7), resolving to Adim, a more sophisticated reharmonization of what otherwise might have been a more pedestrian iii or vi chord.
» B♭m7
» Gdim7, resolving to Gdim, serving as a dominant ♭9.
» A♭ major, our first simple triad.
» D♭/F, with a passing major seventh.
» Gm7♭5, or "half-diminished," serving as a colorful dominant movement toward the C dominant chord on the next bar.
» D♭major7♭5, a sort-of tritone substitution of the previous chord. The voicing is particularly interesting and full of tension: a semitone cluster in the bottom, and a full-tone cluster on the top.

That's a lot of harmonic movement for only two bars of music, and something almost-unheard-of at the time.

Following this (and remember, we're still only at the third bar), we see another signature of the Freshmen: a pedal tone, decorated by moving inner parts. They didn't invent this: the "post" or pedal note with inner movement is a staple of barbershop, but they've repurposed its use in a jazz context. Normally in barbershop, this would be a resolution with the post often on the tonic, or at the very least, on the tonic chord. Here we're on III. This would normally be a passing chord meant to take us somewhere new. Instead this becomes a spot of rest, letting the harmonic tension last longer, with an eventual release as we start the piece in earnest on the following bar (not shown).

If all this sounds very familiar, it is . . . now. Nearly every vocal jazz ballad chart available today, including such arrangers as Kirby Shaw, Roger Emerson, and others, uses these conventions.

But, there's more. The following example is dense with new and innovative arranging techniques.

The contrast of close and open voicings isn't new, but barbershop writing typically has a quick transition from one style to another, usually with wide leaps in the bass (and less-wide leaps in the baritone) to join the top two voices to become the bottom of a close harmony stack. Evolving from this, the Freshmen in the second measure (and throughout the piece) use contrapuntal motion in the bass and T1 to create a gradual expansion and collapsing of voicings, in this case bringing the voices from open to closed voicing. Not only that, but the number of voices themselves briefly diminish from four to three. This is used well to dynamic and dramatic effect, using closer and fewer voices to "hush" moments of the chart, or to build excitement when expanding from closed to open.

The next bar sees some serious reharmonization not yet heard in vocal jazz writing. The phrase "on a hill where robins sing" is typically harmonized with a standard I-vi-ii-V progression. The Freshmen take us on a harmonic whirlwind, with something like iii-vi-♭VImaj7-♭IImaj7-IIImaj7-i-♭II7♯11. If that's enough to make your head spin, let's break it down:

"Hill where"
basic harmony: I
reharmonization: iii-vi

Here we're splitting a tonic chord into two tonic-functioning chords. So far, so good.

"Ro-bins"
basic harmony: vi
reharmonization: ♭VImaj7-♭IImaj7

Here, we have the jazz convention of a "ii-V a semitone away." It's common practice in jazz to add harmonic density by turning a V7 chord into a ii-V7 mini-progression, in a sense "splitting" the chord into two. To add another layer of complexity, depending on the melody, this can be done a semitone higher or lower. In this case, they've chosen a semitone lower. They've added another level of abstraction by taking this semitone-away ii-V, and instead of making the quality of the chords minor-to-dominant, they make the chords both sparkly major sevenths, supporting the melody.

"Sing" (first two beats)
basic harmony: ii
reharmonization: ♭IIImaj7- i

This can be seen as a continuation of the reharmonization above. The progression above becomes a "back-door ii-V" into a new temporary key center: C, or ♭III. This doesn't last, though: we pass quickly into i, before landing on . . .

"Sing" (third beat)

basic harmony: V7

reharmonization: ♭II7♯11

This whole journey ends on a straightforward tritone substitution for V7 . . . though we're left in limbo, as we never resolve back to I.

The Four Freshman represent a great leap forward in a cappella writing, and all the vocal jazz-pop examples that follow, from Gene Puerling to Take 6, take their cues from here. And if you ever want to hear them live . . . as of 2024, they were still touring (with newer members, of course), over seventy-five years later.

Gene Puerling and the Singers Unlimited

Gene Puerling is to vocal arranging what Duke Ellington is to big band writing. There's arguably no one in the vocal jazz world who has had a larger impact, and whose influence is still felt as strongly today.

Puerling's first well-known vocal group was the Hi-Los, most active in the 1950s and 1960s. Though not a cappella, they represented a new way of approaching vocal jazz harmony, blending barbershop-quality blend and balance with big band close-harmony writing. In this way, they were similar to the Four Freshmen mentioned above, and they carry a similar influence among vocal jazz writers. While the Hi-Los are deserving of a chapter of their own, we'll focus on the group that Puerling formed after the Hi-Los: the Singers Unlimited.

The Singers Unlimited was a quartet originally formed in 1971 for singing commercial jingles and soundtracks, but they were later encouraged to record and release their own albums. The group didn't perform live: rather, Puerling used the nascent multi-tracking abilities of the recording studio to turn the quartet into a larger group, with many of his arrangements written for six to eight parts, or even more. This gave Puerling "unlimited" arranging possibilities, and in turn, it expanded the harmonic and textural vocabulary even further. In his innovative use of the studio, Gene Puerling did for a cappella music what the Beatles did for pop recording: he freed it from the confines and expectations of live performance to take full advantage of the studio's creative potential.

We're going to take a look at one of Puerling's most adventurous arrangements, the Beatles' classic "Fool on the Hill." In this, one of his first experimentations with multi-tracking, Puerling pretty much abandons the notion of a fixed number of voices, and he uses voice allocation to great dynamic effect, from solo voice, to lead-plus-pad textures, to rich eight-voice homophonic harmonies, to multiple textures and layers previously unimaginable in contemporary a cappella writing, which was usually designed either for live performance or live-around-the-mic recording.

A signature of Puerling's arranging style is the use of harmonic journeys to start, develop, or end a piece. Where the Four Freshman and other jazz groups followed a well-developed vocabulary of jazz harmonic progressions and colors developed from instrumental jazz, Puerling's harmonic adventures are flights of fancy, unencumbered by traditional functional harmony, or even a direct harmonic or thematic correlation to what follows. Take, for example, the opening to "Fool on the Hill":

Fool On The Hill

Lennon/McCartney
Arranged by Gene Puerling

Based on this opening (and without looking at the notated key signature), do you have any idea what the key of the song is?

It's actually in the key of F—once the verse starts, after this section—but the tonal center of the introduction is roughly A♭ mixolydian, and there's no sense of movement toward the eventual key center of F: instead, the final chord progression is G♭7sus to G♭ add9 . . . then it just drops, without any preparation, into F maj7 immediately following this excerpt. This opening is dreamy, detached from the song itself, much like the eponymous fool on the hill. It's a beautiful example of symphonic, programmatic writing not yet seen in the vocal jazz world.

Getting into technical details, we notice the following:

» The relationship of key centers between the intro and the upcoming verse is a minor third: A♭ to F. The third-away (major or minor) is a key association often used by Puerling. Here, the minor-third relationship gives it a more modal feel, rather than a ii–V, logical-sequence connection as found in more straightforward jazz writing. It is more connected to the modal jazz coming out of the 1960s than the big band writing of the 1950s that influenced vocal jazz to date.

» The voicing structures are broken into two main components: an open fifth in the two lower voices, and a four-part, largely triadic structure in the top voices, thickening to six as the intro develops. In this case, the upper voices float, alone, while the lower voices eventually join in, giving a rich, orchestral texture comparable to instrumental sections: say, trumpets versus lower brass in a jazz band, or strings and horns in an orchestra.

» This voicing structure, in addition to following the harmonic series nicely with wider intervals in the bottom and closer intervals at the top, is also very pianistic. Puerling often wrote from the piano, and he didn't always notate his arrangements: rather, he played the full voicings from the piano, and the singers picked out their parts as they went, following his fingers to find their voice-leading.

» Puerling is the master of the "harmonic surprise," offering sudden unexpected color shifts or chromatic movement. Here, he lulls us into the dreamy land of A♭ mixolydian, then surprises us with a shift to G♭7sus on beat three of measure four . . . and then again, beyond this excerpt, with a clean break into F major. No matter how many times you hear it, it's still unexpected.

The end of the piece is a study in harmonic dexterity and free-floating word-painting. The phrase "see the world" is nearly impossible to add a blow-by-blow chord analysis on paper, so the chords are identified in the notation. It could best be described as a "barbershop tag on LSD." It contains a post note in the soprano with moving parts underneath, which are driven by a mostly-chromatic-descending bass line. But we have six moving parts, not three as in barbershop, so the harmonies get quite dense. The chord progression pretty much defies standard harmonic analysis. If I (Dylan) had to take an educated guess, I'd suggest that Puerling's process was likely something like this:

» Determine the start chord.
» Determine the end chord.
» Write a bass line to get from one to the other.
» "Fill in the blanks"—all six of them—using trial and error until something works.

I've used this technique in my own writing sometimes, and it's amazing what can come out of it.

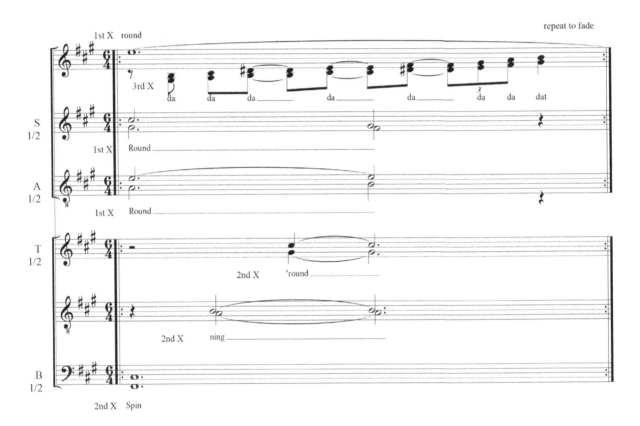

Moving to the ending, Puerling paints an exquisite portrait of the "world spinning 'round." The arrangement breaks from a seven-part, largely homophonic structure in the previous bar to a multi-textured thirteen-voice kaleidoscope, roughly divided into three textures:

» The "spinners," the two bottom staves singing an arpeggiated "spinning 'round," and providing the harmonic foundation.
» The "pads," seesawing between two voicings, with a single held note anchoring both.
» The "fools," singing a swinging little scale, in thirds. This represents some continuity from earlier in the chart (not represented here), which included a simple "da-dat, da-dah" representation of the original recorder solo from the Beatles' version.

These textures are layered in one by one: the pads, the spinners, and finally the fools. Despite the complexity of the spinning textures, they are harmonically static: after the density and angularity of the previous bars, Puerling opens up the skies and leaves us whirling on a single chord and key center, F♯ minor: again, barely connected to our original key of F.

It's nearly impossible to overstate the influence of Gene Puerling on the arrangers who came after him. From Take 6 to the Real Group, from the harmonic dexterity of Kerry Marsh to the thematic, symphonic creations of Roger Treece, every pop-jazz arranger owes his or her craft, in part, to Gene Puerling.

Take 6

When Take 6's eponymous album dropped in 1988, it took the musical world by storm and immediately launched the band into stardom. The sound was brand-new, a fusion of traditional gospel, spirituals, and originals sung with sophisticated jazz harmonies, big band swing, and the passion and groove of R&B. The singing was precise yet soulful, swinging yet reverent. Ask many vocal arrangers (including ourselves), and they can probably tell you exactly where and when they first heard the sound of Take 6.

The main arrangers for Take 6 are/were Mervyn Warren, Cedric Dent, and Mark Kibble, of whom Kibble is the only current member. Each member of the group has considerable training in music as well as an instrumental background, and this is apparent in both the writing and the singing of their arrangements.

An interesting note is that while all members are fluent readers and writers of music, the charts were often not written down at first. Much like Gene Puerling's process, the arrangers would often play the full voicings on the piano, and the singers would "follow the fingers" to learn their part and the voice-leading. The music is largely learned by ear, and with the singers all having extensive theoretical understanding of the functions of the notes they are singing, they can pitch and blend to a high level of precision. More importantly, with such a deep understanding and internalization of how the parts work, each singer knows exactly not only where to keep a note pure, but where there is room to add R&B-style soloistic flourishes in between the functional notes. This is rare in vocal jazz singing, where the complexity of the chords usually allows singers little room for variation: deviate too much, and the harmonic structure becomes shaky or even falls apart. The members of Take 6 know exactly when and where they can play. The result is a performance that is complex, but breathes; it's tight, but loose; it has the precision and purity of Duke Ellington with the slinky soul of Stevie Wonder. To hear this in effect, take a listen to the recorded version of "Get Away, Jordan." It's clean and precise. Then find a live version online. Years later, the arrangement and performance has matured like fine wine: the singers have found all the nuance and places they can play, and the arrangement has even greater depth and soul.

So, what makes a Take 6 arrangement? Some aspects can be pretty well-defined.

» *Six voices.* Unlike the Singers Unlimited, whose artistry and arranging style was shaped by the studio, nearly all Take 6 arrangements are designed for live performance. There can be moments of four voices (usually still sung by six people, with some notes doubled), even moving to unison, but the maximum number is usually six.

» *"Vocal big band."* Many of their up-tempo swinging jazz charts borrow from the vocabulary of big band writing. The bass part walks, and the melody is voiced top-down like a horn section. Sometimes the group splits into two textures: triadic voicings on the top, and three-part open voicings on the bottom. More on this later.

» That said, *the timbres are still vocal*, rather than a "vocal band" attempting to imitate instruments. Though their arrangements may occasionally include some guitar-like rhythm parts and sometimes direct horn imitation, they largely represent the function of those instruments, rather than mimicking the sounds themselves. Horn-like shots and accents are sung with vocal-scat "ba-doo-bop!"–type syllables rather than straight imitation.

» *Sophisticated, but functional jazz harmony*, drawing directly from the big band era and from vocal jazz groups that preceded them, such as the Hi-Los and the Four Freshmen.

Repertoire-wise, the source is largely gospel, spirituals, or original gospel music. There are covers of contemporary pop and R&B songs—and they have lent their voices to recording artists beyond these genres, such as pop-country music artist k.d. lang—but their home is gospel.

With these general notes, let's look at some detail. First up, a look at their use of harmony. This example is taken from their first album and is their jazzy take on the spiritual "Get Away, Jordan." This is a transitional section leading up to a big key change and a dramatic drop in tempo.

Get Away, Jordan

Arr. Mark Kibble

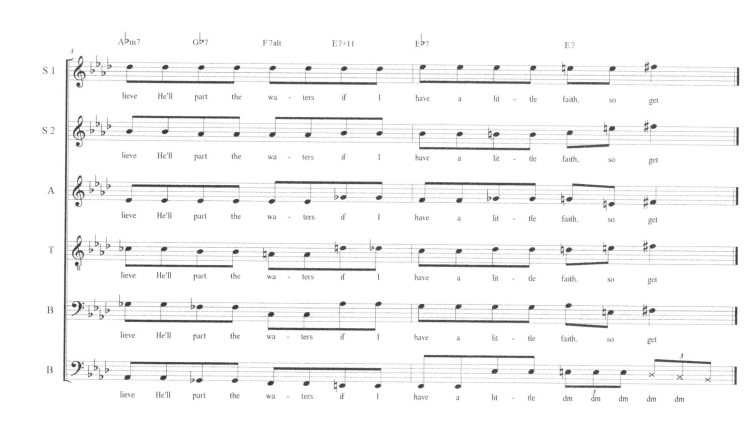

As you can see by the chord changes provided in the score, Kibble is using a combination of a simple pedal tone–type melody in the soprano, with the other five parts harmonizing around it. The harmonies follow a fairly conventional pattern of two main progressions per bar: I7-IV7-♭VII7-V-i-VI7-V7-V7 (new key). This follows our usual circle-of-fifths harmonic progression, but Kibble adds some extra variety. First, he makes frequent use of tritone substitutions as seen in the bass. Second, the inner voices often move so that a tritone substitution also includes differently altered upper partials, with plenty of suspensions, ♭9, ♯11, and ♭13 colorations.

You can also see a division in the function of the parts: upper voices and lower voices. The upper three voices largely cover triadic or quartal stacks, which by themselves are quite harmonically stable, and despite the amount of color and use of upper partials, they are not overly difficult to sing and voice-lead well. The lower three voices (sometimes referred to by Take 6 as "the meat locker") cover the functional tones: roots, thirds, fifths, and sevenths. The three-plus-three combination of foundation and color, basic harmony and chromaticism, is a hallmark of Kibble's writing and serves as an ideal textbook for jazz arranging.

Also, you'll notice something interesting beyond the voice-leading: the second soprano provides something like a countermelody to the static first soprano. This goes beyond adding harmonic color and stands out in places as its own melodic fragment. The use of the second soprano part in particular to add interest and "juicy notes" is typical of Kibble's writing: ask anyone who has sung Take 6 charts which part is the most interesting, and they'll likely say the second soprano. Coincidentally, that's the part Kibble largely sings in Take 6: he gives the best part to himself!

Moving into the final section, Kibble follows a classic big band convention: a semitone-up key change and a dramatic slowdown into a swaggering "strut-tempo."

Get Away, Jordan

Arranged by Mark Kibble

The writing here is straight-up big band style. The harmonies are jazzy but not overly complex. Kibble gives the bass a standard walking bass line (to which Alvin Chea adds some extra skips for rhythmic emphasis, especially useful since Take 6 rarely uses dedicated vocal percussion), and the remaining five voices act as a giant horn block complete with wide vibrato horn-shakes. The soprano takes the role of first trumpet, adding additional soloistic shakes and color. To fill out the big band feeling, the four middle voices peel off to add their own sax section–like tumbling response ("gotta get across") before joining the first trumpet again for the following phrase.

For those of us getting our start in the 1990s and beyond, Take 6 was a touchstone, a common frame of reference, and a musical arranging course rolled into one. Groups that followed, such as M-Pact, Accent, and even Dylan's own group, Cadence, borrowed and adapted what techniques we could to suit our own ensembles. Not since Gene Puerling has any group had such a profound influence on a cappella vocal jazz arranging, and it may be a long time before anyone else does.

CHAPTER 14

Around the World

Vocal Sampling, The Swingles, Rajaton, Ladysmith Black Mambazo

So far, most of the groups we have analyzed come from the United States. This is no surprise, given that a) much contemporary a cappella originates from North America, and b) we're American and Canadian, and we know our own backyard the best.

The explosion of contemporary a cappella music over the past few decades means there is plenty to discover around the world. There's not enough room in this book to name-check every single excellent group, so instead we'll focus on a few international groups that have influenced a cappella writing to date. Each of these groups represents some of the best of their geographic area or style, enough that if someone asks, "Can you arrange like so and so, from such-a-place?" we can at least provide a reference point to start you off. Our criteria for each group/arranger includes the following:

» Represents an innovative arranging style.
» Has had an influence on the a cappella genre as a whole.
» Roughly falls in a contemporary vein, but may include a fusion/synthesis of national styles and traditions with contemporary flavor.
» We're deliberately sidestepping the folk/indigenous music of particular countries or areas: a "how-to" on these would be beyond our realm of expertise.

Pack your bags, and here we go!

Vocal Sampling

Instrumental imitation is at the heart of much contemporary a cappella music, and we're all familiar with vocal representations of guitars, horns, and drums in rock/pop arrangements. But you haven't heard anything until you've heard the sound of an a cappella salsa band.

Vocal Sampling is based in Cuba, having started out as many vocal groups did—in school. Composed of instrumentalists, their six-voice a cappella group was formed in part by the simple game of "how do we do this with just our voices?" Their 1995 album, *Una Forma Mas*, put them on the map, and international tours and acclaim soon followed.

To arrange in a similar manner, it is important to understand the language of a Cuban salsa band. A salsa band typically has the following elements:

» *A percussion section* consisting of (at minimum) congas, clave, and shakers, and usually including cowbell and/or agogo bell, guiro, bongos, and timbales. These may be played by a single percussionist, but more often several. There is no drum kit in traditional salsa bands, though modern bands may use one along with the above-mentioned percussion.

» *The bass*, usually acoustic. The tone is warm, with little overtone, and a quick decay.

» *At least one chordal instrument*, which could include guitar, tres (a guitar-like an instrument with three pairs of strings, tuned like the top three strings of a guitar), and/or piano.

» *Horns*, from one to many, but often three.

» *Lead vocals plus harmonies*, usually sung by band members rather than dedicated background singers. Harmonies are often sung, like a horn section, in call and response to the lead, or they can be used as a triadic "group lead vocal" particularly in choruses.

As instrumentalists themselves, the members of Vocal Sampling are experts in the role of each instrument, and therefore they know how to translate that into voices. In addition, they use body percussion to represent certain sounds, such as the ubiquitous clave. Rather than a vocal representation, the "clave" player (often the vocal percussionist) makes a loose fist with the fingers not fully curled, leaving a hole in the fist. The palm of the other hand is slapped against the fist where the hole is, creating the high wooden clave tone. The benefit of this (and other body percussion) is that you can add percussive elements and still sing a vocal part!

Here's an example from Vocal Sampling's self-introduction song, "Montuno Sampling":

Montuno Sampling

Vocal Sampling

The voices are allocated much like our salsa band above:

» *Percussion*: high and low conga, clave, shaker/guiro, and agogo bells. In this studio version, there are two levels of percussion: in live performance they are performed by one person, with other singers occasionally pitching in where possible.

» *Bass*, sung with a round-sounding "thm" with little brightness or overtone, mimicking the salsa bass tone mentioned above. The bass follows a typical tumbao pattern, propelling the band over beats one and three instead of emphasizing them.

» *A middle voice*, acting as a cross between a montuno instrument (based on the pattern) and a lower horn such as a baritone sax (based on the range and vowel choice).

» *Three voices*, acting as guitar/tres (based on the pattern) and/or a horn section (based on the vowel choice).

You'll see based on some of these "either/or" descriptions that Vocal Sampling is often blending function and timbre to create a hybrid vocal part that covers multiple aspects of the salsa band. In the first two bars, the top three voices use a smooth, neutral "ve-ve-veh" vowel, which could be lower horns or guitar, but they clearly change to a horn section by the third measure, with a nasal "bap-ba-dap."

This intro uses several other signature salsa conventions, such as the bright horn melodies and the quick bass breakdown, ending with the final unison shots before launching into the first verse immediately following this excerpt.

In the chorus, Vocal Sampling continues with the salsa conventions:

seis hom - bres in - stru - men - tos   Que'el vien - to no se lle - vó   ni se lle - va - ra

» *The two-voice "group lead."* This would normally be a three-voice group with instrumentalists singing. But as an a cappella band, they need other voices to cover the instrument parts. The result is "hollowed-out triads" of fifths and sixths, omitting the middle note. Fortunately, thanks to clever arranging and "part math," those middle notes are largely covered by . . .

» *Horns.* Again, this might often be three horns, but two is not unusual. In this active chorus, the horns are quite busy, offering a rhythmic countermelody and running commentary to the group vocal lead. Vocal Sampling uses vowel color to help distinguish between the group lead—sung in a barrel-chested, high-soft-palate manner—and the horns, sung in a thinner, nasal tone.

» *More active bass.* Now that we're in the higher-energy chorus, the bass keeps the main tumbao pattern, but embellishes the rhythm more.

» *Percussion*, which continues the patterns established in the intro, with the occasional improvised timbale flourish.

It's not possible to arrange salsa (or other specific Latin genres) without knowing the genres themselves. But if you want to learn Cuban musical styles, and add additional flavors to your arranging palette, give Vocal Sampling a deep listen, and you'll find that they are the masters.

The Swingles

The Swingles (formerly the Swingle Singers) are one of the longest-running a cappella ensembles around, now at sixty years and counting. Beginning in 1962 as an eight-voice studio-session ensemble, their unique approach to jazzing-up classical material made them a household name, earning five Grammy awards and countless other accolades. In addition to their live performance and recording activity, their often-lyric-less recordings made their music ideal for television and movie scores, and to this day, the "Swingle sound" is a well-understood reference among producers, jingle writers, and other commercial music-making types. As an arranger, you'll want these techniques in your toolkit.

Since the 2010s, The Swingles have expanded far beyond their classical-with-a-jazz-twist sound to incorporate modern contemporary music of many genres, placing them among the world's best contemporary a cappella groups. That said, when people refer to the "Swingle sound" (including anyone who might be commissioning you to write in the style!), they are likely talking about the "classic Swingle Singers" of the 1960s to 2000s, so this is the style on which we will focus here.

Ward Swingle's arranging style and choice of repertoire took a novel approach: take instrumental classical material, especially the music of Johann Sebastian Bach, adapt it for voices, add a jazz rhythm section of bass and drums (later, vocal bass and drums), and *voilà* . . . a new classical-jazz crossover genre appears. Though The Swingles often performed with bass and drums in the early years, this was done in part to "jazzify" the feel: the vocal parts covered all the melodic and harmonic material, and many later arrangements were sung completely a cappella. The sound was instantly popular, blending familiar classics with the popular sound of jazz. Like Liberace did with his onstage theatrics, The Swingles helped bridge the classical-popular divide, reframing classical material and making it accessible to a wider audience.

Here's how it is done.

1. Choose a piece of instrumental classical music. Bach works especially well: his harmonic progressions already have a strong jazzy feel, the chord changes are the bedrock on which most contemporary music is built, and he is the master of voice-leading, so the music translates to contemporary vocal ensembles quite well. That said, The Swingles also covered composers such as Rimsky-Korsakov, Debussy, and others.

2. Decide on your ensemble. Note that The Swingles were eight voices, often covering music that originally had four parts or less. You'll still need more than four voices: see below for why. In addition, the singers will need to be fluent in the following skills:

   » Classical choral blending techniques.
   » Straight-tone singing, with no vibrato.
   » Strong vocal technique, wide vocal range, and smooth, consistent sound through the entire vocal range.
   » Music-reading skills, while not essential, are very helpful. These types of parts are not easy to learn by ear.

3. Find a key that works reasonably well. In a Bach fugue, find a key that allows each section to sing the main melody either at the tonic or at the dominant: this is the common *modus operandi* of fugal writing. A four-voice fugue, for

example, might have sopranos and tenors singing at the tonic and basses and altos singing at the dominant.

4. Transcribe the parts.

5. Make adjustments as needed. This is instrumental music, and it may not always adhere to what is singable. Some lines may be too high, too low, too jumpy, or cover too wide a range for a single voice. This is why you'll want a six- to eight-voice ensemble: a long, rangy line can be broken up and spread across two vocal parts. Some parts may sound better down/up an octave: a squeaky-high countermelody might sound better down the octave as an inner alto part, or a rumbling lower part might sound more agile sung up an octave by the tenors, keeping it out of the way of a walking bass line. And speaking of which, save a voice or two for your "rhythm section."

6. Add syllables. These should be neutral and light, with soft articulations that can be sung at fast tempi. The classic Swingle syllables are "ba-va-da." Bs and Ds offer a clear articulation without the extra effort of an aspirated consonant. The "va" syllable in between is softer and even easier to sing, and it has the added bonus of giving the sound a little light swing if wanted.

   To demonstrate this, try singing a scale to "ba-ba-da-ba-da-ba-da." It's doable, but gets exhausting after a while and the phrasing is a bit rigid. Now try the same scale to "ba-va-da-va-da-va-da." You'll immediately notice that it's easy to sing, it can be sung at any tempo, and the phrasing is light and nimble. It can be sung straight or swung. For a different color, especially for any accompaniment parts with rapid sixteenth notes that are static background parts, keep the same consonants and change the vowel sound. In a high-energy Bach fugue, "ba-va-da" is open and transparent: in the rapid-fire but soft "Flight of the Bumblebee," "doo-va-doo" or "div-va-div" is quieter and even captures a bit of the buzzing sound characteristic of the piece.

7. Add a bassline (optional). If you're looking at an a cappella arrangement of a Bach fugue, for example, a walking bass line adds more jazz flavor. The jazz feel of a Ward Swingle arrangement comes from the feel as much as the sound. The syllables, while scat-like, are still neutral: there's no jazzy or hornlike "shoo-ba-doo-wop bop bow!" syllables to define the genre. Instead, much of the feel comes from the walking bass.

The tone of singing is non-classical. The singing can be light and amplified by close-micing, rather than projected acoustically, which allows for use of the bass and alto's low range without getting lost over the soprano.

Here is a little piece of The Swingles' "Fugue in G minor" (popularly known as the "little fugue"), originally written for organ. We start near the beginning, as the alto states the theme at the fifth, and the soprano states the countertheme.

Fugue in G Minor BVW 578

J.S. Bach

Arr. Ward Swingle

First off, you'll notice the title doesn't match the key signature: Ward Swingle dropped the key to E minor to suit the voices, and you'll see the ranges work nicely: the soprano's highest note is a very-reasonable F♯ (the highest note in the whole piece is A), and the alto's statement of the theme fits well in a low alto range with the bottom note F♯.

The next thing to note is the bass line. The original organ fugue is in three "voices," or independent parts. Fugue voices are usually added one by one and at this point in the organ fugue, there is no bass, only the soprano and alto: Swingle adds a walking bass line from the very beginning to establish the jazz feel. Later, there is a bass voice in the organ fugue, and Swingle deftly blends it in to the walking bass line, using "dm" syllables for harmonic function and "ba va da" syllables to bring the bass voice to the fore when stating a theme or countertheme.

In the third and fourth bars, Swingle divides the sopranos. In the organ fugue, this is one voice, but it would be vocally difficult to execute. Split this way, it is much more feasible to sing well, and when sung properly, it seamlessly sounds like one voice, with the added benefit of a little crossover between the voices, gluing the harmonies together.

In this next section, where the tenors state the theme in the relative major, Swingle takes a few more liberties for the sake of good vocal writing:

Remember, this is a three-voice fugue, but we have as many as five parts at once! In the three-voice fugue, the lowest voice gets the theme: instead, Swingle gives it to the tenors, which works well for two reasons. First, it sits well in the tenor range, and the tenor hasn't made much thematic action apart from the first statement of the theme a while back. Second, it allows the bass to continue its dual-function of walking bass and lowest fugue-voice.

Swingle also strengthens the texture and dynamic in the vocal arrangement by having the bass double the tenor down the octave three bars into the melody. This gives a nice pedal tone quality at this point, and this part of the theme works well as both bass line and melody. Once again, Swingle splits a jumpy vocal part, but this time using two combinations of voices: soprano 1 and 2, then soprano and alto.

The Swingles have had an interesting influence on a cappella writing. While no group has really tried to follow in their footsteps—they are still active, after all—their signature sound is well-known and well-used. It is easily woven into arrangements, and it has been for decades. There is no sound quite like it.

Rajaton

The Nordic countries have produced so many innovative groups that it's hard to choose just one. Sweden's the Real Group, formed in 1984, was a staple for many a cappella artists (including the authors) coming up at the end of the last century and beyond. Denmark's Vocal Line brought a Nordic sound to pop music and gave rise to other groups such as Postyr. But the Nordic group that first made us, as arrangers, sit up and say, "I never would have thought of doing it like that!" was probably Finland's Rajaton.

The name *Rajaton* translates as "boundless," and that's an apt description of the group and its sound. Their dynamic and stylistic breadth is astounding, from jazz and pop to Finnish folk music and originals, from disciplined blend to wild abandon.

There are a few standout characteristics of Rajaton's sound:

» *Blend with individualism.* Our usual definition of "vocal blend" has to do with matching timbres, sacrificing a little vocal individualism for the goal of a smooth collective sound. Rajaton can certainly do this . . . but often, they don't. Each singer has a voice unlike the other, and the result is a rich sound with more complex texture than a silky-smooth, homogeneous blend. Because they phrase so well together, the ensemble sound is fat, but still in sync.

» *The "bright Nordic sound."* Whether it's the high cheekbones or the bright vowels of the languages, groups from this part of the world often have an amazing vocal resonance, and Rajaton is no exception. When those bright tones blend, there's nothing quite like it. Vocal phrases might include sizzly "ee" vowels, or broad "hi-ya-da-dn-da" phrasing.

» *Freewheeling changes in texture.* Some groups sing homophonically most of the time. Some groups assign "instruments" or functions to their singers, establishing textures and largely sticking with them through the song. Rajaton freely switches up groupings from section to section, sometimes even from bar to bar. Textures are functional, but not specifically instrumental.

» *Many voices, or few.* Rajaton may have six singers, but they often don't use all of them. While some arrangers feel the need to use every voice all the time, Rajaton often uses changes in density to achieve dynamic range. Frequently they will sing entire sections with lead, bass, and one voice acting as a "thread" between them. This also allows for difference in texture: a lead can be "double-tracked" in live performance with two singers in unison, then split into harmony. When a new section comes in, the full use of all six voices offers a dramatic contrast.

» *They don't rely on a vocal drummer.* Bass Jussi Chydenius often adds backbeat and occasionally some "beat bassing," but the other parts often contain enough rhythmic drive that a dedicated drummer isn't needed.

We can find some examples of this in Soila Sariola's original piece "Pakkanen," which translates to English as "frost." We'll start at the beginning with the first bold phrase:

Pakkanen

Soila Sariola

This is the call of the piece: for nearly a minute, nothing else happens. Just this phrase, called out into a cold, reverberant soundscape four times, with nothing else but ambient wind sounds and the occasional lonely solo vocal phrase. The verse begins, one voice only, then is joined by the bass line and the "thread," which we'll see in the following chorus. We're well into the song, and there are only three parts! Another voice is added to sing in harmony with the lead, and finally we open up at the chorus and hook of the song.

The bass line, complete with chest-slapping backbeat and octave leaps, is a McFerrin-like one-person rhythm section. The thread acts like a rhythm guitar, but it only holds a single fifth throughout: the common tones tie the lead block and the bass line together. The texture is thicker now: we have a three-part block singing bright, open non-lyrical syllables and a two-voice thread. The "Ah-eh-oh" call is now developed into a full melodic phrase. The harmonies in this phrase add a nice surprising twist with the chromatic shifting across parts in the group lead vocal, blurring major and minor. The thread (second staff) keeps the rhythm driving with a largely off-beat part, but it cleverly works around the group lead by switching to on-beats when the group lead syncopates, keeping every eighth note active between the two textures.

After another verse and chorus, the song takes a hard left turn with a new section, starting slowly and gradually speeding up like a Russian folk song. Finally, we arrive at the final section, tying all these parts together.

The "ah-eh-oh" trio is now a duo, with a two-part descant replacing the origi-nal melody, and the focus is now on a two-voice counterpart with a rapid-fire rush of lyrics. The bass line, the one constant in the piece, continues. The thread keeps going: two voices in octaves on recording, represented by one voice (as notated here) live. There are now four independent textures being created with only six voices, an amazingly resourceful bit of arranging.

Overall it's quite an adventure, and this can be said of many of Rajaton's ar-rangements. If you find yourself stuck and need to think outside the box, Rajaton's unconventional writing style will inspire you.

Ladysmith Black Mambazo

Everyone in the Western world knows "The Lion Sleeps Tonight," but few know the original "Mbube" by Solomon Linda that sparked an entire style of a cappella in South Africa called "mbube," resulting in decades of a cappella competitions in the townships that would stretch until dawn. This soaring style and tradition in South Africa morphed into the smoother and mellower isicathamiya, an a cappella tradition with a lead singer backed up by an a cappella ensemble, with lots of call and response and beautifully sonorous chords. Few in the West had heard this music until Paul Simon's *Graceland* album introduced Ladysmith Black Mambazo to the West in 1986. The song "Homeless" on this album starts with an extended introduction in Zulu by the ensemble:

Homeless

The particulars of the phrasing and vowel placement cannot be captured in sheet music, but the notes can: clear, cleanly voiced triads that maximize tuning, a series of four-part block chords on lyrics in response to the lead singer's call. There are small stepwise variations within these chords, but for the most part they hew to the root, third, and fifth of each chord. The performance is smooth, the effect calming.

Later in the song, once Paul Simon enters, we get a different texture:

The "ih-hih-ih-hih-ih" has an effect almost like vocal percussion, and the parallel descending harmonies on "hello hello hello" and "why why why" aren't the block chords from before, but they are all diatonic and triadic. Coupled with this music is a series of stylized movements, as the competitions judged appearance and movement alongside the lead vocalist's prowess and the backing group's clean harmonies.

To arrange like Ladysmith is not only to follow their harmonic language, but it is to listen to their vowels and phrasing, which is essential in capturing their clean, resonant sound.

SECTION V

Reimagining Arrangements

Most of this book is about discussing and teaching various specific techniques. These are all tools of the craft, parts of the vocabulary that all arrangers have at their disposal. We've done our best, in this book and in our previous one, to teach you all the "what" and "how" we can.

Now, what do you do?

We started the book with all the "soft skills" of creative work, exploring the overarching principles. Between these, and the practical skills, there's a gap in the middle: understanding the process. Analyzing the works in Section Four got us part of the way there. Now we'll take you through the process itself, taking you along with us as we work on our own arrangements, and explain what we did and the choices we made.

This section is less about teaching new skills; it shows you how we put them in action. Chapter 15, "Medleys and Mashups," shows the practical skills of this complex task, but at its heart, the "task" is really a meta-process where you're not just arranging, but you're arranging the arrangement. This level of arranging can't be told . . . it has to be shown.

Chapter 16, "Reimagining a Song," takes this even further. Arranging is part craft, part art, a mixture of the practical and the inspired. Here, we take you through arrangements that went beyond a straightforward "translation" of an original work and became a reimagining of that work to become something very different. The reasons for this are varied, from "it's what the client wanted" to "I got bored with my own chart!" and you'll likely have found yourself in many of these circumstances yourself.

Enjoy the ride as we take you into our own arranging journeys: we hope you enjoy the experience!

CHAPTER 15

Medleys and Mashups

Before diving into creating mashups, we should begin with a clear definition of what a mashup is, as the word is sometimes misunderstood or misused. In its most basic sense, a *mashup* is when two or more songs are overlaid or intertwined. This is distinct from a *medley*, which is the term for songs that happen in succession, one after another, without a break for applause. There are medleys that end in a mashup of the songs at the end, which is an effective way to build energy and put a satisfying button on the succession of songs, but the most notable mashups weave songs together throughout.

Considerations

Mashing up two or more songs requires considering some of the fundamental theoretical aspects of the songs being considered. First of all, the tempo is essential, as mashing up two songs with very different beats per minute (BPM) will result in one feeling very slow, or the other frenetic. Ideally the songs being considered are within a few BPM of each other, or they unfold at a pace that can be accelerated or decelerated. The best way to tell if the songs will work at a specific tempo is to get out a metronome and sing them. Often, there's a workable happy medium to be found between the tempi of the songs, and if you find yourself in a tough place, err on the side of going too slow as opposed to too fast, as there is a top speed at which lyrics can be sung before they become a garbled, unsingable mess.

The keys of the songs also have to be considered, not because there's a specific ideal key for songs, but rather because the vocal range of the melodies in question should be considered. A song for a high vocal range might need to be moved downward, for instance, and you don't want to lose a song's character by changing its tessitura. Other songs likely can't be moved much, such as the melody to A-ha's "Take on Me," which ranges from low to very high falsetto, covering two and a half octaves by one singer. When mashing up a song like this, you're going to have to adjust the key of the other song. Note that there are sometimes other considerations when choosing a key, such as the bass line in "Under Pressure" (which we'll discuss later in this chapter): the signature bass line is one of the most recognizable elements of the song, repeating on a tonic note then dropping down to the fifth. You cannot transpose this fifth up an octave, as the identifiable hook will be lost.

The shape of both melodies is an important consideration, as well. Very lyrically dense, constant melodies—such as those written by Lin-Manuel Miranda of *Hamilton* fame—are harder to mash up than melodies with fewer words and notes. Any space in the melody, especially between lines and stanzas, creates an opportunity for the other song to be featured. A great example of this is Simon and Garfunkel's "Scarborough Fair/Canticle," better known to some as "Parsley, Sage, Rosemary, and Thyme." The two songs alternate back and forth, handing off focus line by line, which is an excellent way to intertwine and showcase both songs. Note: "Canticle" is actually a Paul Simon song entitled "The Side of a Hill," which makes it a bit easier of a lift, as he could alter his own song to his heart's content without anyone feeling as though it had been shortchanged.

You may find yourself listening to some of the end-of-year mashups created by DJs such as DJ Earworm, but remember: production elements don't always translate to voices, and therefore, they can't be relied upon. Basic elements such as harmonic progression, melody, and lyrics will hold when sung by voices, but the timbre of a specific synthesizer, or other studio effects, may not. For instance, Darude's "Sandstorm" has an immediately recognizable sound that will announce itself in an instant. Just a second of it will remind listeners of the original, whereas voices singing those few notes wouldn't be sufficient to ensure listeners knew and remembered the song being referenced. It would take establishing more of the song, and including other elements, such as vocal percussion, to represent the song. There's not a clear demarcation line between what voices can and can't easily reproduce; it depends on the specific group, voices, ability to mimic timbres, and so on.

First Steps

If you're looking to arrange a mashup for the first time, we recommend you don't just pick two songs that you'd like to interweave, clever as they may be. Instead, first learn the mechanics and nuances of the process by attempting a few mock arrangements, even if only a section of the song.

To begin, we recommend you choose two songs that are built on the same chord progression, using the same tempo, feel, and even hook. How is this possible? In a world in which sampling is prevalent, it's not very difficult. For instance, Queen and David Bowie's "Under Pressure" was sampled by Vanilla Ice for his hit "Ice Ice Baby," and weaving those two songs together would be an easy place to start. Let's take a look at how "Under Pressure" and "Ice Ice Baby" interweave.

The choruses of the songs are in the same key and same tempo, as Vanilla Ice dropped his chorus lyric right over a sample of the original (minus the lead vocal singing "Under Pressure"). How do the two fit together when overlaid?

Under Pressure

As you can see, the two hooks—the rap and the original melody—basically sit on top of each other, with a measure and a half long gap between iterations. So, why not take advantage of this space, and push the rap back a half-cycle so that it lays nicely between the original melodic hook, so the listener can hear the two distinctly:

This isn't a necessity, but it's the kind of micro-decision you'll be frequently making when arranging a mashup, as you want to have the two or more songs "play nicely together," directing the audience's attention between the melodies, harmonies, and other recognizable elements in a manner that they can follow and enjoy. Too little interplay, and the audience isn't impressed; too much, and they're confused or will more likely lose many of the clever moments of interplay you've carefully crafted.

If you'd like to continue on this path a little further, another option is "Mary, Mary," originally by the Monkees, sampled by Run DMC. If you want a little more experience in this vein, rather than arranging the entire song, consider creating a chorus that uses elements of both songs. Deciding how much of the melodic elements from the originals to use versus how much of the rap is a matter of taste, and the craft is in figuring out how to deftly maneuver both without including all of either.

In fact, any rap with a relatively simple chorus can be relatively easily mashed into a song with a similar BPM and some space in the melody, which is to say a number of beats between lines where the lead singer is taking a breath and the instrumental figures take focus. If you have a favorite rap, go looking for a song with a similar tempo, and if you can find a song that somehow fits thematically, even better.

Next Steps

Once you're comfortable interweaving a spoken hook with a melodic song, consider arranging two melodic songs that are built on the same chord progression. This is more common than you might think. There are a few places you can begin to look for ideas:

» A classic doo-wop song, with its I-vi-IV-V progression, so long as both songs have a similar tempo. Lists of songs with that progression are easy to find online, including Wikipedia.

» A pair of songs that are referenced in the Axis of Awesome "4 Chord" comedic routine. If you haven't seen it, an Australian comedy act plays several pop songs in rapid succession, possible because so many have been written with the same harmonic structure: I-V-vi-IV. You can watch the video (easily searched online) or look for the list on the Axis of Awesome Wikipedia page. There are forty-seven songs from which to choose, plus another thirty-six are referenced, and additional lists can be found online.

Many pop songs from the past twenty years have been built on loops, and as such, they have the same chord progression throughout: introduction, verse, chorus, etc. If not the same progression as one of the two listed above, then almost certainly another modern song can be found with that same progression, ideally in a similar tempo. Do an online search for the chord progression, and hopefully you'll find a good match, as new songs are being released daily.

Two songs that are similar in feel and flavor are not hard to find. Consider "Blurred Lines" by Robin Thicke, which was so close to Marvin Gaye's "Got to Give It Up" (because it had been written over the same groove) that a jury awarded the Marvin Gaye estate a percentage of the song royalties from "Blurred

Lines." Another very satisfying example is a mashup of Michael Jackson's "Billie Jean" and Justin Timberlake's "Lovestoned" by *The Sing-Off* season one winners, Nota from Puerto Rico. They start with the groove and chords from "Lovestoned" and sing the "Billie Jean" melody over it, then swap, switching to the "Billie Jean" backing parts with the "Lovestoned" melody. There are many songs for which this would work, and in building this mashup, you'll encounter little moments when you have to tweak a melodic line or chord factor due to the differences between the two songs, which is exactly what you'll be doing more of as you build more complex mashups.

Once you have your two songs chosen, the next step is to figure out how you're going to interweave them. Not all melodies have a lot of space in them, so when they don't, see if you can have the melodic lines start at different times, so the audience can notice when each enters. Here's an example, one of the many rejected "pool mashup" moments from the first *Pitch Perfect* film, "She Will Be Loved" by Maroon 5 mashed up with "Waiting for the End" by Linkin Park.

She Will Be Loved / Waiting for the End

Sometimes the meter or feel of one of the songs you're mashing up differs, and you can't always reconcile the differences. Here's another rejected *Pitch Perfect* attempt: "She Will Be Loved" with Kelly Clarkson's "Breakaway," which is in 6/8, presenting a challenge.

She Will Be Loved / Breakaway

Clearly the Linkin Park song in 4/4 is a more natural fit.

And don't worry, Rebel had plenty to sing later in those mashups.

Since we're looking at this moment in *Pitch Perfect*, let's see what challenges other combinations of songs posed. In this example, "Just the Way You Are" by Bruno Mars (one of the two songs that made it to the final version) is interwoven with "Lights" by Ellie Goulding, and both songs are fairly dense once they get started. One way of handling this is to put more people on the melody, or parallel harmonies with the same lyrics as the melody, so the songs become a larger percentage of the overall sound (as opposed to a single melodic line with more voices on the background parts):

Just The Way You Are/Lights

This is, of course, quite busy, so a "softer" version was crafted that leaned on
the melodic lines with primarily whole notes in the background voices . . .

... but ultimately this didn't have the energy and momentum of the others. As you can see, getting it just right took a lot of trial and error, and you can't expect any two songs to necessarily play nicely together. Moreover, if you have a specific moment or mood you're trying to create, as we were in the film, you may find yourself attempting and discarding several versions before you find the right pairing. If you'd like to see the sheet music for the full final version from the movie, it's been published; search for "Just the Way You Are/Just a Dream" (arranged by Deke Sharon).

Looking back at the suggested list of ideas above, it's important to note there are other song forms and chord progressions that allow you to easily switch between songs, but if there isn't enough that's unique about the different songs, the mashup won't have the same effect. For instance, many songs use the twelve bar blues formula. Swapping between blues lyrics over the form has the potential of just sounding confused. Another common musical form is "rhythm changes," which means a jazz song written over the chord changes to Gershwin's "I Got Rhythm." Jumping between songs over that chord progression will likely just sound like you're quoting several jazz songs rapidly, as jazz musicians sometimes do, rather than a true mashup that gives audiences the joy of hearing two distinct songs together. This isn't to say that it's impossible to make a mashup work with these forms; rather, be aware that the more distinct the songs, the better the end effect, especially in a cappella, where you're already bringing the songs sonically closer by translating both to voices rather than using the original instruments, effects, and other production elements that would otherwise help set them apart.

While we're on the topic of *Pitch Perfect*, let's consider the show's finale, which was the Bellas' performance at the ICCA finals at Lincoln Center. The song is initially a medley: "Price Tag" followed by "Don't You Forget about Me" followed by "Give Me Everything (Tonight)." There are quick quotes of other songs from earlier in the movie, including "Just the Way You Are," "Party in the USA," and "Turn the Beat Around." Rather than fully integrating these songs, the songs are referenced quickly between or overtop of grooves from the other songs, primarily "Give Me Everything," which provides the glue. When songs are quickly referenced, overlaid, or tucked in, does it make the song a mashup? Not in the truest form, but that's not what was needed for the end of this film, in which the songs had already been established, so a brief flashback sufficed. The lesson here is simply that your choices as an arranger should reflect the needs of your performers, audience, and medium, rather than a strict adherence to a specific form or concept. Whatever works best is what you should do, and never look back.

Telling a Story

One compelling way to utilize a mashup is to weave songs together to better tell a story. The following two examples show how some of the best storytelling songs—from various Disney movies—can complement each other when intertwined.

Frozen was one of the biggest Disney movies in a long time, inspiring a generation of Halloween trick-or-treaters to dress as Nordic princesses named Elsa and Anna. The story was and is a compelling one, in that the primary relationship in the film is not between a princess and a prince, but rather between the two sisters, having recently lost their parents. The older sister struggles with the fact that she can control ice and snow, as told in the mega-hit song "Let It Go," and the younger sister feels abandoned, her attempts to connect with her sister being told in "Do You Want to Build a Snowman?" Might they work together, creating a side-by-side montage of their challenges, reinforcing the conflict between them?

Both songs are in 4/4. "Let It Go" is in the key of A♭, at 137 BPM. "Do You Want to Build a Snowman?" is in E♭ and around 149 BPM. Not ideal, but let's look at the issues that this presents. Dealing first with the tempi, let's recognize that the heavier hitter between the two songs is "Let It Go," and if we want to lean into one of them, that's the choice as it has a stronger emotional message. If the younger sister, Anna, joins her big sister on the chorus, she's able to both empathize while sending the message that she needs to let her own issues go. Also, having Anna sing "Snowman" a little slower than the somewhat childish and frenetic original will give it more of a pensive, plaintive character. So we'll go with the "Let It Go" tempo.

When it comes to the key, it should be noted that the Lopezes wrote "Let It Go" for Idina Menzel, a woman with a notoriously high vocal range, especially the top of her belt, which most people couldn't begin to match. Since we want to arrange for mere mortals, even fantastic professional ones, dropping it a step or two would benefit everyone involved. "Snowman" isn't particularly high or low, nor is it "rangy" (it doesn't have a large vocal range), so moving it up a step isn't a problem. When posed with a chance to arrange a song in F or F♯, we recommend you go with the former, unless there's a specific note or range you're arranging for (such as a group with young basses who have a low F♯ but not a low F). Fewer accidentals generally a happier singer makes.

Thankfully, both songs are in a major key, and neither song's melody or chord progression engages many accidentals, so it's possible to overlap the melodies rather straightforwardly, allowing a back-and-forth between the different songs that presents as a dialogue between them:

Let It Go / Do You Want To Build a Snowman

This is the arrangement for, and sung by, DCappella on their eponymous debut album.

As you can see, the BGs are 100 percent "Let It Go." Anna is telling her story in Elsa's world, and the audience is along for the ride as they're expecting the song, from the introduction, to be "Let It Go" (which, at this point, most everyone will recognize the second they hear the opening figure). By placing "Do You Want to Build a Snowman?" into the context of this song—same key, same tempo, same background chords, and in the gaps between melodic lines, the audience is immediately able to grasp what's going on. This transparency is beneficial in this case, as we're not trying to show off or be clever; we're just trying to tell a story in the most compelling and emotionally impactful way possible. One song with the melody of the other song placed gently into/onto it goes down very easily.

Now, when it comes time for the pre-chorus, the "Don't let them in, don't let them feel . . ." passage, I could have them sing together . . . wait, no, that's a bad idea. I want the two of them singing the same lyrics together in two-part harmony to feel like a revelation, the beginning of their connection, so instead I have the alto join our Elsa, and I leave Anna alone, silent. More effective theatrically this way, with Anna replying, "We used to be best buddies, but now we're not . . ." as we see she's left out, and the first chorus is sung by Elsa alone, with Anna simply interjecting, "I wish you would tell me why," and so forth, pleading for a reason for her isolation.

If at this point it seems as much thought has gone into the theatricality as the musicality of the way the songs are intertwined, you're correct. Ultimately a powerful piece of music is one that conveys feelings, and in the case of these songs, if we're going to first set up then resolve the conflict between these sisters, each choice we make lyrically and experientially should be just as carefully considered as the key and tempo. If you're wondering if an audience picks up on these elements, they most certainly do, and if you do it well, they won't just understand it; it will wash over them emotionally like a great movie as the technical aspects fall away and they're taken into the storytelling. Anytime you can do this, you should, even if you're tempted to tip your hand and show off how clever you are. A great arrangement is one that's so natural and so compelling that people just love it, and we're sorry to say, most people will never consider the craft behind it any more than you consider how carefully the chips were designed in your phone, or how carefully lit a certain scene was in the last theatrical production you saw. Some will immediately appreciate your magnificent handiwork, but most people will just really like the song, and that's how it should be.

Back to the song. So far, it has been Elsa's song with Anna reacting to her in the gaps. We do want to give Anna her spotlight, her day in court, if you will, to make her emotional message, so that when we fully bring the two together, we had a chance to live in each of their worlds. We also will benefit from a departure from "Let It Go" so that we can excitedly return to it. So, after the end of the first chorus, we shift into "Do You Want to Build a Snowman?" Same key, same tempo, but the BGs will now outline the other song. The vowels are the same, just a little more of an attack, morphing from the "oo" and "noo" at the beginning of "Let It Go" to "doo" for the chorus and then into "Snowman," continuing the same timbre. The shift is as minimal as possible, as we're looking at the same scene, just from a different perspective.

We don't want to disrupt the audience's attention or emotional state; we want the change to be as subtle as possible. And so it continues through the verse of "Snowman," so that Anna has a chance to have her say, and then it's time to shift back to the pre-chorus of "Let It Go" with Elsa on her melody, and Anna joining for a few words at the end of lines, as though she's beginning to align, but not entirely yet. Why? Because we want that big moment to happen on the chorus … and not the second chorus. The two of them singing as sisters again, that needs to be our big catharsis, our last chorus. To give that away too soon would rob us of the biggest statement we can make: the sisters, once divided, are reunited. Yes, we could modulate up, we could have them get even louder, but there's not much more of a powerful statement of reunion than parallel two-part harmony. So, we continue the dialogue in the second chorus:

We're telling the full story, giving them the entire song, so after this second chorus in which they echo each other, circling back and forth vocally, we dive into the bridge of "Let It Go," where Elsa sings, "My power flurries through the air . . ." and Anna replies, "What are we gonna do?" over and over, which in this context begins to sound as though she's taking on Elsa's problem, seeing it as her own. The sisters confront both problems by Anna listening to and helping Elsa. Of course, this is a simplification; when sung powerfully, the song makes its own statement better than text can, which, of course, is the reason we turn to a song in a musical theater production when speech will no longer suffice. And then, finally, after 105 measures of isolation, parallel declarations followed by gradual interplay, we have the chorus we wanted from the start:

The sisters are one, and our ears experience the thing we've wanted to hear as well as feel from the beginning. However, it felt like there was one problem: Anna had focused on Elsa's needs, bearing the weight of her plight, but there wasn't much of a return. So, this felt like the right way to wrap it up, as the last chorus calms down to final chords:

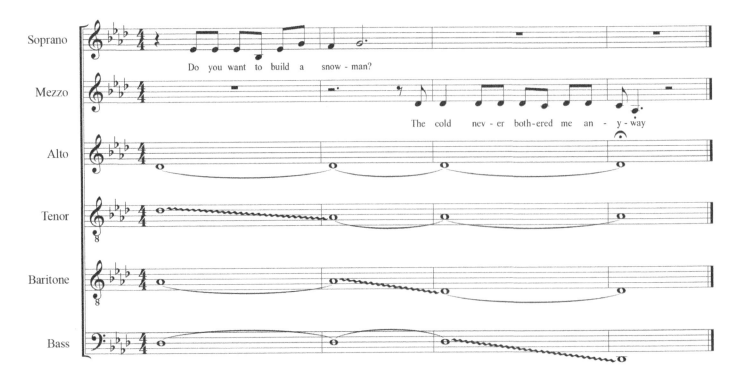

Anna's initial request will be fulfilled; Elsa will, indeed, join her as the cold never bothered her anyway. Naturally when the soloists in DCappella sang this song, they inevitably turned and smiled and hugged as they sang these lines together, an emotional sigh of connection after an emotional journey.

Not all songs interweave this effectively, but I would caution you from assuming that two songs can't tell as powerful a story when intertwined. The choices laid out above didn't just unravel effortlessly; they were the result of careful and repeated trial and error, pasting and replacing until the pacing felt right and the lyrics revealed the story in the best way possible. Not all songs will want to be assembled this way; the key is to follow the story, the lyrics, the melodies, and your own instincts. There is a profound feeling of excitement and accomplishment when you unlock the potential for mashups to recombine beloved songs into a powerful new statement.

Now, lest you think this story was a fluke, let's do it again with two other Disney songs from two different movies: "Part of Your World" from *The Little Mermaid* and "A Whole New World" from *Aladdin*. Unlike the previous example, these two songs are from different movies, and they were written years apart. Is there a story to be found between them? Undoubtedly, that's why I chose them to be mashed up: one song is about a person wishing to be a part of a different world, and the other is a song about a person showing another their world. Both songs, written by Alan Menkin (first with Howard Ashman and later Tim Rice), in a way feel like two sides of the same coin, or so it appeared to be when I got the idea to intertwine them. However, ideas are one thing, and actually making a mashup work is quite another, so let's see how it bears out.

Again, both songs are in 4/4. "Part of Your World" is in the key of F at 134 BPM. "A Whole New World" is also in F, but at 124 BPM. A difference of 10 BPM is usually workable, but in this case, it's safer to go with the slower tempo as the *Little Mermaid* song is almost spoke-sung in parts, and a bit frenetic: there's no room to speed it up. Here we're looking for a classic Disney ballad feel, and 124 feels good.

So, where should we start? Let's think about the story: one song is about wanting to go somewhere; the other unfolds while the person is being shown around; and logic dictates that we want to hear about the desire before it's fulfilled. As with the *Frozen* mashup, we'd like to take the audience with us on this journey of blending songs, so let's start with Ariel's desires, then float in brief moments of Aladdin's offer starting in the verse and moving into the pre-chorus:

Part of Your Whole New World

Unlike in *Frozen*, the songs aren't specifically telling a story about two singers/ characters who are disenfranchised from each other, so we don't have to assume they're standing onstage back to back, but our baritone, Aladdin, can be approaching and singing to Ariel. His offer can increase as his song's lyrics promise more, and as an arranger, we can have the lyrics begin to increase in frequency, even overlapping at times, as the intensity builds. Then to build some "sympatico" between the two singers, I have Aladdin echo Ariel on "but who cares" and "no big deal" between her lines, which builds intensity, as well.

But wait, there's a problem. If you're a fan of *The Little Mermaid*, you might recall that the chorus of "Part of Your World" pulls way back, sung sotto voce as the orchestration dies to almost nothing: "I wanna be where the people are . . ." and so on. We don't have to imitate the original, we can keep building, but here at the chorus is, in fact, a good time to swap songs:

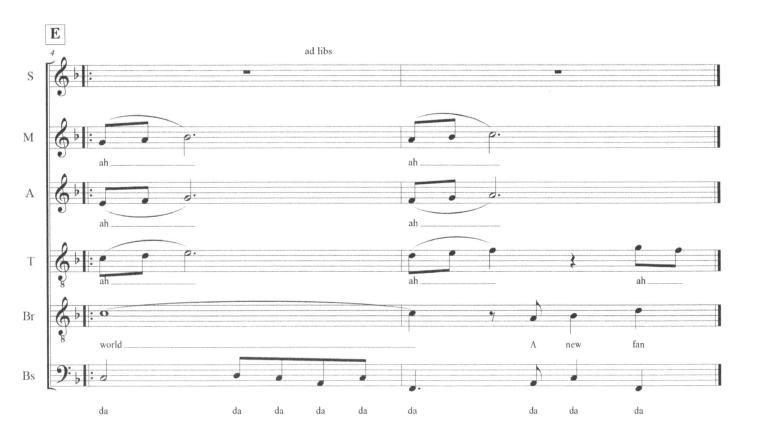

The chord progression swap from one song to the other is rather effortless, which is a bit of good luck we'll always take (don't always expect to be so lucky). However, I wasn't ready to completely abandon Ariel's world—I wanted a way to keep her universe engaged—but I couldn't find anything from within the song that dovetailed well in this moment, so I looked elsewhere. Aha! That song Ariel sings when Ursula, the Sea Witch, takes her voice! A solo line isn't enough, we need harmony to fill out the song, so that's what we'll create: make the melodic lines into parallel harmonies landing on the chords we need for "A Whole New World" placing them atop the original bass line (more or less, there's always room for little tweaks to passing tones and such so that all the parts align well).

Truth be told, I don't know that anyone in DCappella even noticed that I'd stolen that moment from later in the movie, but in the end it doesn't matter. Being familiar with an entire work, or the context a song comes from (be it a movie, a musical, an album, etc.) can give you additional ideas you can draw from and elements you can use. Even if people don't notice what you've done, the pieces will work because they're complementary, and perhaps subconsciously, it will have the effect you've consciously and carefully ascribed to it.

I decided to have Ariel sing the second half of the chorus melody, getting excited: "A whole new world, a dazzling place I never knew," which is the original lyric; it didn't need to be changed to embrace her perspective seeing everything for the first time. Then I have the two of them join on the lyric:

Way up here, it's crystal clear
That now I'm in a whole new world with you

At this point, the singers are happy as they're falling in love, the songs are working well together, and yet you have a nagging feeling you're leaving something out: the chorus of "Part of Your World." Can we add it now, about how Ariel wants to be a part of the world where the people are? Frankly, it doesn't make sense. It's temporally a step backward. So, we leave it on the cutting room floor, never looking back. This may seem like a bad idea to you as an arranger—"How can you leave out one of the best-known parts of the song?"—but ultimately, the rest of the song is doing everything that needs to be done, the story is getting told, and you don't have to use everything. If you do, you'll end up with a lengthy and ungainly piece of music that will feel laborious as you have to keep going back and forth to include everything.

A common axiom in creative work is that you sometimes have to "kill your darlings," which means to eliminate any character, sentences, or piece of a story that you may feel attached to but ultimately isn't serving the overall story. Technically, in this case you're killing someone else's darling, but the idea is the same. Nothing is too precious; your job is to serve the overall audience experience, and what I learned from seeing this song performed in front of audiences in different parts of the world is that never—not a single time—did anyone come up to me afterward complaining that the chorus was missing. Chances are, they never noticed.

So, if we leave out the chorus, where should we go instead? How about the bridge of Ariel's song: "What would I give, if I could live out of these waters . . ." With some of Aladdin's second-verse lyrics woven in the gaps—"Unbelievable sights," "Indescribable feeling," and so forth—the songs continue to play back and forth well. Repeat the chorus, and we've got a song.

But how should we end it? What will give us the most satisfying ending? One choice would be to have the two sing the ending of "A Whole New World":

A whole new world, that's where we'll be
A thrilling chase, a wonderous place, for you and me

. . . and that's what most people probably would have done. It's nice, romantic, safe, and feels like the proper ending of a Disney love song. However, it felt too pat for me, too safe and not as satisfyingly dramatic as the *Frozen* sisters finally reconciling as they stand side by side. I felt like Ariel when she sings, "but who cares, no big deal, I want more."

And what is that "more"? After wrapping up the second chorus in which the two sing together, I decided to end on a different dramatic note, with Ariel's last lines . . .

Out of the sea, wish I could be
Part of your world

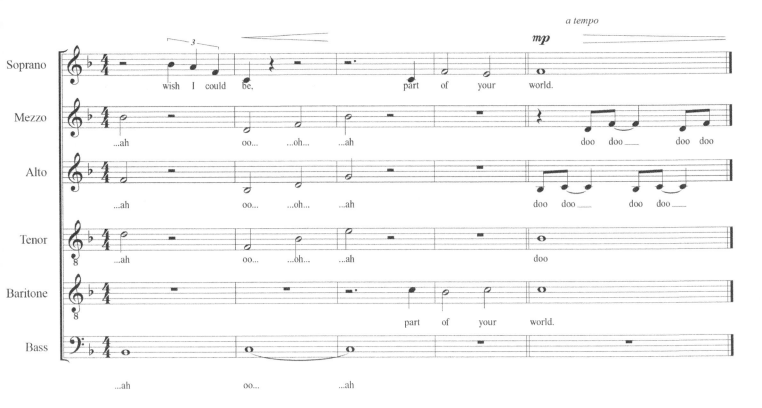

. . . and end with the arpeggiated chords that started her song. How would this work dramatically? Rather than end together, in each other's arms, the two who had a moment together were instead pulled apart, as if the previous measures were a dream, returning to the opposite sides of the stage where they began. I had them holding their notes for an almost impossibly long time (eight measures, with an optional fermata at the end)—not loud, just not wanting to give up the moment—as the rest of the song rolled to its conclusion.

It made the ending of the song bittersweet, the longing unfulfilled. This ending felt and still feels more poignant to me, which is my point: you don't always have to take the easy road and make the obvious choices. People like surprises, and they want to be taken on an emotional journey that won't always end where they expect. I hope you as an arranger sometimes choose the road less taken: the world will be a richer place for it.

Alas, most mashups are not to be found in print as a compulsory license doesn't exist for them and getting the rights is a legal headache, but these "Let It Go/Snowman" and "Part of Your Whole New World" mashups are in print, thanks to Disney. Both can be found online for sale across the internet.

We were rapidly approaching the first "COVID winter" of 2020, when I got a call from my friends in Straight No Chaser, looking for something special that could capture the complicated feelings we all felt during that season. Their manager, David Britz, approached me with an idea—a song by Counting Crows called "A Long December," which wasn't really about the holiday season; it was more about loss, and it just happened to use December as the setting. I loved the song, but I was worried that it didn't have enough of an anchor as a holiday song to really nail their intent, so I thought about it and decided to imagine the lead vocalist walking down lonely streets, hearing carols emanating from the houses he passes, and it hit me: I could weave Christmas carols into the arrangement, throughout the piece, as background parts.

I've arranged for the group for over a decade, and produced two of their albums, so I know their voices and personalities well. My favorite configuration for the ten of them (now nine) was and is to have a soloist, bass, VP, and then two trios, each acting as their own independent unit. I could use one to reflect and support the core harmony and feel of the song, and have the other be the "carolers." In fact, I decided to start the entire song with the sound of carolers, and then have the song kick in:

A Long December

Once the melody starts, I keep listeners focused on the melody and save the quotes for spaces between lyrics:

I urge you to listen to their recording of the song (and/or watch their lovely video) as the effect of these carols floating in and out isn't accurately or adequately reflected in sheet music. The idea is clear, but on the page everything looks as though it's the same, all balanced equally, and moreover the vibe isn't apparent. The guys did a stunning job singing this one, and of course, the fact that they all had to record themselves remotely only added to the poignancy of their performances.

One last bit to show: the very end of the song. After the chorus, which has twice as many quotes throughout, there's a post-chorus, in which the lead singer is on "la," which weaves in beautifully with other carols, a kind of pop song meets traditional holiday counterpoint. When we get to the last iteration of this, I wanted to end the song with a poignant quote, a song that would reflect how we all felt, with the intention of giving the listener chills while reminding them how much we all needed to keep singing. So, I ended with:

"...and heaven and nature sing."

Now, you may be wondering about the legality of mashing in so many holiday songs. Is it legal? Is the price of recording this song (at ten cents per quoted song) going to be cost-prohibitive? Thankfully holiday carols are an enormous gift to all harmony singers in more ways than one, as they don't only fuel many a lucrative singing season, but many of them are also in the public domain, which means you don't owe anyone anything. I decided to quote more than a dozen different carols throughout the piece—reflecting the flavor of passing so many different houses with different songs in each—and in a way, it becomes a bit of a game to the clever listener, as they try to name them all (with rare exception, I only used neutral syllables, not lyrics, so they didn't crowd the core song). It's fun to listen and hear all the quotes, but of course, cleverness should never trump emotion, and throughout, my unwavering focus and purpose was to deliver all the feels.

Expert Level

So far, so good? We must admit, it might almost seem like mashups are easy at this point, or at least not all that challenging. If we've given you that impression, please forgive us: nothing could be further from the truth. Sometimes you start down a path to weave together two songs that are infuriatingly uncooperative. Rather than leave you with the impression that everything is easy for us, we'd rather take you on a journey down to Dante's Inferno, in hopes we all return.

Everyone has a tough day at work, and the same holds in the music industry. I got a call from Disney as they wanted my group DCappella to do a mashup of the biggest Disney songs about friendship, and they needed a thirty-second clip of it, including all three, so they could create a (hopefully) viral TikTok dance for two friends to do together.

Now, mashing two songs together is not a given, but there's often a way. When you get to three songs, you have an additional challenge as they all have to play nicely together. What were the songs they wanted?

» "Friend Like Me": key of D, 196 BPM (which can be cut in half to be 98)
» "You've Got a Friend in Me": E♭, 116 BPM
» "We're All in This Together": D♭, 116 BPM

All are in 4/4. The key doesn't seem to present a problem, and DCappella had seven members—soprano, mezzo, alto, tenor, baritone, bass, and vocal percussion—so I could bounce the melody part around as needed. No worries there.

But the different tempi were concerning—the distance between 116 and 98 is pretty large, as a difference of more than ten BPM usually means one has to be sped up or slowed down far too much to feel like the original song . . . and it's the feel of the original songs that presents the biggest problem.

"Friend Like Me" is a big band tune, with a swing feel, initially written to feel like a classic Cab Calloway showstopper. "You've Got a Friend in Me" is classic Randy Newman: a swampy Louisiana stride piano piece of Americana. "We're All in This Together" is underpinned with marching-band drums and a cheerleader chant. In short, the songs don't adhere one bit to a similar style or formula. Moreover, to lean heavily on one song's style would make the others in this case feel like fish out of water, as all three are so iconic and decidedly different from one another.

It became clear that I needed a different angle, so I went hunting on the pop charts. It was 2021, and the charts were filled with songs built on four-chord loops (as mentioned above), so I wondered if I could create a loop that could serve all three songs, reframing them all as a modern pop chart-topper. What did I find?

Doja Cat's "Say So" was everywhere, and unlike many of the current batch of four-chord loop songs, this chord progression was more interesting:

ii7   V11   Imaj7   VIadd9

Em7   G/A   Dmaj7   Badd9

I find the progression interesting for a few reasons. It's a ii-V-I progression, which you just don't hear in pop music very much anymore: it feels more like a Great American Songbook or showtune progression, as dominant chords that resolve to the tonic are increasingly rare nowadays. I also liked the number of extended chords, as it created a larger playing field; more notes in each chord means more melodic notes will find their way into the chord. And I liked the turnaround on the last chord, a secondary dominant with an added chord factor that would give us a little more character.

However, I didn't want to base this on just one song, so I kept hunting. Dua Lipa's "Don't Start Now" was a similarly huge hit, with a fantastic syncopated bass line jumping the octave often.

When I put the two together, I ended up with something like this:

I decided on the key of D, being the midpoint between the originals' three keys, and the Doja Cat key. As for the tempo, I was stuck. I needed to figure out the two songs that agreed, then I'd deal with the outlier. After much thought and singing through it all in my head, I felt the 116 BPM tempo that the two had in common was too slow, and even giving it the 3 BPM "a cappella bump" (songs often need to be sped up a tad when sung a cappella to feel the same as the original), they were still a bit slower than the fun, up-tempo pop tune I had in my head. Plus, the average tempo of top songs in 2020 was 122 BPM, which was the fastest in a decade. Perhaps people needed to feel happier while being stuck isolating at home, who knows. The 122 BPM just felt right.

So, let's see how one of the songs would lay in this groove:

Okay, that worked. It was clearly a different song, with a different feel, but the melody wasn't fighting this new vibe. I wanted to have the *Toy Story* song be the first in this groove because it shared the message from the very first line, and it felt like the right way to lead off. Plus, of the three songs, my sense was that it was the best-known across all generations.

A few issues arose. The first was that the B chord on the fourth measure meant a slight melodic tweak on the lyric "nice warm bed" at the end of the eighth measure would be needed to contend with the D♯. Since the chord progression would have been set up and looped a couple times by then, I thought we could get away with it:

The other was that the song didn't fit squarely in a four-chord loop, so at the end, for the last "you've got a friend in me," I would need an extra two measures. No problem—a little break from the loop would honestly make me happy:

You might notice that little "We're" in the top corner; indeed, I decided it was time to reestablish the loop, but to change the BGs a bit. The groove stayed the same, the bass line stayed the same, the chords and tempo stayed the same, but to give the song a bit of a nudge and make it grow, I changed the background texture and tossed the melody up into the soprano part.

The idea was that the song needed to keep churning forward. The brief two-measure pause notwithstanding, these songs would feel more like they were where they should have been—not shoved into a different chord progression and groove—if everyone's neck kept bobbing and the cycle continued. "We're All in This Together" has a very simple melody with just a few notes. The one twist was that the melody had to shift onto a D♯ in the fourth measure on the word "stars," but at that point, it was feeling more like a feature than a bug as it was elevating a lyric both in the first song and now here, that is served well by being underlined.

You may recognize the background voices' pattern: this is the Doja Cat feel, whereas the previous song was over a pattern reminiscent of Dua Lipa. Neither is exact: they're close enough to remind people, but not exact copies. How should you decide what to make the same and what should vary? It really depends on the overall groove, the melody that's going to lay in, and what feels right. Build the parts in your notation software or DAW and sing along. See what fits. Your taste is what makes your arrangements unique, and you should trust it, especially when you're out on a limb like this.

Now is perhaps a good time to point out that this might not be the only workable solution. You might have a better one in your head, and that's good. We want nothing more than for everyone reading this to far exceed what we're able to do as arrangers, and continue to bring new ideas and freshness to an ever-growing a cappella community. Moreover, this is neither science nor math (although elements of both apply to music), and as such, there is never only one correct way to arrange. If it doesn't work for your singers, it's not right, so change it until it does. A cappella is nothing more than people, and if those people aren't "feeling" a particular musical choice, make another one. What we do—what we always do—is make the best decision we can, and we continue to develop and grow as music and the world at large changes.

Speaking of changes, there aren't enough changes in a four-chord loop. That's just my personal taste, having been raised on the music of the 1960s, 1970s, and 1980s, a time when popular music embraced complex chord progressions (e.g., the band Steely Dan) and songs that broke the mold (e.g., "Bohemian Rhapsody"). I can't help wanting more variety, so rather than continue with the third song over the loop, I decided to toss in the chant from the beginning of "We're All in This Together," which feels like a bridge, or a B section if you consider this arrangement as an AABA form.

You'll notice I floated the third song—"Friend Like Me"—in over the chant. I decided on half-time, as with our faster tempo, it was just too quick otherwise; you couldn't get the lyrics out, and it felt frenetic. We wanted this to be fun, and never distract from the overall vibe by making people start to think about any aspect of any song not fitting. And I put it in the mezzo voice for good reason: I wanted to have all three melodies overlapping later in the song, and by establishing each with a specific voice, it would help people identify the songs with the singers and minimize changes so the overlapping/mashing would be as smooth as possible.

You'll see there was nothing for the baritone, who was free to ad-lib here and make it feel like a party. The vibe would be great, reminiscent of the original, and a nice, loose, freeing break from the cool groove we set up before. But was it enough to establish this third song? No, it was not. We needed something more.

What could we do? We knew the melody needed to be slower as the double-time tempo was too fast to get the words out. Did we want to slow things down mid-song? No, that was not in keeping with the feel of modern pop music. But we could create an introduction that felt out of time:

Friend Mashup

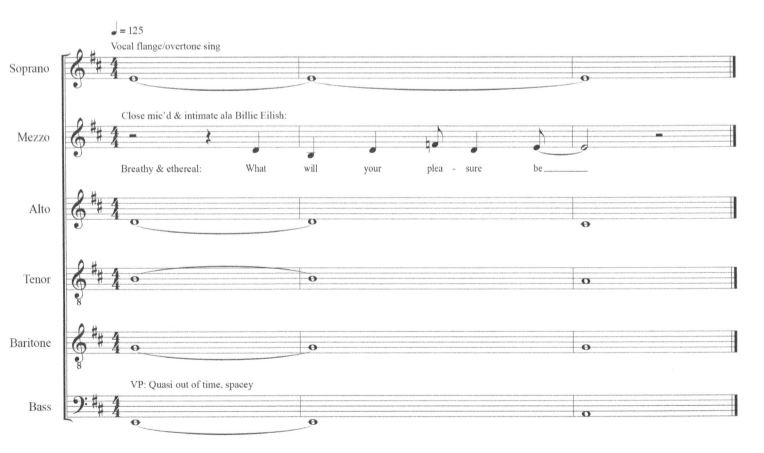

So, I started the song with some long-held notes and "Friend Like Me" floating over it. I liked starting with this part of the song's lyric . . .

What will your pleasure be? C'mon whisper what it is you want
You ain't never had a friend like me

. . . because the beginning of it worked perfectly over an ethereal vocal pad, and as soon as we hear "Friend Like Me," we can kick into a groove—just bass and percussion for a loop—then we were ready for verse one.

Rather than go with the harmonic rhythm of the core of the groove, which was one chord per measure, I decided to give it a half-time feel and change the chords half as often, so the opening eight measures had the four-chord pattern just once. This slower progression set up the chords, and made it feel like our singing the melody slowly at the top wasn't a fluke, but rather it was intentional. People don't need to know the order in which you're making decisions; the key is that it all flows naturally once you're done.

Speaking of flow, let's look at the form thus far:

» "Friend in Me" slow intro: eight measures
» Bass and drum groove: four measures
» "You've Got a Friend in Me" over groove with BGs: eight measures times three plus two measure addition
» "We're All in This Together" over groove with BGs: eight measures times two
» Together chant with "Friend in Me": eight measures

It was now time to weave all three songs together. Our goal was thirty seconds of all three overlapped, which we could do three times with a little cushion. Let's start with the bass and VP groove with just one song, then add a second and then the third. Which first? "We're All in This Together" felt right since we'd been living in that song for a while, chant included, then "You've Got a Friend in Me," then finally, the slow "Friend in Me":

Friend Mashup

The bass and alto were free and could ad-lib broad lines to help it all hold together, following their ears, so long as they didn't get in the way of the three melodies. Once all three parts were in the song, they could just keep repeating, vamp and fade, with the ad-libs providing some variety. Mission accomplished.

You can see the result on the internet—"Mickey's Friendship Mashup"— including the thirty-second TikTok excerpt. I must admit, when I watch the video, with all the clips of Mickey playing with his friends, and the happy faces of DCappella, it all seems so . . . easy. Effortless, even. Which is precisely what you want in an arrangement, especially a mashup: never let them see you sweat.

The problem is that once you make something seem easy, people just assume it to be so, and it wasn't long before I got another Disney mission, this time to weave together three different princess songs for the Princess Team. (Yes, Disney has a team of people who focus entirely on princesses. Are you surprised?) They gave me a couple of choices of three song groupings, and I decided on this one:

» "How Far I'll Go" from *Moana*
» "Into the Unknown" from *Frozen 2*
» "Almost There" from *The Princess and the Frog*

This was the most recent trio of songs they offered, and like the previous mashup, all of them are distinct in their structure:

» "How Far I'll Go": 83 BPM, E major, with a characteristically wordy Lin-Manuel Miranda lyric
» "Into the Unknown": 145 BPM, B♭ minor, a soaring and haunting feel by the Lopezes
» "Almost There": 79 BPM, C major, another Randy Newman composition, this one with a Dixieland flavor

However, to make things even more complicated, they introduced an additional element: they had recently commissioned pop star Brandy to write a song for this Princess campaign called "Starting Now," and they wanted that song featured alongside the other three. So, in essence, it was to be a four-song mashup, with one of the songs new and relatively unknown. I don't mention this to disparage Brandy at all—it's a fine song—but rather, I want to point out that you don't have as much flexibility when mashing up a song that's new and/or relatively unknown. If you don't present large enough pieces of it in a context in which it can be appreciated as itself, distinct and clear, it's going to seem like an unfamiliar and disjointed collection of notes and lyrics.

So, what are the stats for "Starting Now"? G major, 125 BPM, straight-ahead modern pop song with a four-chord loop:

vi	IV	I	V
Em	C	G	D

Before "Mickey's Friendship Mashup," I might have thought the four songs impossible to interweave, but now I see this additional song and its four-bar loop as a lifeline, the glue that will potentially tie together the other songs, if none have to be bent too far to make it work.

Knowing there was a music video to be made, and knowing the theme was princesses, I wanted to assign one song to each of DCappella's three female singers:

» "How Far I'll Go" = soprano
» "Into the Unknown" = mezzo
» "Almost There" = alto

Like in the previous mashup, this would give us an opportunity to create some consistency and clarity, with one voice representing one song throughout. But then who would sing the fourth song, "Starting Now"? I would give it to the baritone, so the other three parts could remain consistent. Plus, the lyric was written largely in the third person, so it didn't feel like it had to be a woman singing it:

Starting now, there's no room left for wondering
Got a new vision of yourself, and she's who you wanna be

Now, that was the easy part. The challenge began when we started to look at each song, and what we could realistically use. None of the princess songs was short and sweet; they all took some time to develop, with choruses that ranged rather than repeated in an easy way. The good news was that they were all big Disney movies, and being presented by Disney, the people who were listening would be those who knew at least one of the songs well, if not all three. But they wouldn't know the new Brandy song.

So, I decided that instead of developing a piece of each song initially, I would make this mashup be a pastiche, featuring sections of our three iconic princess songs, built upon this new four-chord pop song. Where should we start? The chorus, of course, being the most important part of any song.

Following the Ten Step Method laid out in our first book, *A Cappella Arranging*, I listened to the songs repeatedly, got sheet music and midi files ready, skipped the overall form for now as I knew there would be questions I could answer more easily later, and dove into the chorus, laying out the melody. But now the melody was in the baritone voice. Plus, some of the ranges of the original songs were very high (especially "Into the Unknown"), so I decided to drop the song a fifth, down to C major:

vi	IV	I	V
Am	F	C	G

This put the baritone in a nice range, and the group's bass had low Cs for days, so the song could have a powerful low tonic note every third measure. I wrote the melody in the baritone line, then wrote in the bass line. The two held together well, but we were just getting started. Now I needed snippets, well-known pieces of the three princess songs that would play nicely together, not sit on top of each other too much, and land on chord factors needed to flesh out the overall harmonic progression, knowing I only had one additional voice—the tenor—to provide one more piece of the puzzle.

I started with the alto, and the start of her chorus fit nicely. The melody in the original sat on the sixth of the key, as the chord progression chromatically descended beneath it, whereas here it just reinforced the fact that the chord was, in fact, vi, followed by IV. A bit of good luck. Then the next line traced out an A minor triad landing on a D; if we think of the A as a passing note, the C and E land perfectly over the C chord, and the melody resolves down to a D over the G chord. So far, so good. Those three sounded good together.

Next up, let's look at "Into the Unknown." The chorus moved all over the place, climbing higher and higher, and it would likely have been distracting if we'd dropped it in here, so let's look at the first verse. It weaved diatonically around the tonic, which, when we placed it in the key of C, gave us a note that fit well into the first three chords, but then it moved down to an A in the fourth measure, which as an add9 over the G chord should have been okay if we got the other chord factors covered convincingly enough.

"How Far I'll Go" remained, and we definitely couldn't just start at the beginning of the chorus, as the other three songs were already crowding that space. We needed a line that would start in the second measure, and it was the pre-chorus that provided us with "Every turn I take, every trail I track," which worked well lyrically, underscoring the theme of all four songs: progress through perseverance. It played primarily between the A and C, which would work well over the bass F. Then when we got to measure 4 it was outlining G, A, and D, which was fine over the G chord, a little more of the add9 than I ideally wanted, but they didn't fight each other.

Where did that leave us with the tenor line? Clearly what we needed was just that: a line, so I wrote in a slow-moving half-note figure that gave some cohesiveness to the other parts, remaining diatonic. At this point, my writing was a bit of trial and error, looking for something singable that would sound good with the other parts. You can lean into your music theory knowledge all you want, but in the end, it has to sound good, and with so much going on—four songs overlapped—your ear is exactly what you should trust to make sure it all comes together, just like a chef putting the final touches on a meal. The end result:

Princess Mashup:
How Far I'll Go, Into the Unknown, Almost There & Starting Now

Tackling the second half of the chorus meant completing the expectation we'd set up, except where it didn't work, which was in a few places.

Most importantly, the "Starting Now" melody alone in the baritone felt a bit unimpressive by the end of the chorus. We wanted to really announce this new song, leaning into it rather than feeling like we're apologizing for it. Also, if the princesses were all going to be doing their own thing through most of the arrangement, it would've been nice to have had a point at which they convened and sang together. So, the two measures of the chorus was just the place, putting a powerful button there, and giving our baritone the freedom to toss an ad-lib over their held chords on "Now."

The alto could restate "Almost There," and it worked just as it did the first time, an A over an A minor chord. The soprano "How Far I'll Go" pre-chorus melody did work, although it was a tight fit to get into the "Starting Now" harmony, and she had time to breathe in the previous measure. But the mezzo line just didn't work, as the original melody, "There's a thousand reasons I should go about my day," jumped around too much, and it didn't dovetail well into the three-part harmony, so I went looking and decided to grab the haunting "ah" hook that started and reoccurred throughout the song, a short musical figure that could easily be inserted without feeling out of place. Plus it gave us a C over that A minor chord, which we needed. And the tenor created some consistency and unity, but repeating the same figure. Put it together and we had this:

I'll admit, it looks like a mess on the page, out of context. But I learned an important lesson when making *Pitch Perfect*, which is that visuals can help contextualize song fragments and quotes that would otherwise feel too frenetic and disjointed. I knew there would be a video with lots of princess clips that would sell the idea of all these princess themes happening concurrently, as well as closeups of the singers on their different melodies to help listeners isolate and contextualize. Moreover, having control of the final mix, I knew we could put the different songs in different parts of the stereo space so they were not sitting right on top of each other.

I wouldn't have arranged this mashup this way if it had been for a collegiate group that liked Disney songs and was primarily going to sing it live, as it's nearly impossible to get all of the levels, stereo placement, EQ, and clarity just right in a live environment, plus the audience wouldn't have had their focus so clearly directed as happens on a screen with edits. It's always essential to know your audience, your singers, and how the song will be presented. A studio recording and professional multi-camera, well-edited video is a world away from an amateur live performance, and when you have it, take advantage of it.

As forgiving as this medium is, it was still a lot of information, and we needed to carefully build up to all four songs happening concurrently. Also, we wanted to establish that the song would be a pastiche, so we wanted to introduce little hooks from each of our princesses, ones that would also underscore the overall message of progress and perseverance the princess campaign was focusing on.

Before action comes contemplation, so I decided to look at the first few lines of "How Far I'll Go":

I've been staring at the edge of the water, 'long as I can remember
Never really knowing why

And the chorus:

See the line where the sky meets the sea?
It calls me, and no one knows how far it goes

To find the right lyric snippets. I settled on "I've been staring" and "It calls me," adding an echo after each line to underscore them and establish a mood. The BGs would hold long, flanging notes to focus all attention on the lyric.

So far, so good. Now it was time to introduce the other two songs, and rather than go one at a time, to get us ready for all four at once, I decided upon layering the other two. But what lyrics would make the most sense? There's a line in "Almost There" that's perfect: "I know exactly where I'm going," and I put the title phrase of "Into the Unknown" between them, building the tension and anticipation lyrically as well as musically. The BGs here would start to establish the tone and feel of the Brandy song, continuing the chord progression.

From the first measures quoting Moana through this duet, plus a little additional build, we arrived at our chorus at around the :38 mark, and it felt like an arrival as the bass line went from whole notes to a syncopated pattern, the vocal percussion kicked into a full groove, and the baritone sang the full chorus melody (as opposed to short lyrical fragments). Where should we go from here?

My instinct told me we needed a little more of the quoted princess songs, so the focus could move to each of them for a little while, making more complete statements before returning inevitably to the chorus, which we wanted to restate rather than change, as there was plenty going on, and each time you listen, you can focus on a different layer. My intention was to make this feel like a second verse, in that it was still part of the same song, a continuation of the idea we'd established.

To do this, I looked for melodic lines and lyrical statements that would work over the chord progression, and ideally work together. Of the three songs, "How Far I'll Go" was the most similar in style and form to "Starting Now," so I grabbed the chorus, dropped it over the continuing chord progression where it fit nicely, and built around it: mezzo echoing, bass line wanted to simplify from the chorus but not go all the way back to whole notes, so I settled on steady quarters, and the other parts outlined chords with a vocal slide on "hoo." Once I put all that in place, it felt like it had stepped down from four melodies at once a bit too much, so I grabbed the "trials and tribulations" lyric from "Almost There," and we had the beginning of a second verse.

Now it was time to move to a second song. We've quoted a little "Almost There," so I remained there, and since my instinct definitely yearned for some departure from the loop, I decided to lean into the Randy Newman chords for a moment, under "closer and closer every day," doubling down on the character of that song.

I'm not sure younger arrangers are as compelled to depart from the loop, and they should follow their instincts just as I followed mine. Knowing we were going to have clips of various Disney movies, I knew leaning into one of the original songs a bit wouldn't disrupt the feel or flavor of our overall vibe at this point.

Then we were back to the chorus, which at this point, even though it was the same on paper, would sound and feel a bit different as we were more accustomed to the sound of this song and many layers, so listeners' ears could start to dig into the various melodic layers more. They wanted a full length song, so we'd want another chorus after this one, but two of them back to back felt too staid, too boring to me: I wanted some kind of a release, a bridge, a departure before returning. We hadn't spent as much time with "Into the Unknown," a song with many powerful passages, so I decided to lean into one, completely changing the feel for a few measures between chorus 2 and 3:

This was quite a departure as the texture changed, the song leaned on powerful off-beats, there was the first three-part harmony since the chorus ended, and the whole song announced a complete change, almost a wakeup alarm before returning back to the chorus one last time. This energy helped to propel the last chorus to a higher level, which benefitted the song form.

Then, once we'd had our third chorus, how should we end? I didn't want a vamp and fade; we'd already heard this chorus three times. I also didn't think we needed to introduce something else entirely new. What felt most comfortable was to bookend the song, returning to the calming, ethereal vibe of the beginning. The guys dropped back to whole notes, and the soprano returned to the opening "I've been staring/It calls me" with echoes. However, I gave the mezzo a line that underscored the increased empowerment of Disney princesses—"as I feel my power grow"—and we ended with the alto singing, "now things for sure are goin' my way," a suitably uplifting line that signaled the progress wasn't finished.

You can find the DCappella "Starting Now" mashup online, as well. The video is fun to watch—with clips of various Disney princesses from the past eighty years of classic Disney movies, alongside DCappella performing, as well as a distracting amount of shiny lip gloss.

So, at this point, we've given you several ways you can figure out how to make multiple songs work together, but by no means are our examples comprehensive. There's an expression in American football when talking about defenses: "Bend, don't break," which is to say you can give up some yardage, just don't let the other team in your end zone, where they can gain points. By the same token, you're going to find yourself needing to push tempi to the edge (be it fast or slow), wrestle melody lines to work over chords that don't want to play nice, and find ways to make moments work. Just remember that it's what you already do as an arranger; it's just a bit more of a challenge since you're having to fit square pegs in round holes. There is usually a solution, somehow, and when you find it, you'll feel the well-deserved exhilaration of a victor.

Remember that J. S. Bach was able to write a new chorale every Sunday, finding a way to make just four parts work together in new ways, and he said of the practice that it was within constraints that true creativity came to life. Then again, he was able to improvise four-part fugues, so if you're like us—mere mortals—and the songs just aren't working together, sleep on it and see if your subconscious works out the problem as you do. If you're still unable, don't blame yourself; just remember that not every food works as an ice cream topping and pick a new pairing.

Getting Ideas

When you talk about mashups, unless you're talking to a fellow a cappella singer, they're probably not thinking a cappella; they're thinking DJ remixes, where most mashups are created and shared. If you're looking for some inspiration and clever ideas, check out the BEST OF THE BOOTIES series, which you can find in CD form or online. DJs would send in remixes as they made them, and periodically the best would be compiled into a recording as well as enjoyed live at clubs around the United States. "Never Gonna Wake You Up" is a good example of one, with the beat from one song, the melody from another, and the background hook from a third.

If you'd like to hear some astounding mashing up, look for DJ Earworm's annual release mashing up the top-twenty biggest songs of the year. He ends up chopping the songs into such small pieces you have to concentrate to hear all twenty, an exercise in listening for all the signature elements of popular songs, not just the melodies and hooks.

One thing to remember when you're listening to and analyzing DJ remixes is that they're using original recordings (or very close copies of them), and as such, they're able to lean on elements that we can't as a cappella arrangers: the sound of the original lead singer's voice, the actual guitar riff, the production choices that make a specific piano part stand out, and so on. When dissecting and recombining songs in a cappella, we're not using elements of an original recording, but rather vocal re-creations of them, which in some ways is easier (we don't have to make different recordings sound good together when they are recorded in different eras and keys), and in some ways it is harder (we can't rely on a snippet of a track to be immediately identified as a piece of a song; we need longer and clearer sections). If this point isn't clear, consider creating a DJ Earworm–esque year-end best of the top-twenty songs. You can't just use a single element, such as one chord from a song to represent/remind people of a song (e.g., the last chord of "A Day in the Life" by the Beatles). If you hear the original recording, you'll recognize it as a unique sound. But when sung, it's just a chord.

Sure, a mashup is still technically a mashup if you use different elements from different songs, but if the audience isn't coming with you on the journey, if they can't hear the magic of the songs woven together, then you've made a rabbit disappear that no one saw in the first place. Make sure the choices you're making invite the audience to hear how and when the songs intersect, ideally in a way that's both compelling and artistically satisfying, without taking away from the overall song's emotional impact. It's a fine line to walk—too much focus on showing your work and you're showing off, too little and the audience can't tell it's a mashup. What's the right amount? That's something we can't answer, as it will depend on your audience and the way in which the song is presented. Whatever your choices, never lose sight of the fact that all music is, at its best, a powerful emotional transference from performer to audience, and ultimately it's better to have some miss the fact that you've created a mashup than have some walk away feeling nothing.

CHAPTER 16

Reimagining a Song

There are many terms for this: some people call it "flipping" a song; others call it "restyling" or even "transforming." Whatever the nomenclature, there is often a strong desire within arrangers to find a cool new context or style for a song. When Earth Wind & Fire covered the Beatles' "Got to Get You into My Life," they made the song their own, giving it a 1970s R&B groove that breathed new life into the classic. And Joe Cocker's version of the Beatles' "With a Little Help from My Friends" might possibly be pop music's most successful transformation, from lilting pop song to grinding power anthem.

When a group performs their own version of someone else's song, it's referred to as a "cover." There are some cover versions of songs that are so successful you don't even realize there was an earlier version. Dolly Parton wrote and performed "I Will Always Love You" almost two decades before Whitney Houston made it the biggest song of the early 1990s, and it sat at number one on the Billboard Hot 100 for a record-breaking fourteen weeks. Neil Diamond's version of his song "Red Red Wine" was a melancholy ballad before UB40 made it a bouncy reggae hit. Soft Cell turned the original R&B version of "Tainted Love" by Gloria Jones into a 1980s synth-pop anthem. Johnny Cash added mariachi horns to Anita Carter's "Ring of Fire," and Aretha Franklin's best-known song "Respect" was originally Otis Redding's. The list goes on and on, but the message is clear: in many a great song lies an even greater song, if only we arrangers can unlock it.

When an artist first records an original song, it's brand-new. It's known to no one, and it hasn't yet had the benefit of years—or decades—of collective listening, for millions of ears and minds and hearts to mine all the richness it may contain. Put another way: if the song was software, the first recording is version 1.0. Many a song can be altered, customized, or even improved, with future upgrades.

But how?

Bring the Song to the Group

This was the music staff's mantra on *The Sing-Off*, as week after week, groups were assigned new songs, and the temptation was there to have the group simply "vocally translate" the song to voices and be done with it. This usually resulted in a group going home. The best moments from the show were when a group found the best way to take a song and make it their own, matching their style and personality.

To do this, you can start by taking inventory of the group you're arranging for: the people, the character, the ranges, skills, sounds . . . everything. Then think about how you might lean into some aspect of the group's greatness, their unique identity and sound—a tenor's high range, an alto's ability to sing a heartbreaking ballad—by taking the song in a different direction.

Get to Know the Song

Get to know the song deeply, and think about how you can emphasize a song's greatest assets. Let's be honest: not every chord or every lyric is genius, even within great songs. There's almost always room for improvement, and in a way, that's exactly what we're doing as arrangers. We decide which sections get more focus and which are cut, which lyrics get emphasized and repeated and which are cast aside. Chords can be reharmonized, melodies reshaped. Imagine you were in a songwriting session before the song was released. What changes would you have suggested?

Message and Meaning

As time passes, and the present becomes the past, message and meaning can change, from the way sentiments are expressed, to social perception and context. When Annie Lennox recorded "Keep Young and Beautiful" on her debut solo album *Diva*, she decided to not change a thing about the original lyric:

> Keep young and beautiful, it's your duty to be beautiful
> Keep young, beautiful, if you want to be loved

This lyric is, to put it bluntly, an abhorrent and anachronistic sexist statement reducing women to their appearance and age. The first line of the song wastes no time making this point:

> What's cute about a little cutie?
> It's her beauty, not brains

Her choice to record this song, without changing it, made and still makes a powerful statement about sexism and perception in modern society. We mention this song to give an obvious example of the simple reality: society changes, and a song's lyric and meaning therefore gets re-contextualized as time passes. This song may have been perceived as irony and social criticism at the time. Today, it still may be perceived that way . . . or it may be so offensive on its face that no one cares about the spirit in which it may be presented. And let's not forget, it matters who sings it. Sung by a woman, this song may be commentary or satire. Sung by a man, and it's straight-up misogynistic.

This is something you need to be aware of, as we often experience a song as we first heard it, and it is when listening to a song with younger listeners that we're able to hear it as they hear it, understand it as they understand it.

There is no precise guide to considering a song's social context, as societies differ from region to region, and societal goalposts rapidly shift, so we simply offer this advice: be aware, be mindful, and when in doubt, find some trusted people whom you can consult and discuss freely as to whether there appears to be anything questionable or problematic. Great music makes a statement; we're just recommending you make sure that the statement you're planning to make will be received as you intend it.

Experimentation Is Your Friend

Don't expect to simply have brilliant ideas every time you dive into a new project. Sometimes a wrong note in a close harmony arrangement ends up being something you like better. Think about all the different parameters of music you can play with—for instance: tempo, texture, timbre, tessitura, and plenty of others that don't start with the letter "t"—and splash around. Lest you feel this is a kind of cheating or sloppy work, no one needs to know your process, and moreover, it's not the way you come upon the ideas that's a measure of your talent; it's your ability to identify and utilize those ideas in an effective way that will be your measure (pun intended).

>> *Deke Says: I can't help but wonder if some of Gene Puerling's most unusual chord choices were stumbled on this way, since he told me that's exactly what he did sometimes. I initially thought he was being coy, but now it strikes me as a good strategy.*

Turn on the Radio

Popular music is forever changing, year after year, as the same words and same notes get recombined into new sounds and styles, be it disco beats in current pop tunes, or samples of classic R&B tracks that form the foundation of something new. Our minds view art and culture in reference to everything we've experienced, so it makes sense that borrowing from things that have been created—both old and new—is an excellent kernel upon which your new work can be based.

Practice Makes Perfect

Creativity isn't a divine, ephemeral spirit; it's a muscle, improved with regular use. Billy Joel and Stevie Wonder and Randy Newman became legendary songwriters by sitting down in front of the piano every day for years, forcing themselves to write a song. The more you do it, the better you'll get, and the more you'll naturally understand what changing tempo will do, what changing keys will do, what changing style will do, and so on. You will start to be able to hear these changes in your head and forecast which will work better without spending time sketching it out.

Reimagining a song is as much art as it is science. It's not one single technique, but rather, it draws on all your available skill sets and personal experiences. As such, this chapter won't be a discussion of individual techniques, but rather an anecdotal analysis of the process behind our reimagined arrangements: the inspiration (or direction), the problems, the solutions, and the creative techniques and decisions that got us there. Put another way, this chapter isn't a "How-To," but rather a "How We Did It." Let's dive in.

Updating a Classic: "The Most Wonderful Time of the Year" (Deke)

My work with DCappella has been a joy, as the Disney Music Group has given me free rein to do whatever I'd like to modernize classic Disney songs "so long as it works." The key to making it work is to lean into aspects of the song that you love and think will translate well into a current or recent pop idiom, and find a way to alter other elements without losing the fundamental beloved characteristics of the song. People want to smile in recognition when they hear it, which won't happen if enough of the original isn't retained, or the way in which you've changed the song goes "against the grain," feeling forced rather than feeling like a natural choice.

One arrangement I was asked to do for DCappella was not a Disney song at all, but rather a holiday classic: "The Most Wonderful Time of the Year," made popular by Andy Williams and many others. The song is very well-known, and it has been used in commercials, as well. No matter what version of the song I hear, it's always the same lilting, 3/4 time signature. The song has also been done a cappella, most notably by Pentatonix, in an arrangement very reminiscent of the original, and the very last thing you want to do with an a cappella group looking to have their own versions of a cappella songs is to do anything like a PTX version, as it will be seen as derivative.

So, I needed to find a way to take a song that was always done the same way and do it very differently, modernizing it in the same stroke. My first thought was that I needed to find a way to make it work in 4/4, as pretty much every song that's been on the pop charts in the past decade has been in 4/4. So, as I recommend to others: listen to the radio, go looking for recent pop hits, and see if anything can provide inspiration and direction.

I had to look no further than the number-one slot. Harry Styles's hit song "As It Was" was the biggest song of 2022. It's not a Christmas song, nor does it have a warm and fuzzy vibe, but it does have drive and a very compelling beat that's stripped right out of the 1980s (akin to A-ha's "Take on Me"). The lyrics of the song are a bit of a downer, but the song production and timbre is uplifting, and that's what I was interested in.

In this case, it was not the chorus itself that I wanted to start with, but a new figure for the song—an introduction that could serve as interlude/post-chorus between each section. Why? Well, the original was in AABA form, and each section was rather long. Not a problem for a holiday song, but I wanted to create a sound, a vibe, and a hooky musical passage that people could hear and hang on to, before launching into the core of the song to establish the 4/4 feel and overall flavor. When moving a song far away from its original mooring, it's sometimes a good idea to really establish the new sonic world before casting the new melody and harmony into it. To start too quickly into the meat of a song that's been changed significantly can be disorienting to a listener, as they are used to hearing it a certain way, and you want them to be tapping their toes and humming along with your musical vision, then introduce the song they know, which instead of being disorienting, can bring a smile. Sell them on the groove first: then give them the surprise.

So, what was the new musical world I was creating? It was a four-chord loop, eight-measure pattern. I would take a couple lyrics from the original and weave them into a texture that was basically an entirely new song of my own creation:

At this point in the arranging process, I wasn't arranging; I was composing. I was creating something completely new and unique, inspired by a modern pop song, that was to be the bed of an arrangement. And so, what was once entirely mine was now the bed for this Christmas classic:

It's the Most Wonderful Time of the Year

The ii-V-I progression, which comprised the first three of four chords in my four-chord loop, was, of course, chosen to be a comfortable music bed for that exact melodic line. Then, since we had a compelling texture that had been well-established, we could continue to "spin it out" to finish the rest of the A section. Here's a bit from later on:

I kept the bass line, soprano line, and VP on the same figure, but for a little variety, I went with an echo, one measure behind, in the mezzo and bari lines. When panned in stereo space, it sounded great.

Between the two A sections, I added in the eight-measure loop again, our baseline for the song, a return to the groove that felt like a modern pop song built on a four-chord loop. We had to depart to follow the original's harmonic progression as it was essential to the melodic shape, so returning to this as our home base returned the song to feeling like a modern pop hit before venturing into the second A section.

Then it was time for the B section, and my ear wanted a break from this groove. Modern pop songs would move into a rap, but this song was too melodic, and that might have felt like a send-up/parody, and that was not what we wanted, so we needed to keep the melody . . . but what about a release in the form of a half-time feel, giving the melody to the background voices in three-part harmony? Slow down the drum groove and simplify the bass line:

Then, after we were through the B section, our original groove would feel fresh again once we returned, which was exactly the point of a bridge. And that was pretty much the arrangement, as once we returned to our A section, we knew what we would do—interpolating between our intro figure and the A section.

The coda, like in modern pop songs, was, indeed, that intro figure again. I like to leave a voice free—in this case, the lead vocalist—so they can ad-lib, providing some variety to what can feel very repetitious to my ears, but to modern sensibilities is exactly right. Finding the "Venn diagram overlap" between what I like and what modern ears are used to can sometimes be challenging, but I know that when I find it, I'm creating something that is compelling to multiple generations and tastes. Ideally, you'll never have to declare finished an arrangement that you know will be effective yet you don't particularly like; always strive to be appropriate to both the client and the audience's needs, while remaining compelling to your own ear.

Fast to Slow: "Overkill" (Dylan)

When FreePlay travels to a new country, we love to take a well-known song from that area and "give it back" to the audience there: it's a great way to tip our hat to audiences around the world. Often, we like to offer a unique spin on the piece as an added bonus.

I'm a child of the 1980s, and one of my favorite bands from that era is the Australian band Men at Work. As usual, when choosing a song to transform, we decided to move past the most obvious choices, such as "Down Under" and "Who Can It Be Now?" (well, mostly . . . see below!), and we settled on "Overkill," a song well-known enough to be familiar to many audiences, but not the first song that comes to mind, nor something overdone.

"Overkill" also comes with an interesting built-in contradiction. Like many early 1980s rock/pop songs, it has a peppy tempo, 140 BPM, driven by bouncing, eighth-note guitars and a rapid vocal delivery. But the lyrics defy the musical setting: they're about anxiety, loneliness, and alienation. It's as if someone put the wrong song to the lyrics.

As mentioned earlier, an arranger can often dig deep into a song and pull out elements—musical, artistic, and emotional—that weren't as obvious in the original version. This is the approach we took with "Overkill." We started with the lyrics: melancholy, dark, and somber, and we decided to create a musical setting that fit. The original chipper 140 BPM was brought down significantly to a languid, reflective 102 BPM (or 56 BPM at half-time feel, as notated). To create a sense of suspension and groundlessness, there's no solid backbeat at the beginning, and no clear harmonic outline. Only this:

Overkill

Colin Hay

This is a live-looping arrangement, so the parts come in one at a time—alto, tenor, then soprano—and it takes a while for the parts to be heard as a cohesive structure. More importantly, the bass line, which contextualizes the guitar parts above, is held back: it doesn't come in until the second half of the verse, keeping the whole piece unmoored until then.

The lead is divided between the two singers, who stand on opposite sides of the stage, not looking at each other. In a song about loneliness and separation, each singer appears unaware of the other. After splitting the first two verses, it is only in the third verse that the singers finally sing to each other, sharing their pain, in unison:

> I can't get to sleep: I think about the implications
> Of diving in too deep, and possibly the complications

The chorus is sung three times in the song, and being a live-looping arrangement, it is layered each time:

» First chorus: sung together, in harmony (staves two and four).
» Second chorus: bass line is added, as well as a passing inner part, quoting another famous Men at Work song, "Who Can It Be Now?" (staves three and six).
» Third chorus: harmonies are thickened, as well as an additional responsive line (staves one and five).

The result, particularly in the third chorus, adds complex harmonic clusters to create tension and dramatic effect. The minor sixth on the second bar is one of the saddest and most wistful sonorities, and the added suspension over the V major chord on the third bar blurs any optimism a good-old dominant chord normally offers.

The final line of the chorus is then stretched into an extended coda in the form of a two-bar loop. The lyrics about ghosts are given a wispy, ethereal feeling utilizing polyphony with staggered entries and trailing lines, in this order:

» Lead vocals, in harmony (from first chorus: staves five and six).
» Alto 1 and bass, filling out the chords. The bass entry is staggered, entering one beat later (from second chorus: staves three and nine).
» Baritone and soprano 1, adding more harmonic depth (staves one and eight).
» Alto 2 and tenor countermelody (staves four and seven).
» Tenor countermelody continues, and melody sung up the octave (soprano staff two).
» One pass with the lyrics whispered.

You can almost hear the ghosts flying around the room.

Once these are established, the two singers improvise: long, wailing, haunted lines swirling around each other. The other parts fade out slowly, leaving the two singers, again at opposite sides of the stage, once again alone, singing:

Ghosts appear, and fade away . . .

The up-tempo rock song is long gone, supplanted by a musical setting that amplifies, rather than obscures, the beautiful and tragic lyrics.

Normally a "live" arrangement may be considerably embellished for a studio version: we were so happy with this arrangement that, when it came time to record, we didn't change a single part. We added three additional elements: more whisper tracks and breathy "wind noise" throughout, a lofi, heartbeat-sounding kick drum, and a subtle backbeat, articulated as a short gasp, to heighten the anxiety ever-present in the lyrics.

Fast to Slow: "If I Only Had a Brain" (Deke)

As a freshman at the New England Conservatory as well as Tufts, not yet a member of the Beelzebubs, I'd spend many a long night waiting for everyone to leave the main building, and then I'd break into the theater so I could pound on the grand piano in the wee hours of the morning singing the Great American Songbook at the top of my lungs. Excellent endorphins—I highly recommend it. While singing through these songs, I'd often play around and see if I could spin a song in a new way, and one I hit upon and loved was the Scarecrow's song "If I Only Had a Brain" from *The Wizard of Oz*, which works beautifully as a ballad—so beautifully, in fact, that when I heard it on a Harry Connick Jr. album the same way almost two decades later, I nodded in agreement while quickly dismissing the obvious hubris-laden thought that he'd had a secret recorder in my collegiate sessions. The song has a fundamental melancholy about it, and the harmonic language holds up well when morphed from an oom-pah into a languid piano ballad. Years later, I turned it into an a cappella arrangement, as I am wont to do. First, I set up a groove:

If I Only Had A Brain / Heart

To establish this feel, I would set up a bit more of a groove than I'd use in the verse, which made for a nice contrast as an interlude between the mellower, solo-driven sections:

You'll notice it's no longer "If I Only Had a Brain," but the Tin Man's "If I Only Had a Heart," and now it's a female solo, not for an aspiring young collegiate second tenor who over-sings at 2 a.m. Some ideas can be improved upon with age and wisdom. One more peek at later in the song:

I built the song so there was a nice long scat solo (or vocal instrumental, if you dare), and then when we come back to the head again, I used the intro chords and feel to drive the last A section, giving it more momentum.

These examples are merely to help whet your appetite for your own journey into the classics, late at night, ideally in an empty building. Happy hunting.

Finding a New Spin: "Heigh-Ho" (Deke)

Some Disney songs are very short. The meat of the song "Heigh-Ho" in the original *Snow White* is about a minute in length. It's a lovely moment as the seven dwarves are marching home from work, whistling and chanting, but it's hardly a meal—more of an appetizer. The mission from the Disney Music Group was to create a full pop song from this tune, so not only did I need to find a style that would work, I'd need to find a way to stretch it to fill three minutes.

What musical forms have very few lyrics? Dance tunes. Sometimes there's only a line or two declared over an insistent four-on-the-floor beat, and it's repeated over and over again. But what dance style should I choose for this tune? A modern dance style? Late 1970s disco, which underpins so much modern pop music? I suppose any of these would have worked, but for some reason, I got an idea that stuck with me: early 1990s dance music *à la* C&C Music Factory.

That was an iconic period for dance music, a time when samples and technology wove hooks over drum machines with a powerful lead vocal wailing over it all.

"Heigh-ho, Heigh-ho, it's off to work we go" (or "home from work we go") is about all you need to make this style of music work, as songs like "Gonna Make You Sweat (Everybody Dance Now)" relied on one simple, repeated lyrical hook, or Black Box's "Everybody Everybody," Technotronic's "Pump Up the Jam," and Marky Mark and the Funky Bunch's "Good Vibrations." Less is more.

But before we get to the wailing hook, let's see if we can make the core of the song work. I wanted to go for a bit of a more modern dance texture here, so I had the harmonic parts on off-beats, replicating heavy sidechain compression. Knowing there would be reverb and each note would carry over, rather than have the singers sing every eighth and hit the off-beats harder, I just had them focus on the off-beats:

Heigh Ho

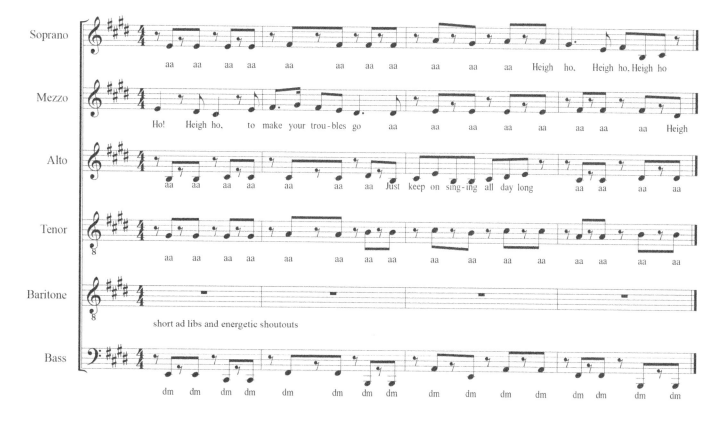

Once we were done with it in the studio, over a heavy beat, it sounded great. Also, as you can see, I had the melody jump between the three female voices, which changes the vocal color throughout the line. Why? I'm not sure I know consciously: it just felt right. Maybe it's because I wanted to make it somehow different, maybe it's because the melody when sung by one person feels a bit wooden or old-timey, but when you bounce it between voices, it has more motion, or maybe I just wanted to try something new. I can't think of the last time I split up a melodic line like that, less than a measure before jumping to another voice. It's usually a terrible idea, but here it works, and I like to try something new in every arrangement if I can. I'm never finished experimenting.

Now it was time to make sure the song's signature wailing could work. That was all going to be ad-libbed, but was there a place where you could cut a female vocalist free to go over the top? Absolutely, over the original time you hear the lyric "Heigh-ho" when the dwarves first sing it: an octave leap, then a long-held note.

It's ultimately unsatisfying looking at notation for this, as the most important factor—that wailing—isn't notated. However, it can't be; it shouldn't be. The best vocal performance you're going to get for that will be improvised, and if you have the singers, we highly urge you to leave some space for them to improvise in arrangements where it's appropriate.

By the way, you can hear a little bit of the original's character in this, the whistling figure in the mezzo line. It's stylized, staccato, and different from the original recording, but whistling is such a representative and iconic element in the original, I felt I had to weave it in somewhere.

Another reason I liked the early 1990s pop-dance style is that those songs often feature a rap, something I wanted to use, as "Heigh-ho" also has a little-remembered verse that happens a couple minutes earlier in the film:

> We dig dig dig dig dig dig dig in our mine the whole day through
> To dig dig dig dig dig dig dig is what we really like to do

In particular, the style of rap from 1990s pop-dance was often very emphatic, yet spoken rather low in the male register: think Freedom Williams from C&C Music Factory, or even, dare I say it, Vanilla Ice in "Ice Ice Baby." "Heigh-Ho" was written back in 1937, almost a century ago, and the melody isn't anywhere approaching modern. I've taken melodies and reworked them with a rhythmic tweak here and a melodic nudge there to approximate something from another decade, but this melody is such a heavy lift, why not just remove it altogether? So many of DCappella's songs are melodic; this is a chance to reach for something very different.

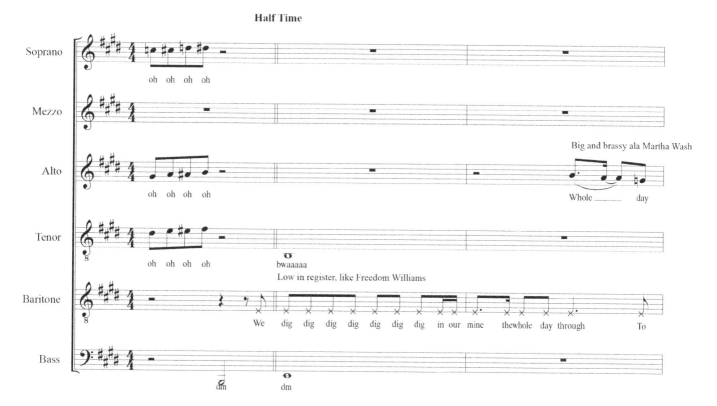

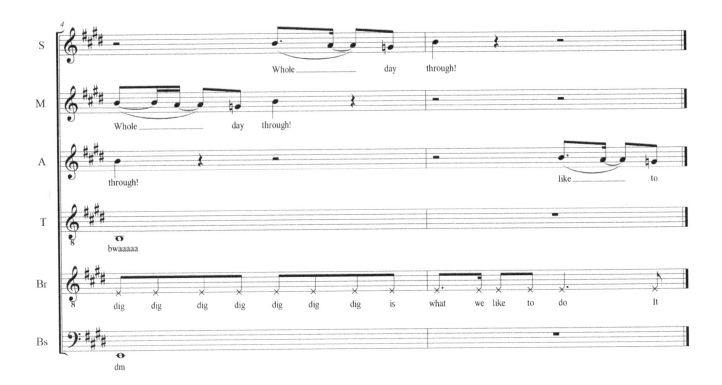

And so on. There are other figures in this song, such as the "dig! dig!" chant at the top, that to hear it all fit together, you'll have to listen to the original recording. Suffice it to say that this reimagining works, but it's not the only thing that could have worked—a different era of dance track, as I mentioned, is another very solid option. Many Daft Punk tracks have only a few lyrics. When it comes to other options, "The Fez" by Steely Dan has few lyrics, so you could turn this song into a cool jazz-pop jam. The Beatles' "She's So Heavy" and "Why Don't We Do It in the Road?" have few lyrics, so a rock anthem direction is possible. Heck, "Tequila" has only one word, and it's pretty much a perfect song that everyone loves. Most of the time, when you're feeling like you're painted into a corner, you likely have more exits and options than you realize. Just step back and think bigger.

Finding a New Spin: "Dreamboat Annie" (Dylan)

We've said earlier in this chapter that it may take years or even decades before the undiscovered treasures of a song can be unearthed, and this is what happened for me with "Dreamboat Annie." Sometimes the "new spin" on an arrangement comes from external factors: inspiration from other songs, a particular performance or writing technique you have in mind, or directions from the client. In this case, all the inspiration came from within the song and the sound of the ensemble for whom I was writing.

The Ault Sisters are a wonderful young Canadian SSA all-sisters trio. Much of their repertoire is inspired by groups such as the Andrews Sisters, backed by a jazz rhythm section, but they are also skilled a cappella singers, and the family blend is magical. When they asked me to arrange "Dreamboat Annie," a piece of 1970s classic rock by Heart, I decided to arrange it a cappella, and transform it in the process.

The original is an up-tempo, gently driving acoustic-rock number. When putting on my arranger's hat, the first thing I noticed, like "Overkill" mentioned earlier, is that the setting didn't match the lyrics. The groove and feel sounded like a jaunty drive along a country road, but the lyrics, "Oh Annie, Dreamboat Annie, my little ship of dreams" and "riding on the diamond waves, little darling one" suggested, obviously, water. This piece doesn't want to chug along: it wants to float.

SSA is one of the "floatiest" vocal configurations you can have. Three unchanged voices means there aren't enough voices to establish driving textures (it's not impossible, of course, just not inherent in the sound), and the lack of natural bass makes it easy for the voices to shimmer, swoop, float, and fly. It's perfect for the sound of floating on water.

The original piece is in four, but I wanted a gently rocking feeling, which led me to reimagine it in three: think of the number of lullabies in 3/4, and you'll see what I mean. The original song establishes the truck-along-the-dirt-road groove right away: instead, I created lilting ocean waves, cresting and receding. This eventually settles into a soft pulse, like a small boat drifting in the ocean:

Dreamboat Annie

o.p.b. Heart
Arranged by: Dylan Bell

No one knows what the song is yet: this section is my own composition. But it sets a mood for the first verse. Note the phrasing in mm. 8–9: the four-over-three cross-rhythm emphasizes the feeling of the ocean waves.

The original is in the key of C. Some people associate keys with colors or feelings: for me, C is a bland, neutral color, like beige. In the same way that beige is almost a non-color, I don't think of C as a key so much as an absence of a key, and I'm not all that fond of it. The melody is in warm-alto range, from low-alto G to high alto/mezzo C. The chord changes firmly establish the key, with the verse starting with a definitive ii-V-I pattern. Typically the melodic phrases end on the tonic chord, with the melody on the fifth, as grounded as that dirt road they drive on. In keeping with the floating-on-water feeling I wanted, I abandoned all of this. I moved the key center up a fourth, a big key change usually associated with a changed-voice to unchanged-voice difference in singer, such as tenor to alto. Here, it's alto to soprano, but still an unusually big change in key for roughly the same voice type. But I wanted the melody to float, rather than be grounded.

Furthermore, I made a modal shift, taking a nice major melody, with lots of stable thirds and fifths, and reframing it as a Dorian-sounding melody with lots of ethereal-sounding seconds and fourths. Instead of the melody sitting under a ii-V-I progression, it is now re-harmonized so that the melody is now reimagined (without changing a note!) like this:

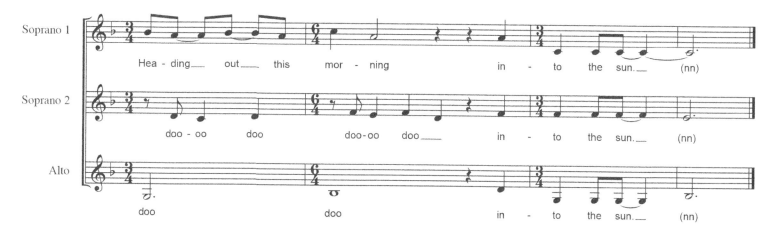

What is this? It's hard to tell, isn't it? We can call this key center "Roughly F," in which case the chord progression, rather than ii-V-I, now rocks between ii and IV. Chord-wise, we have Gm-B♭maj7♯11-Gsus4-B♭maj7♯11, with some nice quartal stacks and some quintessential SSA-type clusters. Yet, despite the jazzy-sounding chord names and voicings, it's nothing like jazz. It's just ambiguous, misty, ungrounded.

In fact, in this Roughly F tonality, we never get a clear F major chord. The closest we get is at the end of the song:

At the end, I reprise the ocean waves (the motif appears in fragments elsewhere in the arrangement, but more fully here), and end on a clustery . . . what? Fadd9? Gsus2? Was this song ever in Roughly F, or is it really G minor? Call it whatever you like, the result is the same: an arrangement that floats and glimmers, true to the title, the lyrics, and the wonderful SSA group for whom it was written.

From This to That: "Supercalifragilisticexpialidocious" (Deke)

Everyone knows this beloved song: it is the cornerstone of the movie as well as the Mary Poppins character. It is one of those Disney songs that you wouldn't find anywhere else: silly, nonsensical, and utterly charming. However, what it isn't is cool. Or modern. It was created for, and remains tethered to, the film in a way that makes it hard to reinvent, and yet that is exactly what I was asked to do.

When considering how to modernize a song, if an idea or alternate style doesn't jump out to me right away, I strip the song down to its most basic components. Let's distill out the polka/oom-pah feel, forget the harmonic progression for a moment, and look at just the melody—notes and rhythm. The melody lives primarily on the third, fifth, and sixth—feels a bit pentatonic. That brings to mind folk songs, but to go that direction would slow it down, and this song would take forever to get through. The word itself is cumbersome. We need it to move along quickly. So, let's look at the rhythm of each line of the chorus, which is basically twelve eighth notes followed by two quarter notes. If we need to keep it moving, let's speed it up, see how quickly we can reasonably get through the word just speaking it . . . something like 180 BPM. And as I did this, chanting the word to myself, I started to hear a beat underneath, almost like a rap tune, but not quite. Almost like a cheerleader chant, and then I realized I was in the realm of Avril Lavigne's "Girlfriend":

Hey hey, you you, I don't like your girlfriend
No way no way, I think you need a new one

And Taylor Swift's "Shake It Off":

Players gonna play play play play play
And the haters gonna hate hate hate hate hate

A little like Gwen Stefani's "Hollaback Girl," but faster, more of a driving beat. This direction gives a modern underpinning, a groove, and a sensibility that can reframe a lyric and melodic line that is more hurdy-gurdy than hip-hop. In fact, when arranging the chorus, which I always do first when flipping a song (because the chorus is the most important part, and if it doesn't work, you'll need a new direction), I realized it wants not only to be sung, but to have a spoken/rapped layer, as well, plus an ad-lib over the top of it all. Good, but not quite, still a little clunky, so I decided to start the melodic parts, which I turned into a three-part figure, an eighth note late, on sixteenth notes, but have the rap say straight:

Supercalifragilisticexpialidocious

The harmonic progression works fine without reharmonization, but to really make it feel like a modern pop song, the beat will need to be very strong, so I went with a combination vocal percussion and body percussion loop. I rarely notate vocal percussion; it's usually pretty obvious, and the people I work with are amazing, but this one I was careful to spell out as the two elements needed to work together in a specific complex pattern reminiscent of the songs mentioned above:

So far, so good. When it came to the verses, I decided less was more: a cheer-leader chant/rap approach to the verse lines would be better than having them sung, as the melody itself drags you back into the world of London circa 1910, and the choruses feel fresher when they're sung after a rapped verse.

And that's about it for the song. I made the verses a bit more complex in the background harmonies as the song progressed, but not much. One of the hardest things to do when you're a young arranger is to know when to stop, and to feel comfortable letting an arrangement be simple when simple is right. As you work more, you realize that unnecessary complexity just takes longer to learn and makes a group more uncertain onstage. Sometimes it's exactly right, but between those songs, it's great to have some numbers that are easy to learn and easy to sing so the group can just have fun and perform without having to worry about nuances and complexities. This arrangement was very successful, and it works great as a set opener or closer, as it has energy and is very well-received: it's a song people love but really never hear in any version other than the original . . . until now.

From This to That: "Summer in the City" (Dylan)

In 2020, during the pandemic, I was fortunate enough to be isolated with my musical (and life) partner, Suba, the other half of FreePlay. This meant we could keep performing, at least virtually, and we produced over fifty episodes of our livestream concert series *FreePlay Fridays at Four!* We never repeated a full concert program, so we were always on the lookout for new songs and new ideas.

One sweltering summer week, we decided on a "Beat the Heat"–themed show, and this spawned two of the tracks on our next album, *Talk to Me*: "Conga" and "Summer in the City." "Conga" is a pretty faithful arrangement of the Miami Sound Machine original (with a few twists), but "Summer in the City" was a creative transformation.

The original Lovin' Spoonful version is a frenetic 1960s rock song, and the musical setting suits the lyrics well: you can feel the steamy sidewalks, the blaring traffic, the buzz and impatience of the people. But the verses contrast with the choruses, which talk about the nighttime calm, and maybe a little romance. I decided to lean into the relaxed chorus lyrics and find a mirror to fast rock: relaxed samba-jazz.

Though the genre is quite different, samba-jazz suits the ethos of the piece: it evokes thoughts of hot summer days, it's also often associated with the 1960s, and depending on the tempo, it can evoke either energetic street dancing or relaxed sensuality. And like most genres, it comes with a clear musical grammar to follow.

I started by relaxing the tempo, from a driving-backbeat 104 BPM to a gentle "walking samba" feel of 90 BPM. The driving electric piano and organ parts were replaced by a gently picked guitar and some light Brazilian percussion, and a mellow alto lead.

Summer In The City

J. Sebastian, M. Sebastian
S. Boone

The original version has a chorus with more relaxed lyrics, but the instruments keep driving with the same intensity. I decided to create a clear contrast from the (still-relaxed) samba, by removing all percussion and groove, and "floating" the first half of the chorus over some rich vocal-jazz-ensemble BGs, in half-notes. The contrast is deepened by switching to tenor lead and alto harmony.

In the original version, after the verse and chorus, there is a bridge of sorts. It's a short, four-bar instrumental break with a two-bar repeated guitar riff, with implied harmonies of Cm to A♭7. Then it's gone, and we're back to the original feel. Oddly, the original has no return to the vocals: the band plays through the changes of the verse, and the first half of the chorus, then fades out. The original song is under 2:45 . . . lots of room to add new material. There's so much more to explore here, especially with that short interlude, so I started there.

Instead of a guitar riff, I used some samba-vocabulary and turned it into a horn section. But I didn't want a big, bright Cuban-sounding horn section: I wanted something Brazilian-sounding—warm, smooth, and a little bit slinky—so I opted for a trombone quartet.

I started like the original, with a breakdown, but I harmonized the riff with the top two parts. On the second repeat, we added the bass trombone and a tenor trombone counterline.

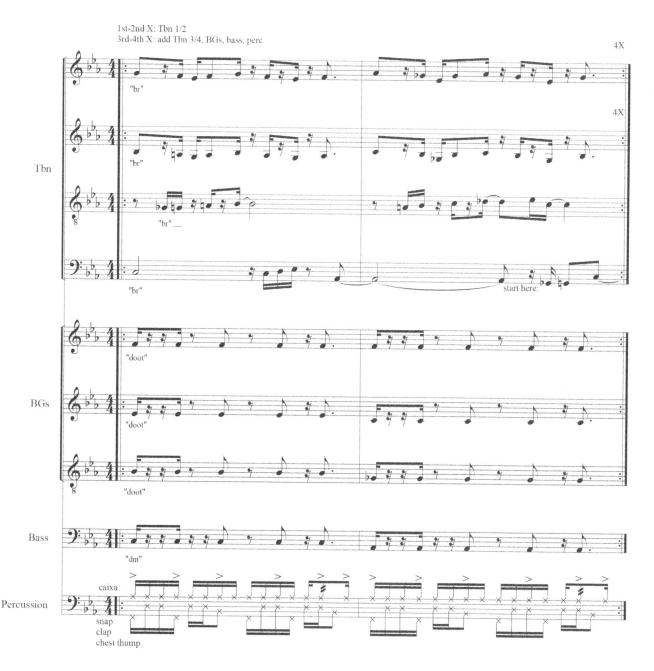

Then, off to the races. I decided on a trombone soli, something harmonically and rhythmically hip. I used the same chord changes, now with a jazzier flavor of Cm11 to A♭13, but I upped the intensity level by adding elements of Brazilian MPB (*Música Popular Brasileira*): in this case, 1970s samba-funk. I borrowed the rhythmic feel of a well-known 1970s MPB bass line, added a drum kit part, and went to town.

all percussion
unison

You'll notice a couple of lines that hint at the original melody without actually stating it: they set the stage and give us a place to develop. The whole soli takes us on a sort of adventure. To transition back into the verse recap, I added a samba unison pattern, commonly used to punctuate a section, or to lead to another section of the dance.

In the original song, that's basically it. An instrumental verse, a fadeout on the chorus, and it was done. This seemed unsatisfying to me, though, so I did a recap of the first verse and another chorus, similar to the "return to the head" one would expect after a solo section in a jazz standard.

Now, how could I "take the song home"? I opted to take us on another journey, this time turning the second half of the chorus into an endlessly repeating figure and fadeout. The trombone quartet makes an appearance again, using a repeated figure as a call and response against an improvised vocal solo:

At first, I give the horns center stage, with the soloist singing in the breaks. Then, to kick up the ending a notch, I brought back the MPB funky drums and bass, and the soloist took over. We stay in the space for a while, and the piece fades out, like a gentle Rio sunset.

Classical Crossover: "I'll Make a Man Out of You" (Deke)

There's a pop operatic singer in Britain named Jonathan Antoine, and his dream when shooting his first big television special was to do a Disney song, specifically "I'll Make a Man Out of You," as *Mulan* is his favorite animated movie. He invited DCappella to join him, and he asked me to do something special with the song. Say no more. Classical plus Disney? War? The first idea you have isn't always the best, but when that idea involves "Mars: The Bringer of War" from *The Planets* by Gustav Holst—the piece of music that launched a thousand battle-scene knockoffs, including John Williams's brilliant *Star Wars* scores—I didn't want to look for option number two. I just wanted to make it work. However, there's a hurdle: 5/4. You know the piece I'm talking about, right?

I'll Make a Man Out of You

If you don't, put down this book, grab some headphones, and take a trip to Mars. Once you come back, you'll likely say, "Okay, amazing piece of music, but how the heck do you fit a Disney melody over this, since the meter is completely different?" My answer was to stick with Holst completely and just draw out the melody over it. It's early in the song, so not everyone will necessarily know the Disney song from the first couple of lines, but we'll have a moment of recognition once they do:

And then, once the song was established enough, I'd made my point, classical and pop had been thoroughly crossed over, it was time to shift to the 4/4 song that people (including Jonathan) knew and loved:

Once the pattern was morphed into 4/4, I slowly transitioned into the original groove, and by the top of the second verse, everyone's in full Disney mode (or should I say Donny Osmond mode, as he was the original soloist). This is all to say that you don't have to take an idea and have it drive every aspect or choice within your arrangement(s). Sometimes a fun quote at the top of a song is enough.

Classical Crossover: "Humble Fugue" (Dylan)

Sometimes you get an interesting directive from the client, and with this arrangement for the German eight-part women's chorus Jazzica, their director, Till Kindschus, requested this:

> We want you to arrange "Humble Stance" by the Canadian group Saga. The arrangement shall NOT aim to imitate the sound of that rock band. Rather we want you to do a strange classical crossover.

Well, that was quite an interesting request. But, always up for a challenge, I dove in.

Rather than quote classical material, or mash up the piece with an existing classical work, I decided to use classical writing techniques instead. Much of the piece is "orchestrated" using themes from the original: sort-of classical in style, certainly not rock-sounding. But to drive the classical-crossover point home, I decided a purely classical-sounding centerpiece was needed. For a German choir, what came to mind? Bach, of course. I decided I'd write my own fugue, weaving in melodic material from the rock song, and present it Swingles-style. I dusted off my copy of *The Well-Tempered Clavier* to remind myself of true-to-form fugal-writing techniques and got to work.

Though the rest of the arrangement is in six parts—(SSSAAA)—this is far too dense for a fugue. The sweet spot for a fugue is three "voices" or independent parts: enough for melodic and harmonic interest, but easy enough for the listener to keep score of who's doing what. A fugue has a few basic elements: a subject, presented in imitation through all the voices often at different pitches, episodes involving change of key center, and development through use of a countersubject. Here, the "subject" is taken from a guitar/synth line used as an interlude between verses, and the "countersubject" is the bass/guitar riff.

Here is the fugue section in full, with analysis to follow.

"Humble Fugue"

Dylan Bell

ba dam ba___ ba-dam ba___ ba-dam___ ba ba-da-va da va da va___

ba dam ba___ ba-dam ba___ ba-dam___ ba ba-da-va da va da va___

» Mm. 1–2: exposition, with the subject in voice 2 (S3 and A1) in the tonic key of B minor.
» Mm. 3–4: imitation at the fifth by voice 1 (S1 and S2), with voice 2 complementing with counterlines to support the subject.
» Mm. 5–6: interlude, where the countersubject is introduced in voice 2.
» Mm. 7–8: introduction of voice 3, with statement of subject at the tonic.
» Mm. 9–10: countersubject in voice 1, with modulation to relative major (D).
» Mm. 10–15: interlude, with modulation to F♯ minor, and the subject at the fifth in voice 2.
» Mm. 16–17: subject at the tonic in voice 3, leading to the big finale.
» Mm. 18–20: pedal point. Like any good Bach fugue, the pedal point allows for some interesting harmonic movement, building up tension to the end.

In a Bach fugue, this moment would likely lead up to a recap, or resolve itself to finish. Instead, I leave it holding at the dominant, and after this, the piece goes full-rock, with a rousing "We Will Rock You" *stomp-stomp-clap* chorus as the high point of the song.

I'd never tried to write a full (mini) fugue before, but it was a rewarding experience. It must have been effective, as well: this was my first commission for Jazzica, and more than a decade later, I'm still writing, giving workshops, and performing as a guest artist with them.

Starting from Scratch: "Bibbidi-Bobbidi-Boo" (Deke)

Sometimes you get an assignment that doesn't make sense to you. Maybe it's a request for a song that you don't think works well nowadays in its current form, or a song that's so iconic that to do a straightforward version of it means you'll never get out of another performer or arranger's shadow. That can be a challenge, but at this point in the book, it's hopefully one you're up for. When I work with clients, I say, "The answer is always yes," and then I figure out how to get to yes.

Perhaps the most challenging and frustrating request I've received in the past decade (and quite possibly ever) was when I was asked to arrange "Bibbidi-Bobbidi-Boo" for DCappella. I'd arranged challenging songs, and I'd proven to them I could modernize some very iconic songs, so they didn't think twice when they tossed this song in my lap. However, I cursed under my breath because this song has so many things working against it:

» The entire song, start to finish, is forty-five seconds long.
» The musical style is an old Italian folk-music style called a tarantella, thoroughly unlike any pop music style nowadays.
» It's in a bouncy 6/8 meter, which is difficult to map onto other tempi.
» The lyrics are almost entirely composed of nonsense syllables:

> Salaca doo la menthicka boo la bibbidi-bobbidi-boo
>
> Put 'em together and what have you got? bibbidi-bobbidi-boo!

I can't draw a lyric out of this mess to work with, since the source material is impossibly ridiculous. I definitely can't do anything involving a rap, since that would only lean into the goofiness of the lyrics. The chord progression is basically useless, as it is almost entirely I and V chords in this AABA form (which also doesn't help, not being akin to current pop songwriting) with brief moments of the IV and II7 chords in the B section. And to make things worse, over these simple chords, the melodic shape is both married to the rapid declaration of the lyrics and has many chromatic notes in it (e.g., the first line is 5-#4-5-6-5, then 3-#2-3-4-3). Looking at the meter, I wondered if I could slow it down into a 6/8 ballad and give it a Boyz II Men–style post-doo-wop treatment, but even if I can tweak melodic notes and reharmonize so there's more motion, the lyrics would turn any cool R&B stylings into some kind of weird farce.

I couldn't find a way in.

So, what did I know? I knew I needed to modernize the song, so I was going to have to go with 4/4 at some tempo. The song needed to be a proper full song, so I needed around three minutes of material, which meant I was going to have to write a bunch of it whole cloth rather than arrange it. And there was so very little to work with that I was going to have to either stretch it out or condense it and have most of the song not focus on those forty-five seconds . . . and then it occurred to me: I needed a style of music that could be cool and weird and trippy enough that the lyrics would fit in. It's officially called "The Magic Song" parenthetically, so what might I have been able to do that sounded magical? How about something in the cool trance meets spa music world?

First and foremost, I needed to create that song, that groove. It wouldn't be the original song; it would be something completely different, the way I created a new composition for "Most Wonderful Time" (mentioned above) and then dropped the song into it.

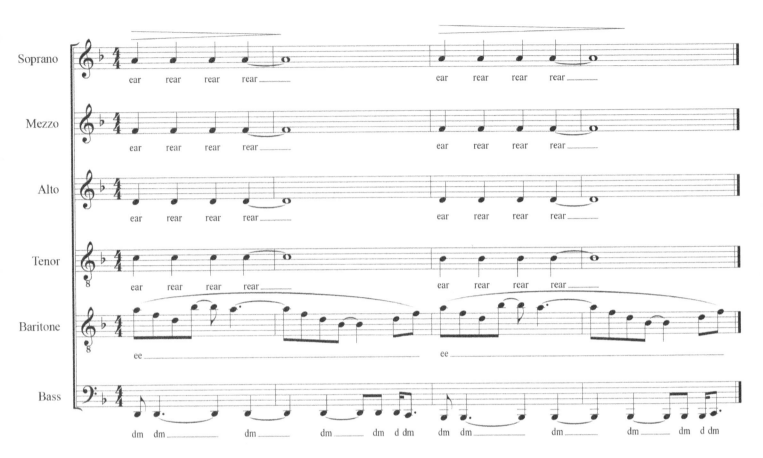

In this case, I wanted a long exposition, one that would unfold and transport the listener to a completely different sonic world, and linger there for a long time. In the final recording, the first lyric doesn't arrive until almost a minute into the recording. Before that point, you have no idea that it's a Disney song, and you can't really tell that it's a cappella, either, as I used very strange vowels ("eer-reer-rear-rear" and "ee") and made sure they were heavily affected. In addition to the written parts, the vocal percussionist, who is an excellent mimic, did a vocal bamboo flute over the top that completed the sonic picture.

These parts came in bit by bit—the upper harmonies first, then the flute, then the baritone falsetto line, and finally the bass line accompanied by the slow VP groove. A wall of sound was slowly built. Only then, after people were relaxed and minds were wandering, did I introduce the melody:

Bibbidi Bobbidi Boo

I decided to keep the triplet from the tarantella, but the melody doesn't start until the third beat, and the melodic lines are spread out, which makes the whole thing feel out of time. By the time you get to the third line, "Bibbidi-bobbidi-boo," the timing is off by three full beats, as the original has downbeats on the first syllable and on "boo," whereas by removing the triplet feel, it sounds as though it's elongated and floating outside the established groove and meter. The tenor and baritone lines created other musical elements that filled out the texture, aligning with the bass and percussion, further emphasizing that the melody was untethered, floating, and when they all sang the melodic lines breathily: ethereal.

When arriving at the B section, after the A sections and additional interlude, I decided to give the song a clearer sense of four, so even though the bass line stretched across two measures with a hemiola flavor, the upper voices aligned, and the melodic line was echoed. The effect was to ground the song, escaping from the floating nature for a while, so we could, of course, return to it. Also, there was more harmonic interest in the B section. Basically, whatever you were doing in previous sections wants to be done differently in the B section or bridge of a song, so you can return to the original figure with it sounding fresh and being heard in a slightly different way, re-contextualized. In this case, rather than using this section to escape from a standard set of elements, it was more of a traditionally aligned passage, so we could untether again when it was done.

The rest played out as you'd expect, with the coda a return to the original texture, and the addition of a cascade of the song's melodic hook out of time:

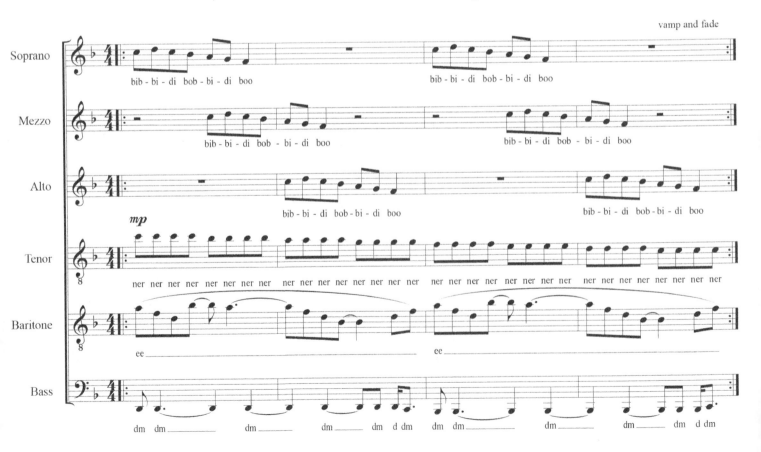

With the three female parts overlapping, the sense of their floating out of time was at its peak, and the song continued this way as it slowly faded.

This is one of my all-time favorite arrangements for DCappella, not because I feel like I pulled a rabbit out of a hat (or more correctly: pulled this song from in front of a speeding train as it was tied to the railroad tracks), but simply because I really like the way it sounds. Creativity always happens within constraints, and sometimes great constraints can push you to find solutions that, under less stressful situations, wouldn't have happened because you'd rely on safer, time-tested choices. I hadn't arranged in this style, I had very rarely used these vowels, and I'd never pushed a song so far away from its original rhythmic underpinnings. The result was beyond what I'd hoped for. Bold choices and big chances sometimes work out.

Starting from Scratch: "What's He Building?" (Dylan)

And speaking of working with next-to-nothing, what if your "song" has no melody or chords at all?

My TTBB quartet, The Watch, was asked to create a new live arrangement for a Tom Waits tribute. The tribute was designed not simply to cover Waits's songs, but to collect a number of different artists who would each put a unique stamp on familiar material. I decided to take that to its logical extreme by essentially "recomposing" a Tom Waits song: "What's He Building?"

The original can barely be described as a song; it's more of a soundscape poem. Tom Waits is already known for his quirky vocal delivery and his exploration of the underbelly of the human experience. In "Building," Waits creates an eerie, junkyard sonic atmosphere reminiscent of *musique concrète*, complete with hammering, grinding metallic sounds, radio static, and creepy whistling. Over this, Waits intones ominous lines, such as:

What the Hell is he building in there?
I'll tell you one thing: he's not building a playhouse for the children . . .

It's a favorite of Tom Waits fans: bizarre, immediately recognizable, and imminently quotable. Just saying the title, in a gravelly voice, is a catchphrase in and of itself.

But it's not a "song," in the normal sense. So, I figured I'd try to blow some minds and turn it into . . . a jazzy, big band number.

The decision to go this route was based on a confluence of factors:

» Tom Waits's music is often affiliated with jazz: it's a genre he borrows from liberally, and many of his studio musicians are jazz players. It's a long way from the soundscape he's built in this song, but not entirely out of character with his overall work.

» The convention of "jazzifying" unlikely rock and contemporary songs is novel, but not unheard of. Paul Anka's 2005 album *Rock Swings* achieved this brilliantly. In short, people understand it, and if done well, will buy into it.

» The Watch's "musical center" is jazz and contemporary music: this would be right in our performance sweet spot.

Now, where to start? First, I decided to create form out of (mostly) nothing. Though it sounds formless on the first few listens, eventually the lines Waits mutters can be distinguished into couplets, and stanzas of a sort. The title phrase is repeated in between, acting as a sort of refrain. I rearranged the order of a few lines, repeated some phrases, removed others, and eventually had material for two verses, one half verse, and a chorus: all the building blocks needed for a song.

Next, melodic material. Again, there was none to begin with. I broke each verse into two sections: part spoken, to retain some of the character of the original, and part sung. The growly spoken parts, combined with jazz, immediately suggested a 1950s, Allen Ginsberg "beatnik" feel: groovy-hepcat spoken poetry over a *film noir* vocal background of walking bass, ride cymbal, bongos, and improvised muted trumpet phrases. Perfect.

For the sung melody, I opted for something with a sly but bouncy feeling, in D minor:

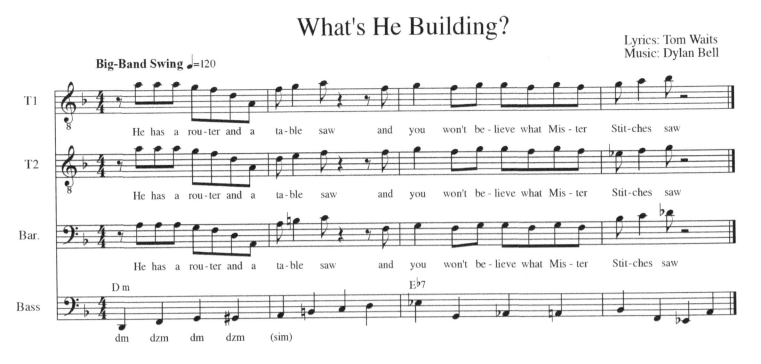

Instead of feeling dark and ominous like the spoken part preceding, it has a conspiratorial levity that gives an interesting juxtaposition to the words. The melody follows a comfortably predictable pattern: a four-bar "opening" and a four bar "closing":

Like any good big band chart, it's arranged with a nice balance of unison/ octave writing, some harmonized ends-of-phrases, and a nice four-part block harmony phrase to conclude.

It's often said that the best creative works simultaneously fulfill and confound our expectations. Put another way: we love a blend of familiarity and surprise, the expected and the unexpected. In this piece, the fact that it's a "song" at all is already surprising, so if we give the audience that much surprise, let's also make it familiar-sounding and enjoyable.

To that end, the chorus is a rousing, swinging melody reminiscent of a 1960s spy thriller, straight out of the Henry Mancini playbook.

All the elements are in place: now it's time to assemble it. The overall form starts like this:

» Intro: no music, just sound effects. The audience is confused, but curious. Then, the creepy whistle comes in. To those who know Waits's music, this is the giveaway: now the strange sound effects make sense.
» The intro has a lower-brass big band build, repeating the title of the song. We know the song, but what is this? A melody? Rhythm? That sure wasn't in the original!
» We settle into verse 1: our spoken beat-poetry section. After some surprise, we now get the words we know, in a music backdrop that suits it. Then, the second half, with melody.
» Chorus 1: Mancini-town!
» Verse 2, and chorus 2: similar.

What next? Waits's material doesn't give us much of a bridge or departure . . . but this is a great time for a solo. Let's amp it up a bit, and include a buildup into a semitone key change to E♭ major. But a straightforward solo might take us out of the character of the song. Instead, let's keep the solo in eccentric-Waits-territory. To do that, I added an instruction to the solo line, one of my favorite musical instructions to date:

In performance, the solo usually ends up as a crazy, double-time, drunken-saxophone-style solo interspersed with improvised lines like "banging nails and stuff on the floor," "something about plutonium," and "does he even have a permit for that?" The rest of the band plays it straight, with walking bass, ride cymbal, conga, and sax-style accompaniment shell-voicing figures. We end the solo by modulating back to the original key of D minor.

After this, we have the half-verse, done as a breakdown, with all voices in close harmony.

One last chorus to round out, with an abrupt pause: here, we re-created the original soundscape intro and creepy whistle. To finish: a coda/buildup similar to the first musical entry, and a nice fat IV7#11 chord—a great jazz substitution for a minor tonic chord—and an over-the-top "horn-splat" glissando to end.

This one became a show-stopping set closer for us. The chart stands on its own if you don't know the original, but if you do know it, it's even more interesting.

Dead End: Now What? "So Danço Samba" (Dylan)

While the transformation of "Overkill" came from a rather highbrow artistic impulse, and "Building" was a full-on recomposition, "So Danço Samba" was flipped simply because I was bored.

FreePlay wanted a nice samba for our album *Go Back Forward*, and we settled on "So Danço Samba," a song that, like "Overkill" for a Men at Work song, was well-known but not an obvious first choice. So far, so good. We have the luxury of our own home recording studio, which meant that rather than coming in with a fully polished arrangement and fully rehearsed, we could come in with something half-done and work it out as we went.

Like many samba-jazz songs, this is a thirty-two-bar, AABA structure that moves fairly quickly through the form. We scratched out some standard four-part trombonesque BGs, added bass, some vocal percussion, and sang the lead in two-part octave unison, with harmony in the bridge. Our first round through the form was complete.

Then, we thought . . . *Now what?*

The next obvious step would be a vocal scat solo over the form. So, always happy to improvise, I jumped in the booth and laid down a couple of takes. It was fine, but it still didn't pique our interest. The arrangement was perfectly acceptable, if a little ordinary. But there was nowhere to go. The final head-out (or recap of the melody, for those not jazz-inclined), then the ending. We were getting bored with our own arrangement, and we hadn't even finished it yet.

I tried again, this time with a whistled solo. I can whistle over changes pretty well, but whistling naturally has a jaunty, sometimes tongue-in-cheek feel to it. I laid down a good, jazzy take, but it had some of that cheeky attitude: a little extra-wide vibrato here, a little exaggerated glissando there. Then it hit me.

Esquivel!

If you haven't heard Esquivel! before (and yes, the exclamation point is often included as part of his artist name), take a moment and look him up. Juan Garcia Esquivel was a genius Mexican composer/arranger best-known for his quirky arranging style, giving his music the name "Space-Age Bachelor Pad Music." The term says it all, but if you can imagine the music from early 1960s TV shows, mixed with Latin big band with some absurd Warner Brothers cartoonlike elements built in, you're getting close. He used lots of over-the-top effects in his orchestration, block-style vocal jazz ensembles singing sophisticated parts to nonsense syllables like "zoo-zoo-zoo" or "ra-ra-ra," and . . . whistled melodies. We now had our spin, our new angle to approach the rest of the piece.

We kept the whistle solo, and the original bass and four-part trombone BGs, and added some Esquivel-inspired elements. In the A sections:

So Danço Samba

A.C. Jobim
V. de Moraes

» You know that song, "The Knuckle Song," you may have learned as a kid on the black keys of the piano? It has a B section: Suba sang that, as a xylophone, in octaves.

» I added a slow countermelody in 1960s-era men's chorus style, deliberately leaning on odd notes (such as the flat fifth, on the second-bar II7 chord . . . sung to "ra-ra-ra").

» Suba added a "Looney Tunes" sliding Hawaiian guitar part in four voices.

In the B section, we kept it smooth, with some more Esquivel vocals:

This looks pretty normal, with one added twist. We took what we like to call the "Henry Mancini" or "horn splat" glissando in the fourth bar and added an Esquivel-inspired technique. Normally, when singing a glissando, you naturally sing softer as the pitch slides down. Now (assuming no one is around nearby) try singing a glissando, getting louder as the pitch goes down. A little bit ludicrous, right? Imagine that in five-part block harmony.

For the next trip around the form, we gave the Esquivel Orchestra a break and added a horn "shout chorus," a little more whistling, and a piece of a conga rhythmic composition from Cuba called the "Cubalinda." This was just enough to give the piece some heavy musical content, while remaining quirky.

For the final head, we brought back the Esquivel vocals, this time with words. Imagine the vocal ensemble sound from the theme to *The Flintstones*, bright and smiley, then take it over the top, and you get this:

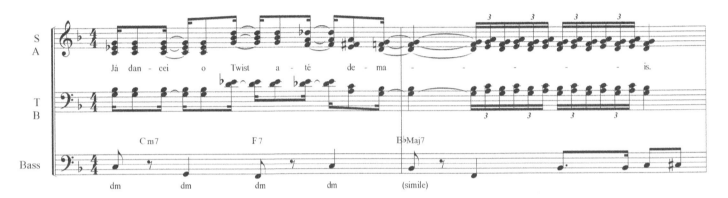

An exaggerated trumpet-style shake, some more silly syllables, and another louder-than-it-should-be glissando, and the picture is complete.

In an album full of fairly serious pieces, this arrangement ended up as a moment of levity and slightly demented fun. And all from getting bored with our own work!

You Want Me to Do *What*? "Prince Ali" (Deke)

I was asked all the time to modernize Disney songs, but I was never given a specific musical style, until I got a phone call asking for "a dubstep version of 'Prince Ali'." This struck me as a particularly odd request, as the year was 2019 and dubstep was definitely out of favor, waxing and waning back in the early 2000s through 2010s, and not old enough to have made a comeback yet. In fact, the request reminded me of the birth of Pentatonix on season three of *The Sing-Off*, where, when directing them in their infancy, they seemed to want to put a dubstep breakdown into the middle of every song. It was cool then, but at this point, Pentatonix had pretty much removed any vestiges of dubstep from their repertoire.

It was also an oddly specific request because the song itself doesn't really lend itself to dubstep. The tempo, chords, melody . . . nothing about it really aligns. Dubstep has been described on Allmusic as "tightly coiled productions with overwhelming bass lines and reverberant drum patterns, clipped samples, and occasional vocals"—but "Prince Ali" is almost constant vocals, the bassline isn't at all the most impressive let alone an overwhelming element of the song, and if the drums are ever reverberant, it's because they're the parade drums at the top of the song, not a carefully layered set of drum samples. Dubstep is pretty much always in the 132–142 BPM range, whereas "Prince Ali" is 97 BPM, and that much of a tempo shift is a nightmare when it comes to lyrics and melody—either far too fast to get the lyrics out, or at half-time ploddingly slow. One thing was clear: we'd need a bass drop. Everything else was going to be a game of inches, dragging the song closer, step by step, to the form.

What do you do when you're in this position? First, you listen to the masters of the genre. A lot. In this case, I listened to Skrillex, Flux Pavilion, Nero, and the rest of the dubstep gang. This isn't music that is translated into a cappella very often (if at all), as it's largely lyric-less and vocal-less, based around synth and sampled drum sounds, and it relies heavily on production elements rather than the human elements at the core of pretty much all a cappella. Tossing a brief dubstep drop into an a cappella arrangement is fun and exciting, but building an entire song in this style is a much heavier lift. It's not a spice; it's not even an ingredient; it's the entire entrée.

And if that wasn't enough, I was not just tasked with creating a studio project: this arrangement needed to be performable live. If it were just for the studio, sounds—percussion, bass, vocal synth sounds—could be so heavily effected as to render them unrecognizable as a human voice, resulting in a timbre that's virtually indistinguishable from other dubstep tracks, which could then be chopped and "flown around" the arrangement to the point where they're treated as samples. It's a fun process, but unworkable because as soon as the recording was done, we'd have to get together in rehearsal and find a way to reproduce it, which would undoubtedly be a disappointment to the singers and to the audience. A solution was needed that could be sung, as well, and any effects used in the studio would have to be more or less reproducible live onstage.

Where could we start? Let's look at the tempo. Speeding up 97 BPM to 132 would make a torrential mess out of the lyric, if it could even be sung at that speed, so the better move was to go with a half-time feel and take a tempo close to 140, at the top of the dubstep range. Faster than that, it no longer sounded like dubstep, so we had to make it work.

Next, let's try to make the chorus/A section work, the part everyone knows. One of DCappella's signature sounds is the women singing in three-part parallel harmony, so let's start there. The bass needed to be as low as possible (thankfully low B♭s are absolutely in Joe's range—a blessing since that's the tonic—so let's move the song from A minor up to B♭ minor for this reason) and on half notes since we wanted to make it all feel like it was intentionally half-time, that the song had been slowed not by necessity, but by design. The percussion would reflect this. That left two parts, and there was plenty of harmonic drive in the women's parts, so I went with something I had heard a good amount of in dubstep recordings: octaves.

It worked. The women would sing with a sultry swagger, so it was cool, not lethargic. Next up, I wanted to craft an introduction that would work, get some momentum going, and the introduction should be one of the easiest parts of the song. While listening to a number of songs, I jotted down notes, and I thought the groove from "Roll with the Punches" would be perfect. There were also a couple of frequent rhythmic motifs I heard in dubstep—one being a series of two sixteenths, then an eighth, another being quarter-note triplets, so I decided to use both, establishing the dubstep character from the very top:

VP similar to "Roll With The Punches " Peverelist - but more varied sounds sprinkled in

You can see the bass note is on for a measure, then off for a measure, something else I heard. Soaring over it all is the baritone singing, "Make way for Prince Ali," which I put in his voice since it needed to be from the fifth of the chord, F above middle C. When you want more tension in a vocal part, remember tessitura: in this case, "high for a baritone" sounded more intense than "midrange for a tenor."

Next I decided to tackle the verse. I was holding off on the post-chorus as that was where the drop needed to happen looking at the overall shape of the song, and I was still trepidatious. That moment needed to be the most impressive, the most dubstep-y, and the most over-the-top, crazy-chopped-up, but I couldn't rely on studio trickery. As we always counsel: jump around when arranging, work on the sections that you are inspired about or able to figure out, and save the harder parts for later, as they'll often reveal themselves once you've figured out the other song sections and the "grammar" for the arrangement becomes established.

The introduction wanted to be over-the-top and powerful, like a call to arms or call to prayer shouted from the highest rooftops, and the chorus was going to have a similar huge energy, so I thought the verses should pull back, be breathier and more ethereal, and give us somewhere to grow. Rather than keep the women in perpetual three-part harmony, I decided to give the melody to one voice and have the others join on just certain notes—the off beats—which was a rhythm well-established in the original recording. I kept the tenor's signature double sixteenth then eighth pattern going, I kept the bass on low whole notes, and I left the baritone free to ad-lib, and I had a texture.

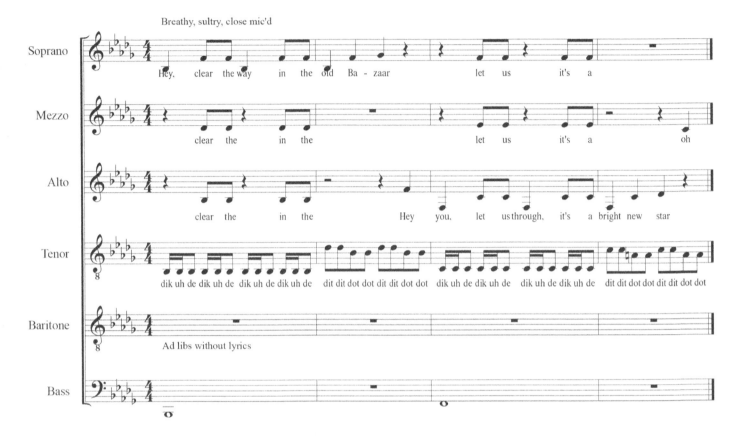

This was not a texture I'd woven before: it might seem unbalanced, but it worked. Everything was elongated, the result of the song being reimagined in this new tempo, and the drive was coming from the tenor and percussion parts, everyone else drawn out. This was also beneficial as it was a low, slow point from which to build, and that was exactly what I did through the verses and choruses, with increasing rhythmic intensity, and lines that went from low vocal range and climbed to the top:

I was pretty certain I'd not spanned two octaves, climbing diatonically before. It wasn't easy to sing the entire line smoothly, and to make matters even more difficult, I was asking for a smooth crescendo across the entire passage. Okay, this was tough, but still singable . . . but wait, it was too clean, too careful. I needed to make one more adjustment: the tenor line needed this shape, but not singing exact pitches. Dubstep has these kind of synth lines that rise and build into the drop (which was exactly what I was setting up). Professional singers spend their entire lives working to sing exact pitches, so it takes a moment to explain how this line should just slide up and only use the written pitches as a general guideline, but once he got it, it worked perfectly.

Remember that music notation is a tool, but it shouldn't be a constraint. You should be thinking about what sound you want, then find a way to shoehorn it into the traditional five-line staff, not create vocal parts that always conform to notation, as it's an unnecessary limitation. There will be times when it's safer to stick to what is expected in traditional notation, like when arranging for an amateur chorus, or when you won't be at the rehearsals to explain "beyond the notes," but when writing for your own ensembles, don't get stuck on the staff; use your imagination, all vocal colors and timbres and rhythms, then figure out how to best sketch it out on paper, later refining it in person.

And now it was time for the drop. We'd built up to it, we had textures that worked, and dubstep has been established as the sound. Now it was time for the kitchen sink, everything I could possibly throw at this moment that could be reproduced on stage. Here we go:

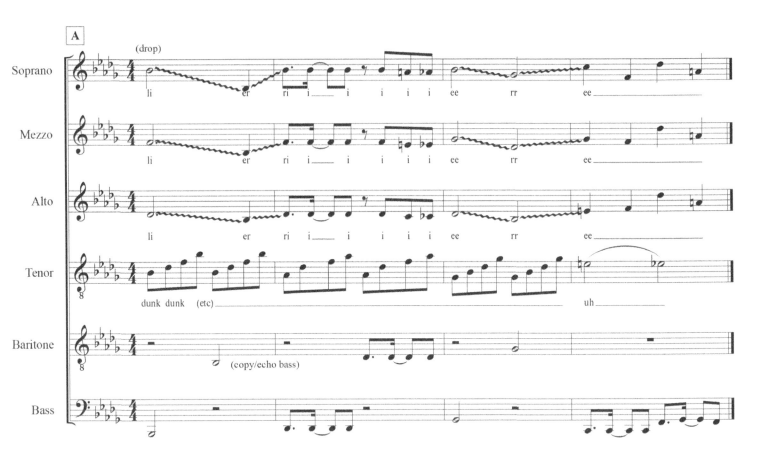

Let's start with the women. I didn't want it to sound like they were singing their part; I wanted it to sound like they were singing, "Why, Prince Ali?" and then the DJ took over, manipulating their voices. This meant sliding and moving their voices as a unit, same spacing from each other (which, in this case, was a second inversion triad, root on the top in the melody). Sometimes when they were moving, they held the same syllable; at other times I had them re-striking it on the "ee" vowel (written as "i-i-i"). And then when I wanted them to all slide down in their voices, I morphed the vowel to an "r" sound, with an "er" as the vowel moving between the two, which sounded like traditional DJ scratching, the sound of the record slowing down and returning to regular speed. I finished the line with them singing the melody in unison, so there was a clear break from effected and non-effected, and so the tag down on the melodic line was very clear.

The bass line was a standard dubstep drop rhythm, while outlining a harmonic progression I whipped up that was reminiscent of a dubstep break. That left the baritone free to echo the bass line an octave higher, and the tenor to outline the chords on a percussive staccato syllable ("dunk"). And so it continued, sliding and breaking: the opposite of traditional a cappella, but it worked. The rest of the arrangement spun out these ideas, played with other textures from dubstep, and leaned into the established electronica character.

The group loved it. It has become some of the members' favorite arrangements for the group ever. It sounds like nothing they've ever done, and like nothing anyone else has ever done. It's cool, weird, playful, and fun. Hard to sing, but satisfying. However, Disney had mixed feelings about this arrangement and recording. They asked for something quite unusual and unexpected, and yet what they received was so outside the box that it was a year before Disney even released it. In fact, it wasn't until the group had an official partnership with Roland (including the BOSS RC-505 loopstation, which we'd already been using) that marketing found a way forward: feature the group along with the gear, build the video around that, and then a story could be told explaining why this song was so . . . electronic.

Now's a great time to say something that's more commerce than creative, but it bears mentioning anyway if you're a professional arranger, or even an amateur who is working at a high level: people do not always know what they want. Even Mickey Mouse. Ideas can look good on paper, and flashes of creativity may present themselves, but how they eventually look on paper, appear onstage, or sound in the recording studio may be different than originally expected. Or, more often, I find that nothing in particular was specifically expected, but the mission itself when taken to completion was bound to land outside the rest of the repertoire. This isn't necessarily a bad thing, and there were people inside of Disney who loved it, but it just didn't have a clear lane in which to move forward.

When you take risks for your group(s), you'll likely encounter moments like this, and it may take time for it all to play out, as frustrating as that may be. Trust in the process, and try not to get too angry with the people who initially asked for a ham sandwich and later say that what they really wanted was turkey. Always remember . . . they're not experts, and they can't hear an idea in their heads: they may need it fully realized before they can make a decision, pro or con. If you have created something really good, they will eventually figure it out.

It's All About the Ending: "River" (Dylan)

This one started as a request for FreePlay, from our dear friends Janis Siegel (the Manhattan Transfer) and Lauren Kinhan (New York Voices). They wanted FreePlay to perform on their online show *Vocal Gumbo*, and they wanted something special for their year-end episode. Their parameters were specific:

> » It had to be a world premiere.
> » It had to be one of our live-looping pieces, not a studio recording.
> » It had to be something Canadian.
> » It had to be a "holiday-adjacent" song—i.e., December-seasonal, but not religious.
> » It had to feature Suba's Carnatic (south Indian) vocal improvising.

Most of this could be taken care of with proper song selection, and we found the perfect match: Joni Mitchell's bittersweet holiday anti-anthem "River." It's a well-loved and well-covered song, so we had to do something special with it so it wouldn't be "just another version." But it's also so beautiful as-is that we didn't want to take it apart and rebuild it. Our solution: we decided to put all our arranging firepower into the final coda, extend it, and make it an entirely new chapter.

In the original, Joni quotes a fragment of "Jingle Bells" on the piano to open the song, taking us into the holiday spirit, but it's lonely and melancholy. At the end, she plays that fragment over and over again, reharmonizing it with her left hand, as the song fades. It has a pensive, spinning quality to it, as if she's skating away on that frozen river, alone. We decided to take this spinning quality and dial it up to eleven. Everything would spin: nothing would be grounded or have an anchor. We wanted to fly away, unsure if we'd ever make it back. We also wanted to take the "Jingle Bells" motif and amplify/modify it, as well. The deadline was approaching: we had two days to finish it. And on Christmas Eve, with the two of us sitting at the piano, we finally found it. And it was something we'd never done before.

To create the sense of spinning, we created three loops:

» Suba's "bells," a ten-beat loop
» Dylan's "bells," a twelve-beat loop
» Dylan's vocals with words, a sixteen-beat loop

These loops would swirl and spin around each other, never matching up (for the math types out there: they align once every sixty bars, but the song is over before then). Each is a planet on its own orbit, never to meet.

We wanted it to feel harmonically ungrounded, as well, with no clear chord progression . . . and besides, with loops that would never meet, a "progression" was effectively impossible. Just what we wanted. Harmony is typically based on stacking thirds, usually a nice diatonic mix of major and minor thirds, to create clear chord qualities: usually major/minor, with some diminished/augmented for passing flavor. Stacks of fourths or fifths, however, lack a center: none of the notes "pull" toward another, so there's no sense of gravity leading toward a particular tonality. But the solid structure of stacked fourths/fifths is hardly cacophonous: it's unusual, a little angular, but not unpleasant.

So, our "bell" loops look like this.

Suba loops them in fourths, ascending.

Dylan loops them in fifths, descending.

The two voices start a fourth apart, and four beats apart, creating what appears at first to be a round. But as Suba ascends and Dylan descends and the loops fall out of sync, the voices pull further and further apart, with a final range of three octaves apart. Suba's bells in alto/soprano range, sung in eighth notes and in stacked fourths, sound like carillon bells. Dylan's bells, in tenor/bass range in open fifths, sung in quarter notes, sound like deep, tolling church bells. No clear key, no real time signature: just spinning. The unwinding effect looks like this: to make it easier to see the visual effect without covering too many bars, I've notated it "half time":

Now, time for Suba's Carnatic solo.

To keep the sense of melodic ambiguity going, Suba chose the raga Hindolam. The basic pitches, in numbers, are:

1   ♭3   4   ♭6   ♭7   8

You'll notice there's no fifth, no natural halfway point in the scale. It sounds ungrounded, or even more like it's sung in the wrong key: start the scale on the fourth, and it sounds like a minor pentatonic scale in the key a fourth away.

We started this arrangement in the key of B♭ major, and the stacked bell-voicings we chose, though harmonically ambiguous, are "relative G minor-ish." Suba sings the raga in G, giving us:

It sounds G-ish, but it also sounds C-ish. You're never really quite sure.

Once Suba gets established with her solo, Dylan's vocal parts are layered in. We already have enough wide range in the bass-baritone bell parts, so Dylan's tenor vocal parts sort of slither in between them in the space also occupied by Suba's solo. We use the melody of the verse, "I wish I had a river . . . ," and we harmonize that in parallel suspended second chords: melody on bottom, parallel fifths next, and finally the suspension.

We stay in this swirling universe for a while as Suba develops her solo. Then, the solo cools down, we fade the other parts into a reverb-filled mist, and we end with a strange but somehow uplifting departure in parallel, shifting major/minor colors:

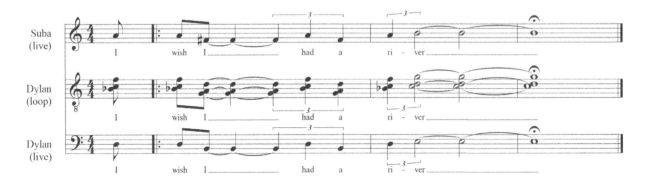

We'd never tried anything quite like this before, and we surprised ourselves with the results. The song is now a staple in our repertoire . . . even outside of the holidays!

In summary, there's no one way, or correct way, to reimagine a song. You need to consider a group's abilities, the audience for whom they'll be performing, the original version's particular strengths and weaknesses, the general stylistic context into which you'd like the new version to fit, and so on. Your inspiration may come from a lyric, a piece of the melody, a modern pop song, or a directive from the client/group themselves. Sometimes it'll be a remarkably easy process as it all unfolds naturally as you go, and other times you'll pull your hair out looking for a good idea, only to have it pop into your head as you're taking a shower and thinking of something else. Or, let's be honest, it could be the result of hard work, several attempts, multiple dead ends, and a final version that sounds to you like the labor you put in, but to everyone else it seems obvious and effortless. You get credit both ways—easy or difficult—and you deserve it either way.

Conclusion

The arranger could very well be called the Invisible Artist.

Do your job as an arranger well once, and no one will know or notice. The group gets all the credit. Do it well a dozen times, and your fellow singers will give you kudos, and maybe other music directors might start seeking you out to arrange for them. Do it well a hundred times, and singers in other groups and other places may start to recognize your name.

Do it well a thousand times and the public might notice. Might.

Think of your favorite recordings, your favorite performances. You likely attribute all their beauty and glory to the original artist. Aretha's the greatest, Frank Sinatra touches your heart, Taylor Swift gives voice to the emotions you can't express with words alone. And if you, an arranger, usually don't consider who has arranged these timeless pop classics, why would a layperson who doesn't even know what arranging is (beyond flowers) even think to acknowledge you?

You must come to terms with this reality because it is a constant. Furthermore, to draw attention to yourself as an arranger is to betray your craft, to stand between the sacred relationship between performer and audience as you cry out, "Look at me!" You may have a Superstar inside you, dying to burst into your arrangements . . . but most of the time, "inside you" is where they belong. If you sever that tie, the moment is lost, the music is ruined. You're the Wizard of Oz and for people to look behind the curtain, or even realize there is a curtain, ruins the magic.

Plus, you don't want people focusing on chord voicings, on horn hits, on technical sleight-of-hand, or on the deep groove. You want them to feel it, to love it, to have it grab them in a way they don't understand. Once music becomes primarily cerebral, you might as well be reading actuarial tables so far as most people are concerned. Like an ostentatious chef who draws attention to the color and display of a dish, the flavor is diminished, if not lost. There may be a visual aspect to food just as there is a cerebral, mechanical element to music, but to make it primary is to destroy the fundamental power of the medium.

What could possibly be the value of discussing and dissecting such a marginal, underappreciated (most people don't know what an arranger does, or even what an arrangement is), under-respected (those who do know what it is usually consider it second-class), under-remunerated (according to US copyright law, arrangers don't even own their arrangements—the original composer and songwriters do) creative act? Many a book has been written about the glorious and highly respected act of composing music, but few have been written simply about the process of arranging—what it is like and how it feels—and to our knowledge, no one else has done this in the a cappella world. In this book, we're not actively addressing this concept as much as creating a variety of snapshots about different aspects of the act of arranging, and yet in composite, we hope the picture becomes clear: this unusual thing we do has a feel, and a flavor, and although it can't easily be described, we all have a similar experience.

One more thought we'd like to leave you with, and that's the concept of choice. Arranging is a perpetual act of choosing: which note, which voice, which syllable, and so on. As for becoming an arranger, perhaps it chooses you. Maybe your need to arrange arose from a desire to create order from chaos; or maybe it came from a place of curiosity, wanting to learn how music works "under the hood"; or perhaps it came simply so you could sing that new song on the radio. A correction is needed, as we don't create complete order, as music is imperfect, be it our equal-tempered Western tuning system, or the fact that a cappella rarely is in perfect tune (despite our best efforts). More correctly, we seek better order, to create something that exists in our voices and only our voices when before it didn't, to say something about the human condition, which itself is neither perfect nor all that orderly.

To be an arranger is to create without much credit or appreciation, unlike the performer or the composer, whose names will be known, and celebrated. We don't do this because we're going to become rich or famous; we do it because we love it. Even though it's not addressed directly, we hope our own love of arranging comes through in every page, and that these words inspire you to infuse your arrangements with a similar love, which will translate into your singers' voices, and eventually the audience's ears. That's the best reason to do anything.

Appendix A
Basic Arranging in Ten Steps

1.   Choose a Song

You're probably thinking, *Wait . . . isn't this obvious? A prerequisite? Should this even be considered a step?* We'd like you to consider song selection as your first major decision as an arranger, because so many of your subsequent decisions will proceed from this first choice.

You're probably also thinking, *Okay, but deciding on a song is easy, isn't it?* If you're a freelance arranger, or just arranging for fun on your own, your decision is usually either made for you, or you have no restrictions. Easy.

But if you're arranging for a specific group with specific needs, you have many nuanced considerations. It's easy to come up with songs that would be fun to arrange, but usually there is a question of what is needed in the repertoire, based on what is currently sung, your group's core style, untapped talent, soloist options, which artists/composers you already have in the repertoire, whom you'll be singing for in upcoming performances, and so on.

We recommend avoiding songs that are performed by other a cappella groups often: doing so will inevitably lead to listeners comparing your group's version of the song to others, rather than listening to your group on its own merits. Conversely, your group will make a name for itself much more quickly if you develop your own sound and your own repertoire. This matters less if you're just starting out in a region with few or no other a cappella groups, and yet if you plan on expanding your fan base and reach, it's a good idea in time to develop your own sound and style.

Regarding your current repertoire, you should be sure that your group has a great first and last song, and a great encore. Usually these songs will be most effective if they are up-tempo, high-energy numbers. You'll likely find your group performing these high-impact numbers most frequently, as you'll sometimes only be singing a few songs (at a party, event, on a street corner, for friends) and want them to leave a lasting impression.

Your group should also have at least one excellent ballad at its disposal. Once you grab an audience with your energy, you want to leave an emotional impression, and one of a cappella's greatest strengths is the ability to render big, beautiful chords.

It should go without saying, but before you settle on a song, be sure you have someone in your group who can sing the solo (if you're planning on a solo line in your arrangement). A great arrangement of a great song with a poor soloist usually appears to the audience as mediocre (or worse). The soloist is the most important vocalist in any song, so you had better be sure that you have the right voice to get the job done.

2.   Listen to the Original Repeatedly

This principle is the same as in foreign language study: listen to the song over and over again until it becomes second nature. While you're concentrating, and while you're not. You will begin to hear sounds, textures, rhythms, and chords that you never heard before, some of which are very subtle and mixed quietly in the background.

Many a cappella arrangements suffer from not integrating the subtle, often almost subliminal, musical elements that define a song. There are times when "doing the obvious thing" in an arrangement isn't the most effective. When you've listened to a song to the point that you can hear it in your head while it's not playing, you've fully integrated it. You want to internalize not only the specific notes and chords, but also the nuances of the song's feel, and this takes time.

And besides, it helps later on when you find you don't need to listen back to the original recording as often.

3.   Look at—and Listen to—Other Arrangements

"What? Isn't that cheating?" Let's put it this way: Would you rather spend your time reinventing the wheel by transcribing the melody and chords, or focusing on the more creative elements of arranging? We thought so.

Stravinsky admitted to "stealing" musical ideas from others and himself, and he wasn't the first great musician to do so. Whereas there is a plagiarism case to be made from someone copying a paragraph out of a book, there's no ownership of a musical texture, or vocal lick, or arranging trick. The artistry is in knowing when and where to use these various elements. It's not cheating; it's research. Conversely, by listening to "what's out there," you can deliberately move in another direction with your arrangement if you wish, and ensure that your version stands out.

You can find a variety of other arrangements in printed music, or in recorded form. Search online for different versions in sheet music (not only a cappella, as a piano/vocal score might provide some insight and save you time if an a cappella version doesn't exist in print), and recordings.

Caveat emptor: often there are mistakes or simplifications in the printed music (yes, even the melody and/or chords), but if you've more or less memorized the song, you'll catch them. All you need is a close approximation of the solo in many cases anyway, as the soloist may want to learn the solo directly from the original recording.

You should be able to find many different recorded versions of songs (again, not only a cappella), providing a variety of different approaches to the core material. This will help you identify which musical elements are most important to your arrangement, and help you assemble a list of effective as well as problematic choices others have made. This provides an initial road map of the song's potential pitfalls and high points.

Other arrangements of a song can be heard on various a cappella albums, and they can be found in a number of places. Although you don't want to lift entire passages note for note (that would be cheating), you can see what decisions the arranger made, appreciate what works, and learn from the less effective sections.

4. Decide on a Form

Sometimes the form is exactly right without alteration, and other times it will take a great deal of creativity to know how to sew together the important sections of a song that has too much "instrumental filler." The longer the original, the more likely you'll have to cut something.

One important thought that we've learned from singing and watching a cappella throughout our lives: listening to and watching a cappella is a heightened experience. It is often more exciting, but also more exhausting. In a sense, everyone's a lead singer, and the audience has many more personalities and faces to watch than in a band, but not so many so that it's like watching a chorus. As a result of this more personal, more intimate performing experience, audience members concentrate and pay attention to a cappella more than most instrumental musical forms, which is why less is often more. Say what needs to be said as poignantly as possible, and avoid unnecessary repetition.

If you don't understand this point, bring a stopwatch to an a cappella show and compare performed song lengths with the originals. A three-minute song onstage comes across as a full 4.5-minute radio tune. Performing "Hey, Jude" at its entire seven-minute length would be incredibly tiresome. Or take a look at any a cappella album: many of the best a cappella albums clock in at thirty-five to forty-five minutes or even less, versus fifty-plus minutes for a modern album with instruments. Your mind can more easily wander when an instrumental passage occurs, whereas your attention is drawn to the sound of voices, which can then result in the listener tiring more easily.

Since many songs are written for and recorded with instruments, there are often instrumental solos, long intros, and transitional passages that may translate poorly to voices. If you've memorized your song completely (and you should have), try singing it through from start to finish, and see where you lose interest. Chances are, your audience will, as well.

Also listen for anything that won't translate well to your singers' voices. Unless your group is well-versed in vocal guitar solos, you may well want to abridge or skip them, unless you come up with an alternate choice for that musical passage.

If you're having a hard time keeping everything organized because there are too many changes in the song's form, you can use technology to help organize your thoughts. If you're familiar with music-recording software, you can import an audio file of the song, then cut it into individual sections. This will allow you to mix and match them, creating different "radio edits."

» *Deke Says: We use this radio-edit technique on* The Sing-Off *before we start every arrangement (especially because we often have to choose the best ninety seconds of a four-minute song), and we call them "cut-downs." Create a couple of versions and compare to see which works best.*

If you're more low-tech, write out a basic road map either on computer or on index cards, and experiment with shuffling the pieces around. By now you know the song well enough that, by seeing the pieces in front of you, you can reorder/cut pieces of the song in your head.

On rare occasions, perhaps if a song is too short, doesn't have a bridge, or relies on too many long guitar passages, you'll find extreme measures are necessary. Options include weaving in another related song, possibly by the same artist, or composing a short transition. You may find that it's just not going to work, no matter what you do. Don't fret—choose another song to arrange now and put this song on the back burner until you find a solution.

5. Prepare Your Materials

Before you get started, you should know that it doesn't matter if you notate music on paper, if you do so on computer, or if you arrange by ear using recording software. Each method has inherent benefits and hurdles, and all can result in superior artistry. It's a matter of personal choice. Whatever method you choose to document your arrangement, it's time to set your foundation.

Before you go any further, you need to decide (at least for now) how many vocal parts your arrangement will have.

If you have a small ensemble (six or fewer), your choice is likely made for you, as you'll want as many notes as you have people, and doubling only one or two parts will likely cause an unwanted imbalance.

If you're arranging for a midsized ensemble (seven to fifteen members, like most collegiate groups), consider leaving at least two people per part unless you really know what you're doing. You'll get a much fuller sound, and you'll hedge your bet against out-of-tune singing. Writing for more parts can get more complicated to manage: try starting with soloist/melody, bass, and two to four background parts, expanding from there as your creativity demands.

Don't forget to factor in the soloist, and any extra parts, such as vocal percussion or duet lines, that need their own designated voice. Once you have your final count, consider how many staves (on paper) or tracks (in your recording program) you need. The solo should be on the top of each staff system, and it may be joined by duet or trio parts. You should avoid having more than two parts per staff, as the inner voices will have difficulty following which notes are theirs. If you're recording, you'll likely have your own track management system, and there is no right or wrong organizational method.

With two parts per staff, the upper voice should have "stems up" through-out, and the lower voice "stems down" (should you need to cross the voices, it'll be apparent). If your final count is three, four, or six staves, you'll want twelve staff-per-page paper, and if you've arrived at five, ten staff-per-page is also available. If you're arranging on a computer, this isn't usually a concern—you can put each voice on its own line and condense later. If you're recording to computer, you can lay out the number of tracks you need in advance.

If it isn't already clear, arranging on computer (via notation program or recording program) is far more flexible than paper, as you can make major changes once you're well into the process without much difficulty. Example: you can move everything up a half step in a computer with the click of a mouse, but on paper you have to rewrite everything laboriously.

Once you've decided on all of the above, "lay out" the song by counting the number of measures, and making a note where each section begins (verse, chorus, bridge, etc.). Next, fill in your clefs and key signatures on paper, or name your tracks in your recording program. When you're done, you'll have a solid foundation that will allow you to work on sections in any order you'd like without any confusion as to where you are or how it fits formally with the rest of the music.

6.   Write Out the Melody

Take your "prepared" paper/computer file/song file and write out/sing the solo line from the first measure through the last, including all rests. Having the solo line written down/recorded will keep you from losing your place while you're arranging—it serves as a "place keeper" and a road map.

Also, for small groups, especially quartets and quintets, the soloist's pitch and rhythm is important to consider at all times. Sometimes the soloist will be the only voice on a certain chord tone, and you'll want to know exactly where the solo will be: pitch, rhythm, and syllable. In these cases, it's worth the extra effort to make sure the solo line is exactly correct, inflections and all.

Also, remember that a soloist sometimes doesn't sing exactly the same notes and rhythms as the original, or even remain consistent each time she sings the song in your rehearsals. For this reason, you should make a note, as you arrange, what sections of the melody need to be sung as-written to make the arrangement work as you intend versus places where the soloist can be more improvisational.

7.   Write Out the Bass Line

Once you have your form and melody, the next most important vocal part is the bass (or second alto, if you're working with all female voices). You may well change the bass line as you're adding other parts, but you should at the very least create what you think you want now.

If the bass line in the original song is unique and/or memorable (a hook, or a clearly definable countermelody), you're probably going to want to duplicate it as closely as possible, knowing that you'll have to leap an octave at times (when the line becomes too low to sing, or too high to still be the lowest voice), and you should choose carefully where to do so without disrupting any signature melodic contours.

If it's not clearly definable, then you're free to weave a bass line of your own. Consider vocal range, roots of the chords, and the rhythmic feel of the original as primary factors. The bass line is the song's "second melody" and is usually the most recognizable line after the solo, so make it melodic, catchy, and wherever possible, fun to sing. A fully engaged singer is a better singer, and a boring bass line will likely result in a boring performance.

Don't forget to take into consideration specific vocal production concerns, like where your bass/bass section is going to breathe, how fast your bass can articulate, and how long he can hold a note. If you're not familiar with bass voices and their sounds and limitations, have your bass sing for you, and listen to a few of the greats, like the Bobs' Richard Greene, Take 6's Alvin Chea, the Persuasions' Jimmy Hayes, and the Nylons' Arnold Robinson. Each has a unique way of phrasing and articulating, and there's much to be learned from their recordings.

8.   Write the Backgrounds ("BGs")

From Rockapella to Take 6 to the Nylons, the background voices ("BGs") are usually treated as a unit in contemporary a cappella arranging, but there are a myriad of things to consider. So many things, in fact, that it's impossible to go into them all in any depth here. To give you a shove in the right direction, some of your considerations should be:

» *Rhythmic variety*: having these voices sing different rhythms from the solo and bass.
» *Syllabic sounds*: words versus sound-syllables.

- » *Voice leading*: making the background lines melodic and avoiding unnecessary jumps.
- » *Duet/trio*: locking into the same words and rhythms as the melody.
- » *Block chords versus counterpoint*: all voices acting as a single unit versus individual, separate lines.
- » *Arpeggiation*: voices working as a unit, but spelling out chords by singing one note at a time, like guitar strings.
- » *Instrumental idioms*: using the voices to imitate instrumental sounds or textures.
- » *Musical styles*: using vocal conventions from classical, doo-wop, close harmony, pop, R&B, etc.

Of all of these ten steps, this will prove the most time-consuming, demanding, and ultimately the most rewarding, as it's here that you get to be your most creative.

9. Make the Final Touches

Now is the time to go back and "sing through" the entire arrangement, out loud if possible (sing a specific line an octave higher or lower if need be).

Where is it too empty or boring to sing? Where might it be too busy, or too complicated? How do the sections fit together? Where do you breathe? Is there a sense of development throughout the chart? Where are the weakest passages, and how can you fix them?

It's best to turn off your "inner editor" when you're originally coming up with ideas, but you do eventually need to turn it back on and look at your arrangement as a whole, and now's the time.

10. Record/Rehearse

If you have the capabilities to do so, it's helpful to record your own arrangement. By singing each part "for real," in more detail than you did in Step Nine, you'll discover whether any parts just don't work, or what parts will need extra attention in rehearsal. You'll be able to "spell-check" your notation properly as you discover any copy errors or places where the notation is unfriendly, or laid out badly. Most importantly, you'll finally hear your arrangement sung by real voices, before taking it to the group. You'll discover if it works as a whole (and save yourself some time and embarrassment if things need to be fixed), and in the process, you'll likely discover some performance nuances that you can bring to the group.

If you thought your job was complete when you copied and distributed your arrangement, you're mistaken. A great arrangement is one that grows and changes with the group that sings it, and a great arranger is one who knows that no arrangement is finished until it is tailor-fitted to a specific group. Do not let your ego get in the way of this crucial step in the arranging process; suggestions from the group, and your own changes after you hear a proper sing-through, will only make the chart better. You will be respected and applauded for your flexibility.

When listening to the sing-through in rehearsal, your focus should in part be on your choices, their interpretation of them, and the distance between. How does the arrangement sound in voices as opposed to in your head? What differs from your expectations, what have they improved upon, and what isn't as good as you'd hoped?

Be honest with yourself, and open to trying a variety of ideas and suggestions. This is when you get to "mold your clay," and it is the most valuable learning experience you'll ever have as an arranger—use this time wisely.

In case you didn't realize it, many renowned composers and arrangers have had the luxury of writing for the best orchestras and choruses in the world, and they could write just about anything they could imagine; you probably can't. Like it or not, you're arranging for your group, and it's your fault (not theirs) if the arrangement doesn't work. It's your job to make them sound their best and your responsibility to maximize their potential through your choices. You can push their limits occasionally, but to push those limits, you have to know them, and work within them.

And just as you'll push your group's limits, you should also push yours. There are plenty of standard arrangements in the world, and you're probably not interested in adding to the pile. To be a great arranger, you have to know how to write a standard arrangement, and also have the creativity and drive to do something new. Most instrumental arrangers approach a song with the initial question, "What am I going to do differently?" whereas many a cappella arrangers approach a song with the quandary, "How can I make this sound the same, but with voices?" Consider putting yourself in a perspective that straddles and makes the most of both ways of thinking. The best arrangements manage to maintain the successful elements of an original version, and also bring to it something new.

Once you're finished, and your arrangement is safely in the repertoire, it's time to go back to Step One . . .

Exercises

» Choose a simple song you know well (say, "Happy Birthday") and arrange it using this method. Notice the ways in which this differs from your usual practice. Are there valuable steps you've been skipping? Are there ways you're used to arranging that are superior to this method?
» Consider the order of these ten steps. Are there some steps you can take in a different order? Do you prefer a different order? Would you add any steps?

» Try arranging a song using a different notational method. If you usually write down your music on paper or in a notation program, try arranging through a recording program by ear, and vice versa.

» Look at some of the first arrangements you've ever done, remember how they sounded, and analyze what you would do differently now.

» Take an arrangement you've done for one group and give it to another group. What do the two groups do differently, and what remains essentially the same between their interpretations?

Appendix B
"Anitra's Dance"

Anitra's Dance

E. Grieg
Arr.Dylan Bell
and Suba Sankaran

doo ba doo ba doo ba doo ba-yoo _____ dm ____ dm ____ dm _____ ba doo ba

doo ba doo ba doo ba doo ba-yoo _____ dm _____ dm _____ dm _____ doo ba doo ba doo ba doo ba-yoo _____

E **Freely,** ♩=69

dee dee dee dee dee dee dee dee dee dee dee dee dee dee

dee dee dee dee dee dee

dee dee dee dee _____ dee dee

dee dee dee dee dee dee dee dee dee dee dee dee dee dee

molto accel.

bahm bahm bahm bahm bahm bahm bahm bahm

ba dum ba dum ba dum ba dum ba dum ba dum ba dum ba dum

Prestissimo

doo ba doo ba doo ba doo ba - yoo ba doo ba doo ba doo ba doot bop

doo ba doo ba doo ba doo ba - yoo ba doo ba doo ba doo ba doot bop

Appendix C
Music Links

If a picture tells a thousand words, a recording tells a thousand notes: notated examples, while giving us the basic essence of arranging, don't always tell the whole story. Sometimes you need to hear it to really get it. And while the rules around Fair Use in publication only allow us to print a few measures at a time (even if they are our own arrangements), it's nice to hear the whole work in context.

Below are web links for nearly every musical reference in the book. Please note that, since we're often talking about a particular arrangement/recording of a song, rather than the composition itself, the word "by" is often used here to mean "as performed by" rather than "as written by."

Chapter 2: The Creative Process

» "The Dry Cleaner from Des Moines" by Cadence:
https://www.acappellaarranging.com/wp-content/uploads/2024/01/05
-The-Dry-Cleaner-from-Des-Moines.mp3
» "I Want a Hippopotamus for Christmas":
https://youtu.be/0Bnq070H3BA?si=D74iUmAu0Ad2hR8U

Chapter 4: Vocal Ranges and Additional Techniques

» The Overtone Music Network:
https://www.overtone.cc
» "Blackbird" by Bobby McFerrin:
https://www.youtube.com/watch?v
=Y5M68ynBMXA
» "Just the Two of Us" by FreePlay:
https://www.youtube.com/watch?v=Tt1ALtSxlzs
» "Vincent" by FreePlay:
https://www.youtube.com/live/Exz4CjItaKs?si=6PsCdpoycyDYjvcP
&t=2159

» "Smile" by FreePlay:
https://freeplayduo.bandcamp.com/track/smile-pavane
» "Anitra's Dance" by FreePlay:
https://freeplayduo.bandcamp.com/track/anitras-dance-excerpted

Chapter 5: Counterpoint, Polyphony, and Two-Voice Writing

» "In My Life" by the Beatles:
https://www.youtube.com/watch?v=YBcdt6DsLQA
» "Thank You Falettinme Be Mice Elf Agin" by Sly and the Family Stone:
https://www.youtube.com/watch?v=N5BP2KlPD4U
» "Old Man" by FreePlay:
https://freeplayduo.bandcamp.com/track/old-man
» "Bohemian Rhapsody" by Carlmont Choirs:
https://www.youtube.com/watch?v=XlYrLgOY6tM
» "Mr. Blue Sky" from *The Sing-Off*:
https://www.youtube.com/watch?v=5Bvnt6g4r2g
» "Signed, Sealed, Delivered" by DePauwCappella:
https://www.youtube.com/watch?v=F-n3UKgzgl8
» "Amazing Grace, Gospel":
https://www.acappellaarranging.com/wp-content/uploads/2024/01
/Fig-21_19-Amazing-Grace-Gospel-FULL.mp3
» "Michael Jackson Dance Medley" by Retrocity:
https://www.acappellaarranging.com/wp-content/uploads/2024/01/MJ
-Dance-Medley-FULL.mp3

Chapter 6: Harmonic Principles and Techniques

» "Amazing Grace, Barbershop":
https://www.acappellaarranging.com/wp-content/uploads/2024/01
/Fig-21_7-Amazing-Grace-BBshop-FULL.mp3
» "Hit That Jive, Jack" by Cadence:
https://www.acappellaarranging.com/wp-content/uploads/2024/01/06
-Hit-That-Jive-Jackl.m4a
» "The Book of Love" by Magnetic Fields:
https://www.youtube.com/watch?v=jkjXr9SrzQE
» "Pachelbel Rant" by Rob Paravonian:
https://www.youtube.com/watch?v=JdxkVQy7QLM
» "I Wish" by Cadence:
https://www.acappellaarranging.com/wp-content/uploads/2024/01
/I-Wish-Full-MX2.mp3

» "Smile/Pavane" by FreePlay:
https://freeplayduo.bandcamp.com/track/smile-pavane
» "God Only Knows" by FreePlay:
https://freeplayduo.bandcamp.com/track/god-only-knows
» "Stairway to Heaven" by Led Zeppelin:
https://www.youtube.com/watch?v=QkF3oxziUI4

Chapter 7: Arranging for the Studio

» "Quiet Moon" by the House Jacks:
https://youtu.be/73BxB0Uv2Gs
» "Wanna Be Startin' Somethin'" by the Watch:
https://www.acappellaarranging.com/wp-content/uploads/2024/01
/Wanna-Be-Startin-Somethin-FULL.mp3
» "Adventure Day" by the House Jacks:
https://youtu.be/lOXuTH-c24I
» "The Dry Cleaner from Des Moines" by Cadence:
https://www.acappellaarranging.com/wp-content/uploads/2024/01/05
-The-Dry-Cleaner-from-Des-Moines.mp3
» "Old Man" by FreePlay:
https://freeplayduo.bandcamp.com/track/old-man
» "Immortals" by DCappella:
https://www.youtube.com/watch?v=BaTf90kcq_A
» "Spider-Man" by the Nylons:
https://www.youtube.com/watch?v=v6uJ89AqjD8
» "Game" by Cadence:
https://youtu.be/qmNZCbPVdhc?si=SX6Ao1PWja57W7Jm
» "After You" by the House Jacks:
https://www.youtube.com/watch?v=nlonEx2We2A
» "Conga" by FreePlay:
https://freeplayduo.bandcamp.com/track/conga
» "Unbroken" by the House Jacks:
https://www.youtube.com/watch?v=k9dE3CiW47A

Chapter 8: Live Looping

» "Fireflies" by FreePlay:
https://www.youtube.com/live/i5X-o9bwZ3M?si=HvNkqIAtXq
-ErHCc&t=4423
» "Step in Time" by DCappella (alto solo):
https://www.youtube.com/watch?v=45nD58wPlWQ

» "Stand by Me" by Ben E. King:
https://youtu.be/pKtLNYNWbBw?si=Pan8SNTVejzsvDrp

Chapter 9: Adapting Arrangements

» "It's Not That I'm Lazy . . ." by Dylan Bell:
https://dylanbell.bandcamp.com/track/its-not-that-im-lazy
» "Sunshine" by Cadence:
https://www.acappellaarranging.com/wp-content/uploads/2024/01/04
-Sunshine.m4a
» "Blues on Sunday" by Cadence:
https://www.acappellaarranging.com/wp-content/uploads/2024/01/09
-Blues-on-Sunday.mp3
» "Goodnight, Sweetheart" by Saint Helens High School SoundFX:
https://www.youtube.com/watch?v=PZ4bcAKPAUI
» "White Christmas" by the Gas House Gang (TTBB):
https://www.youtube.com/watch?v=s6yknrx4WOE
» "White Christmas" by the Mixed Company Singers (SATB):
https://youtu.be/-vhY-aTKNMc
» "Since U Been Gone" by the House Jacks (TTBB):
https://youtu.be/DRXftAVo4iE
» "Since U Been Gone" from *Pitch Perfect* (SSAA):
https://youtu.be/z5oQRpVoKSY

Chapter 10: Instrumental Imitation and Lyric-less Arrangements

» "Sing Like a Trumpet" by Deke Sharon:
https://www.youtube.com/watch?v=50excXOTAuQ
» "Caravan" by the Mills Brothers:
https://www.youtube.com/watch?v=SVBpB7rSn7A
» "I Wish" by Cadence:
https://www.acappellaarranging.com/wp-content/uploads/2024/01
/I-Wish-Full-MX2.mp3
» "Ring of Fire" by Ballard High School Men's Ensemble:
https://www.youtube.com/watch?v=d9kG7LoUtRI
» "Gringo Samba" by Dylan Bell:
https://dylanbell.bandcamp.com/track/gringo-samba
» "'Round Midnight" by Bobby McFerrin and Herbie Hancock:
https://www.youtube.com/watch?v=j2wj1xF8dUo
» "Sing Like a Muted Trumpet" by Deke Sharon:
https://youtu.be/5ol9d9qHfTE

» "Muted Trumpet Demonstration" by Dylan Bell:
https://youtu.be/FFXkJDVfKmM?si=jYxD84ixAZ3QDBOM
» "The Dry Cleaner from Des Moines" by Cadence:
https://www.acappellaarranging.com/wp-content/uploads/2024/01/05
-The-Dry-Cleaner-from-Des-Moines.mp3
» "Hit That Jive, Jack" by Cadence:
https://www.acappellaarranging.com/wp-content/uploads/2024/01/06
-Hit-That-Jive-Jackl.m4a
» "Learn Vocal Sax" by Richard Steighner of the Exchange:
https://youtu.be/1zclsrSEZSc
» "Sing Like a Flute" by Deke Sharon:
https://youtu.be/qdbCO-1pwfI
» "All Away" by Deke Sharon/the House Jacks:
https://www.youtube.com/watch?v=cLwyMkMw1I4
» "Fever" by Vocalosity:
https://www.youtube.com/watch?v=pPEeYlwVjz0
» "Forget About the Boy" by HKA Community Choir:
https://www.youtube.com/watch?v=2xhqCgT1Gcw
» "I Believe" by Take 6:
https://www.youtube.com/watch?v=pZRICH2UORo
» "Diamonds on the Soles of Her Shoes" by Paul Simon:
https://www.youtube.com/watch?v=-I_T3XvzPaM
» "Don't Fix What's Broken" by Cadence:
https://www.acappellaarranging.com/wp-content/uploads/2024/01/02
-Dont-Fix-Whats-Broken.mp3
» "Killer Queen" by Retrocity:
https://youtu.be/ckJ79Z6BoIU?si=GLOX3I3xhJ54lqmQ
» "The Glory Days" by DCappella:
https://www.youtube.com/watch?v=fdP2PNb5ET0
» "The Three Little Pigs" arranged for DCappella:
https://www.youtube.com/watch?v=jyULoYXJV0U
» "Sing, Sing, Sing" by Vocalosity:
https://www.youtube.com/watch?v=CqU9oztZKtY
» "Cantina Song (from *Star Wars*)" by DCappella:
https://www.youtube.com/watch?v=JP-iWGVMFPM
» "Axel F" by Revv52 featuring Peterpot:
https://www.youtube.com/watch?v=RukIgjO8z1w

Chapter 11: The Foundation

» "Good Old A Cappella" by the Persuasions:
https://www.youtube.com/watch?v=_wTabn1HBh8
» "Kiss Him Goodbye" by the Nylons:
https://youtu.be/-foSal5IQmU?si=0yrXIxYN-FMVpgHx

» "Bus Plunge" by The Bobs:
   https://www.youtube.com/watch?v=zgcu3OQX2SM
» "Through the Wall" by The Bobs:
   https://youtu.be/j3hj22suhyM?si=BhAA9sySOTD4hpGD
» "Trash" by The Bobs:
   https://youtu.be/rfpiCAYJmFY?si=EyzQa7a2gfkPwDHc

Chapter 12: The Contemporary Sound

» "Motownphilly" by Boyz II Men:
   https://youtu.be/Rciee-oQLoI?si=BS3kEVEy9jWXSmr5
» "It's So Hard to Say Goodbye to Yesterday" by Boyz II Men:
   https://youtu.be/oK9gLkXe0xw?si=XaUqVpIIKtaZwM-2
» "Thank You" by Boyz II Men:
   https://www.youtube.com/watch?v=y7gnzVuHfdg
» "A Long December" by Straight No Chaser:
   https://www.youtube.com/watch?v=n-ar3GZL6KI
» "Don't Dream It's Over" by Straight No Chaser:
   https://www.youtube.com/watch?v=IiLBOd6fR-c
» "Daft Punk Medley" by Pentatonix:
   https://www.youtube.com/watch?v=3MteSlpxCpo
» "Can't Help Falling in Love" by Pentatonix:
   https://www.youtube.com/watch?v=YSkHIv7GhOM
» "Can You Feel the Love Tonight" by Pentatonix:
   https://www.youtube.com/watch?v=cT1Kzk7akjQ

Chapter 13: Lush Jazz Harmonies

» "Their Hearts Were Full of Spring" by the Four Freshmen:
   https://www.youtube.com/watch?v=djDm2JVMm9Y
» "Fool on the Hill" by the Singers Unlimited:
   https://www.youtube.com/watch?v=Y_NNeeTSRvY
» "Get Away, Jordan" by Take 6:
   https://www.youtube.com/watch?v=BP_Cqo-bteY

Chapter 14: Around the World

» "Montuno Sampling" by Vocal Sampling:
   https://www.youtube.com/watch?v=qz-5NDMYcrE

- » "Fugue in G Minor" by The Swingles:
  https://youtu.be/ax-7kYRA88Q?si=qH0KLlg_y6wCnijs
- » "Pakkanen" by Rajaton:
  https://www.youtube.com/watch?v=fG1duDKUxLc
- » "Homeless" by Ladysmith Black Mambazo:
  https://www.youtube.com/watch?v=gfZxnVQHdgI

Chapter 15: Medleys and Mashups

- » "Scarborough Fair/Canticle" by Simon and Garfunkel:
  https://www.youtube.com/watch?v=-BakWVXHSug
- » "Under Pressure" by Queen and David Bowie:
  https://www.youtube.com/watch?v=a01QQZyl-_I
- » "Ice Ice Baby" by Vanilla Ice:
  https://www.youtube.com/watch?v=rog8ou-ZepE
- » "Mary, Mary" by the Monkees:
  https://www.youtube.com/watch?v=AMNize7s8nc
- » "Mary, Mary" by Run DMC:
  https://www.youtube.com/watch?v=QgmyVLheqkQ
- » "4 Chords" by Axis of Awesome:
  https://www.youtube.com/watch?v=5pidokakU4I
- » "Got to Give It Up" by Marvin Gaye:
  https://www.youtube.com/watch?v=Ayyy-03ITDg
- » "Blurred Lines" by Robin Thicke:
  https://www.youtube.com/watch?v=yyDUC1LUXSU
- » "Billie Jean/Lovestoned" by Nota:
  https://www.youtube.com/watch?v=zueXNTfCYMo
- » "She Will Be Loved" by Maroon 5:
  https://www.youtube.com/watch?v=nIjVuRTm-dc
- » "Waitin' for the End" by Linkin Park:
  https://www.youtube.com/watch?v=5qF_qbaWt3Q
- » "Breakaway" by Kelly Clarkson:
  https://www.youtube.com/watch?v=c-3vPxKdj6o
- » "Just the Way You Are" by Bruno Mars:
  https://www.youtube.com/watch?v=LjhCEhWiKXk
- » "Lights" by Ellie Goulding:
  https://www.youtube.com/watch?v=0NKUpo_xKyQ
- » "Just a Dream" by Nelly:
  https://www.youtube.com/watch?v=N6O2ncUKvlg
- » "Just the Way You Are/Just a Dream" from *Pitch Perfect*:
  https://www.youtube.com/watch?v=g-ByPeSVxyQ
- » "Let It Go/Snowman" by DCappella:
  https://www.youtube.com/watch?v=lu2Q0ouEJ_c

» "Friend Like Me" from Aladdin:
  https://www.youtube.com/watch?v=Qx91ff77yzM
» "You Got a Friend in Me" from *Toy Story*:
  https://www.youtube.com/watch?v=Zy4uiiy0qgA
» "We're All in This Together" from *High School Musical*:
  https://www.youtube.com/watch?v=DykVJl6wr_4
» "Say So" by Doja Cat:
  https://www.youtube.com/watch?v=pok8H_KF1FA
» "Don't Start Now" by Dua Lipa:
  https://www.youtube.com/watch?v=oygrmJFKYZY
» "Mickey's Friendship Mashup" by DCappella:
  https://www.youtube.com/watch?v=HBBJjAP3-po
» "Mickey's Friendship Mashup" TikTok Dance:
  https://www.tiktok.com/music/Mickey%27s-Friendship-Mashup
  -6990257083039877122
» "How Far I'll Go" from *Moana*:
  https://www.youtube.com/watch?v=cPAbx5kgCJo
» "Into the Unknown" from *Frozen 2*:
  https://www.youtube.com/watch?v=gIOyB9ZXn8s
» "Almost There" from *The Princess and the Frog*:
  https://www.youtube.com/watch?v=ThMwHKfzz1I
» "Starting Now" by Brandy:
  https://www.youtube.com/watch?v=7Ms-Y99bAi0
» "Princess/Starting Now Mashup" by DCappella:
  https://www.youtube.com/watch?v=1iLsgHRtyaE
» "Never Gonna Wake You Up" from Best of the Booties:
  https://www.youtube.com/watch?v=oT3mCybbhf0

Chapter 16: Reimagining a Song

» "Got to Get You into My Life" by the Beatles:
  https://www.youtube.com/watch?v=r95-7zfgtLw
» "Got to Get You into My Life" by Earth, Wind & Fire:
  https://www.youtube.com/watch?v=MKskYvTGEHE
» "A Little Help from My Friends" by the Beatles:
  https://www.youtube.com/watch?v=0C58ttB2-Qg
» "A Little Help from My Friends" by Joe Cocker:
  https://www.youtube.com/watch?v=nCrlyX6XbTU
» "I Will Always Love You" by Dolly Parton:
  https://www.youtube.com/watch?v=lKsQR72HY0s
» "I Will Always Love You" by Whitney Houston:
  https://www.youtube.com/watch?v=3JWTaaS7LdU
» "Red Red Wine" by Neil Diamond:
  https://www.youtube.com/watch?v=BeJ55sUacPM

» "Red Red Wine" by UB40:
https://www.youtube.com/watch?v=zXt56MB-3vc
» "Tainted Love" by Gloria Jones:
https://www.youtube.com/watch?v=OJKe2j9Wjh4
» "Tainted Love" by Soft Cell:
https://www.youtube.com/watch?v=XZVpR3Pk-r8
» "Ring of Fire" by Anita Carter:
https://www.youtube.com/watch?v=OlWGsaorj6U
» "Ring of Fire" by Johnny Cash:
https://www.youtube.com/watch?v=1WaV2x8GXj0
» "Respect" by Otis Redding:
https://www.youtube.com/watch?v=KvC9V_lBnDQ
» "Respect" by Aretha Franklin:
https://www.youtube.com/watch?v=9iayJ8u4Qew
» "The Most Wonderful Time of the Year" by Andy Williams:
https://www.youtube.com/watch?v=gFtb3EtjEic
» "The Most Wonderful Time of the Year" by DCappella:
https://www.youtube.com/watch?v=b5IVEoGx2MU
» "Overkill" by Men at Work:
https://www.youtube.com/watch?v=RY7S6EgSlCI
» "Overkill" by FreePlay:
https://freeplayduo.bandcamp.com/track/overkill
» "If I Only Had a Brain" from *The Wizard of Oz*:
https://www.youtube.com/watch?v=nauLgZISozs
» "Heigh-Ho" from *Snow White*:
https://www.youtube.com/watch?v=HI0x0KYChq4
» "Heigh-Ho" by DCappella:
https://www.youtube.com/watch?v=d-1pnKUqD3U
» "Dreamboat Annie" by Heart:
https://www.youtube.com/watch?v=Z5YTF26mkiU
» "Dreamboat Annie" by the Ault Sisters:
https://www.youtube.com/watch?v=nxtwwFcht9c
» "Supercalifragilisticexpialidocious" from *Mary Poppins*:
https://www.youtube.com/watch?v=1Pu1adxqUAg
» "Supercalifragilisticexpialidocious" by DCappella:
https://www.youtube.com/watch?v=D1N61KD6H9M
» "Summer in the City" by Lovin' Spoonful:
https://www.youtube.com/watch?v=5YgevxRGXIU
» "Summer in the City" by FreePlay:
https://freeplayduo.bandcamp.com/track/summer-in-the-city
» "Mars: The Bringer of War" from *The Planets* by Gustav Holst:
https://www.youtube.com/watch?v=4gKHw7KJ7pE
» "I'll Make a Man Out of You" from *Mulan*:
https://www.youtube.com/watch?v=j9MfuWSQoWc
» "Humble Stance" by Saga:
https://www.youtube.com/watch?v=cMLNDBYt-g4

» "Bibbidi-Bobbidi-Boo" from *Cinderella*:
https://www.youtube.com/watch?v=VNKuARjkWEg
» "Bibbidi-Bobbidi-Boo" by DCappella:
https://www.youtube.com/watch?v=R8uXwGBxY2k
» "What's He Building?" by Tom Waits:
https://www.youtube.com/watch?v=04qPdGNA_KM
» "What's He Building?" by the Watch:
https://youtu.be/0hKwy4dPm2Q
» "So Danço Samba" by A.C. Jobim:
https://www.youtube.com/watch?v=2Hh4MZRtP8E
» "So Danço Samba" by FreePlay:
https://freeplayduo.bandcamp.com/track/so-dan-o-samba-2
» "Prince Ali" from *Aladdin*:
https://www.youtube.com/watch?v=mT_8FAMsmCM
» "Prince Ali" by DCappella:
https://www.youtube.com/watch?v=u73LALy9ALw
» "River" by Joni Mitchell:
https://www.youtube.com/watch?v=OLHxxBTl71I
» "River" by FreePlay:
https://www.youtube.com/watch?v=6bFxmIrfDpE

Thank-Yous

We'd like to thank all the groups we've worked with that have inspired the arrangements within these pages, including (but certainly not limited to): Cadence, the House Jacks, Hampton Avenue, the Tufts Beelzebubs, Retrocity, DCappella and the Disney Music Group, Straight No Chaser, The Swingles, Committed, The Nylons, American Vybe, FreePlay, Groove 66, the Ault Sisters, Vocalosity, Wibi A Cappella, Pentatonix and Ben Bram, Stay Tuned, the cast and writers of In Transit, Street Corner Symphony, Janis Siegel and Lauren Kinhan, everyone who sang on *The Sing-Off* (United States, Netherlands, China, and South Africa), and the cast and crew of the *Pitch Perfect* films. We're always learning, and we learn the most from the work we do for you.

Personally, Deke would like to thank his family for their love and support: Heidi, Austin, Cap, Juli, Mary, and Ian. Dylan would like to thank his mom, Susan; his siblings, Megan and Brendan; and his wife and artistic partner-in-crime, Suba.

And finally, we'd like to thank you—for being the lovely people who fill the world with harmony, and for making it possible for so many singers all around the world to sing exactly the songs they want in exactly the way they want. Well, maybe not *exactly* the way they want, but the way they should want, because let's face it: you know best!

About the Authors

Heralded as "The Father of Contemporary A Cappella," performer, arranger, author, producer, and coach **Deke Sharon** is responsible for the current sound of modern a cappella. He has arranged thousands of songs, produced dozens of award-winning albums, and written seven books, as well as produced and music directed movies (*Pitch Perfect* 1, 2, 3) and television shows (*The Sing Off*, *Pitch Slapped*, *Pitch Battle*). He was the vocal orchestrater and a producer of the first a cappella musical on Broadway *In Transit* and the opening number of Andrew Lloyd Webber's new musical *Unmasked*. He has an annual concert at Carnegie Hall each spring and has shared the stage with countless music legends including Ray Charles, James Brown, Crosby Stills & Nash, Run DMC, The Temptations, LL Cool J, and The Four Tops, as well as performed the televised "Monday Night Football Theme" with Hank Williams Jr. through the 2011 NFL season. Deke lives in San Francisco.

Juno-nominated **Dylan Bell** is a vocalist, multi-instrumentalist, composer/arranger, music director, educator, author, and producer/engineer. Since he first discovered his parents' eclectic Beethoven–to–Bob Dylan record collection, Dylan's musical curiosity has kept him effortlessly crossing and blurring musical boundaries. Dylan is a mainstay on the Canadian music scene: he has performed for such luminaries as Nelson Mandela and Bishop Desmond Tutu and has arranged for, produced, or performed with the greatest names in vocal music including Bobby McFerrin, The Nylons, The Swingles, Cadence, the New York Voices, and his own live-looping duo FreePlay. He has played stages in more than twenty countries across six continents, and his compositions and arrangements are performed across the world from Adelaide to Zurich. Dylan lives in Toronto.

Made in the USA
Middletown, DE
21 September 2024

61251468R00250